The American Economy from Roosevelt to Trump

Vittorio Valli

The American Economy from Roosevelt to Trump

palgrave
macmillan

Vittorio Valli
Department of Economics and Statistics "Cognetti De Martiis"
University of Torino
Torino, Italy

ISBN 978-3-319-96952-7   ISBN 978-3-319-96953-4   (eBook)
https://doi.org/10.1007/978-3-319-96953-4

Library of Congress Control Number: 2018954741

© The Editor(s) (if applicable) and The Author(s) 2018
This work is subject to copyright. All rights are solely and exclusively licensed by the Publisher, whether the whole or part of the material is concerned, specifically the rights of translation, reprinting, reuse of illustrations, recitation, broadcasting, reproduction on microfilms or in any other physical way, and transmission or information storage and retrieval, electronic adaptation, computer software, or by similar or dissimilar methodology now known or hereafter developed.
The use of general descriptive names, registered names, trademarks, service marks, etc. in this publication does not imply, even in the absence of a specific statement, that such names are exempt from the relevant protective laws and regulations and therefore free for general use.
The publisher, the authors and the editors are safe to assume that the advice and information in this book are believed to be true and accurate at the date of publication. Neither the publisher nor the authors or the editors give a warranty, express or implied, with respect to the material contained herein or for any errors or omissions that may have been made. The publisher remains neutral with regard to jurisdictional claims in published maps and institutional affiliations.

Cover illustration: Jupiterimages / Getty

This Palgrave Macmillan imprint is published by the registered company Springer Nature Switzerland AG
The registered company address is: Gewerbestrasse 11, 6330 Cham, Switzerland

Preface

In 1978, I published a book on the US economic system. After more than 30 years, I returned to write about the largest and most powerful economy in the world and on its economic and political relations in a very different, but equally important, historical phase. The first edition of this book was published by Carocci in 2010. It was written in Italian and had a considerable success in the relatively restricted Italian market.

This English edition of the volume is not only a fully revised and updated version of the book but a new edition. It adds two important chapters. Chapter 5 is devoted to technical progress and to the strong accumulation of physical capital and knowledge, which have been a distinctive feature of American economic success for over a century. The other new chapter is dedicated to the economic consequences of Donald Trump in the first 18 months of his presidency. Also Obama's presidency and the critical matter of the decline of the American economy have been more fully analyzed.

A remark must be made: the Roosevelt in the title is not Franklin Delano, but Theodore Roosevelt, since my book takes essentially the move from the beginning of the twentieth century.

I have not written a thorough and detailed economic history, but I have tried to give an interpretation of the main long-term economic trends in the country from 1870 up to now. I did not do so as an economic historian, but as a macroeconomist, focusing only on the main changes and some crucial turning points of the economy of the US.

The interpretative line, the red thread of the book, is the following.

In the period 1870–1913, the US had an impressive economic development and a much faster rate of growth than most other countries, becoming the major economy in the world. This had been largely due to the great advantage of the *frontier*, that is, the possibility to move west using untapped natural resources, new lands to cultivate, new pastures, new mines, and so on. This favored large immigration inflows and both extensive and intensive investment, technological progress, and economies of scale, facilitating the rapid growth of the economy.

In the early twentieth century, these benefits gradually weakened. The US, however, could successfully continue its rapid economic ascent because, since 1908, it had gradually replaced those benefits with the ones derived by the *Fordist model of development*.

Despite the great depression undergone by the US economy after the Wall Street crash of 1929 and throughout the lost decade 1929–1939—when the Fordist model worked backwards—the Fordist model could be partially reactivated after the conclusion of the Second World War.

Since the 1950s, the dominating US economy had been slowly losing ground because of the outbreak of some creeping, deep weaknesses in the American development mechanism and in the Fordist model itself. The US had gradually become a large net importer of energy and was growing at a slower pace than several Western and Eastern European economies, the Soviet Union, Japan, and the four Asian tigers. This led the US to try another solution, namely, the attempt at gradually building up *a global economic empire*. Since Bretton Woods, the US had strongly pushed towards the establishment of the dollar as the key currency of the international monetary system; it had made a huge mass of foreign direct investment; it had favored a gradual process of liberalization of the international movements of goods and capitals, sustaining from the early 1970s a growing economic and financial globalization; it had taken part in major wars in Korea, Vietnam, and the Middle East. The dominance in finance, technology, and the internet economy, accompanied by an extensive political and military power, could temporarily relieve the US fears that globalization could, in the long run, destabilize the very sources of its economic hegemony. The crisis of the Soviet Union and of the Soviet bloc in the late 1980s and the beginning of the 1990s seemed to promise the full achievement of the American aims and to mark the *end of history*, with the final prevalence of western liberal democracy.

But history teaches us that history never ends: it has always trends and cycles, reversals of fortune, sudden upheavals, gradual ascents or decline.

Unregulated globalization and technological changes finally led to a *great backlash*. The rapid industrialization and technological catching up of Japan, South Korea, and then China and other emerging countries contributed to accelerate the US deindustrialization and indirectly increase US economic inequalities. We have, moreover, witnessed the passage of part of Eastern Europe to the EU after the dissolution of the Soviet Union; the booming expansion of the Chinese economy and, since 1992, that of India; the growing tensions in the Middle East; the attack on the twin towers on September 11, 2001; the wars in Afghanistan, Iraq, Syria, and Libya; the advent and semi-defeat of ISIS; the desire for resurgence of Russia and of emerging powers; the great recession; the drama of migrants and refugees from Latin America, Middle East, and Africa; the Brexit, and so on.

The reaction to a part of these events has been the brutal recourse to arms and wars of the two Bush administrations, the more nuanced, but undecided, Obama's international policy and the rough avowal of *America first* and of protectionist measures of Trump's populist policy. All this is leading towards an *imperfect multipolar world*, much more difficult and complex than the *asymmetric bi-polarism* prevailing in the 1946–1989 years, frozen by the hard equilibrium of cold war and nuclear terror. A phase of gradual decline of the American economic power had taken its first steps.

In economic matters, the *great recession* of the 2007–2010 years has proved the inner fragility of an economy dominated by banks and multinationals and in which the political decisions are heavily influenced by the interests of the big finance, the big e-corporations, the multinationals, and the super-rich.

In the US, President Obama saved the majority of financial institutions and some big industrial corporations and helped the recovery of the country by stimulus packages. He tried also to put some timid limits to the unruly action of major financial groups and to extend the health coverage to the majority of the population. Finally, he tried to take some steps toward a "green" policy, but at the same time, he favored the expansion of fracking techniques in the extraction of oil and gas, which reduced the US energy dependence but caused severe environmental damage in vast zones of the territory. Obama's major domestic failure is due to his timid reformist and gradualist approach, which could attenuate, but not arrest, the continuing rise of the great fractures in the US economy and society: the rapidly increasing divide between the rich, the poor, and the declining middle class, between races and religions, between immigrants and natives. These fractures have indeed been the culture medium of Donald Trump's populist appeal.

President Trump has announced and then tried to cancel, or reduce, the effects of Obama's policies on health and on green policies. He also proceeded to extend anti-migration walls, to repudiate some multilateral trade agreements and to raise some tariffs, to try reducing off-shoring and attract foreign investment. He finally cut taxation, in particular to corporations and to rich people as himself. His populist policy has helped him to gain the presidential election, but his controversial personality, full of haughtiness and of racist and sexist elements, and his intricate links with the interests of the arm industry, the oil and coal corporations, the construction industry, and big finance, can prelude to even greater social fractures, to trade wars, and to a dangerous scenery in international relations and in the social and environmental arenas.

Torino, Italy   Vittorio Valli

Acknowledgments

During many years of work on the American Economy and on comparative economic development, I have accumulated many intellectual debts. The first one is toward Harvey Leibenstein, Hollis B. Chenery, Gregory Grossman, and Carlo Maria Cipolla. I originally met them in Berkeley in 1966–1967 and then on several other occasions. The first three scholars gave me a taste for the analysis of the problems of economic development and of comparative studies; the fourth, a great economic historian, the pleasure of combining economics and history. Another important debt is toward Angus Maddison and several Italian economists, in particular Paolo Sylos Labini. Of Angus Maddison, I appreciated not only the impressive work of reconstruction and analysis of macro-economic data, widely used in this book, but also the vast knowledge, clarity, and concision in writing. Of Sylos Labini, I greatly appreciated his exceptional capacity of skillfully combining economic theory with social facts and his relevant policy insight and generous civil commitment. A debt is also due to friends and colleagues who read or reviewed the Italian or the English editions of the book and gave me helpful comments and suggestions, and in particular, Nicola Acocella, Giovanni Balcet, Gian Carlo Bisacchi, Terenzio Cozzi, Silvana Dalmazzone, Enrico Filippi, Dino Martellato, Ferdinando Fasce, Angus Maddison, Ignazio Musu, Giuliano Petrovich, Sanjay Reddy, Salvatore Rossi, Marcello Signorelli, Renata Targetti Lenti, Pierangelo Maria Toninelli, Gianni Toniolo, and Maurizio Vaudagna.

Particular thanks are due to Luigi Oddo, who has skillfully provided the updating of most figures and tables for the English edition of the volume.

I finally thank the editors of the publisher Carocci for their important contribution to the Italian edition of the book and Laura Pacey and Clara Heathcock of Palgrave Macmillan for their very kind and competent supervision of the new English edition of the book.

Any errors or omissions are, of course, my complete responsibility.

Contents

1	**The Birth of a Great Economic Power**	1
	1.1 The Economic Ascent of the US	1
	1.2 The Economic Consequences of the Frontier	3
	References	8
2	**The Fordist Model of Economic Development**	11
	2.1 The Concept of Fordism	11
	2.2 The Fordist Model of Economic Development	14
	References	17
3	**The Great Depression and the New Deal**	19
	3.1 The Wall Street Crash	19
	3.2 The Great Depression	22
	3.3 The New Deal	24
	3.4 The Debate on the Great Depression and the New Deal	25
	References	30
4	**Return and Crisis of the Fordist Model of Development**	31
	4.1 The War and Its Consequences	31
	4.2 The Return to the Fordist Model: 1946–1969	32

	4.3	The Crisis of the Second Wave of the Fordist Model	37
	References		43

5 Capital Accumulation, Technological Progress, and Knowledge — 45
  5.1 The Main Determinants of Economic Development — 45
  5.2 Capital Accumulation — 47
  5.3 The Role of Technological Progress — 48
  5.4 The Importance of Knowledge — 52
  5.5 Structural Changes in the US Economy — 55
  5.6 Robots and the E-Economy — 57
  5.7 Summing Up — 59
  References — 62

6 The Global Power of the US — 65
  6.1 After Teheran and Yalta — 65
  6.2 The Main Points of Strength of the US Economy — 68
  6.3 The Economic Consequences of the Wars — 69
  6.4 Economic, Military, and Political Powers — 71
  6.5 The US and the Turin Index of Economic Power — 72
  References — 77

7 Main Weaknesses in the American Economic Power — 79
  7.1 The Dependence on Foreign Oil and Other Raw Materials — 79
  7.2 The Environmental Problem in the US — 82
  7.3 Phases of Ascent and Decline of the US Economy — 83
  7.4 From Surplus to Structural Deficit in the US Balance of Current Accounts — 84
  7.5 The Weakening of the Dollar — 87
  7.6 Rising Inequalities in Wages, Income, and Wealth — 90
  7.7 Terrorism and Organized Crime — 93
  7.8 The Withering of the American Dream — 94
  7.9 The Erosion of Democracy — 96
  References — 101

8 Toward a Global Economic Empire — 103
8.1 The Instruments — 103
8.2 Post-war Aids and the Marshall Plan — 104
8.3 The Path toward Trade Liberalization — 105
8.4 Foreign Direct Investment and the Growth of the US Presence in the World — 108
8.5 The US and the Third Wave of Economic and Financial Globalization — 112
8.6 The Financial Supremacy — 116
8.7 Ideology and the American Lifestyle — 117
8.8 The Influence of Media and Internet — 118
8.9 The Power of Arms and Diplomacy — 118
References — 122

9 The Great Recession — 125
9.1 Why the Great Financial Crises? — 125
9.2 The US Sub-prime Financial Crisis — 126
9.3 The Great Recession — 130
9.4 The Inadequacy of Controls — 134
9.5 Possible Remedies — 135
9.6 A Comparison with the Great Depression — 137
References — 141

10 Obanomics — 143
10.1 Obama's Ideas on Economics — 143
10.2 Obama's Response to the Great Recession — 144
10.3 The Industrial and Innovation Policy — 151
10.4 Obama and the Environment — 152
10.5 Obamacare — 156
10.6 Inequality, Taxation, and the Middle-Class Crunch — 159
References — 161

11	**The Economic Consequences of Donald Trump**	**163**
	11.1 Populism and Trumpism	163
	11.2 Donald Trump's Victory in the 2016 Presidential Election	166
	11.3 The Relations with Economic and Financial Power	167
	11.4 America First	168
	11.5 The Neo-Protectionist Policy	170
	11.6 The Reform Tax Bill	173
	11.7 Trump's Policy on Health Care and Environment	174
	References	179
12	**America's Decline? Toward an Imperfect Multipolar World**	**181**
	12.1 America's Decline?	181
	12.2 China: The Other Economic Giant	185
	12.3 The Role of the European Union	190
	12.4 Russia, Japan, India, and Other Emerging Powers	194
	12.5 The Nongovernmental Powers	200
	12.6 The Fragility of International Organizations	201
	12.7 Conclusions	203
	References	205
Statistical Appendix		**207**
Index		**215**

List of Figures

Fig. 1.1	The economic consequences of the frontier	5
Fig. 2.1	The Fordist model of development in the US	15
Fig. 3.1	The great depression in the US	22
Fig. 3.2	Fascist corporatism versus democratic neo-corporatism	29
Fig. 4.1	US real output per hour and real adjusted hourly earnings: 1950–2017	33
Fig. 5.1	The pyramid of economic development	46
Fig. 6.1	Economic, political, and military powers	72
Fig. 7.1	US oil dependence from abroad: 1949–2017	80
Fig. 7.2	Balance of current accounts in the US economy in percent of GDP: 1960–2016	86
Fig. 7.3	US dollar rates of exchange: 1968–2017	88
Fig. 7.4	The erosion of democracy	99
Fig. 8.1	US exports and imports of goods and services in the US: 1950–2016	107
Fig. 8.2	US outward and inward FDI stocks in selected years: 1980–2016	109
Fig. 9.1	Real GNP in the great depression and in the great recession	137
Fig. 10.1	Ecological Footprint and Bio-capacity in the US: 1961–2014	154
Fig. 12.1	Total GDP in China, Russia, and India: 1978–2017	196
Fig. 12.2	The economic ascent of selected emerging countries: 1978–2017	197

List of Tables

Table 1.1	Population in the US and other selected countries: 1820–1913	4
Table 3.1	Indicators on the great depression in the US	23
Table 4.1	Rates of change of GDP and per capita GDP in selected economies: 1950–1973	35
Table 4.2	Main reasons for the rapid growth of selected economies in the years: 1950–1973	35
Table 5.1	Knowledge indicators in the US and other selected countries	54
Table 5.2	Employment by sector of economic activity in the US (%): 1870–2017	55
Table 6.1	Population, GDP, and per capita GDP in the US, Soviet Union and Russia: 1950–1991	66
Table 6.2	Selected internal indicators in selected countries	73
Table 6.3	Exports, stock of outward FDI, and persons employed in R&D	74
Table 6.4	The TIEP: 1952, 2008, and 2017	75
Table 7.1	Phases of ascent and decline of the US economy: 1870–2017	83
Table 8.1	Selected indicators on economic globalization: 1980–2016	106
Table 8.2	Selected indicators of the US in the third globalization wave	114
Table 9.1	The great recession in the US and in selected EU countries	133

List of Tables

Table 9.2	Real GDP and real per capita GDP in the two US great crises	138
Table 9.3	A comparison between the great depression and the great recession	139
Table 10.1	Annual % rate of change of real GDP in selected areas or countries: 2007–2017	145
Table 10.2	Harmonized % unemployment rates in selected areas or countries: 2007–2017	146
Table 10.3	Federal receipts, outlays, deficits, and debt as percent of GDP: 2007–2019	149
Table 12.1	The US and China: selected indicators	185
Table A1	Population in the US and in the selected countries (million)	207
Table A2	Total GDP in PPP, not adjusted to ICT prices, in the US and in selected countries (US = 100)	208
Table A3	GDP per-capita in PPP, not adjusted to ICT prices, in the US and in selected countries (US = 100)	209
Table A4	Macroeconomic indicators in the US and in selected countries: 1952–2017	210
Table A5	Macroeconomic indicators for the US in the period 1980–2017	211
Table A6	Other indicators for the US in the period 1980–2017	212
Table A7	Full-time and part-time employees by industry in the US: 1950–2017	213

1

The Birth of a Great Economic Power

1.1 The Economic Ascent of the US

In the last decades of the nineteenth century, the US had become the main economic power in the world. According to Maddison's estimates of total Gross Domestic Product (GDP) in purchasing power parities (PPP), in 1872 the US surpassed the main industrial power of those years, the UK.[1] Then it surpassed two poorer but much more populous countries such as India and China in 1876 and around 1886 respectively, becoming the country with the largest total GDP in the world.

While in 1870, China, India, and the UK had a total GDP in PPP larger than the US by 93%, 37%, and 18%, respectively; in 1913, the situation had radically changed: the US had a total GDP in PPPs 2.1 times larger than China, 2.3 times larger than the UK, 2.5 times larger than India.[2]

In the years 1870–1913, the US had accomplished a great *relative economic ascent*. With this concept I mean a prolonged period (two decades at least), in which the rate of growth of the economy, measured by the average annual rate of change of per capita GDP, is significantly higher than the world rate of growth. In those years, the percent annual rate of change of per capita GDP of the US had in fact been 1.82, while the world average had been 1.3.[3] The last quarter of the nineteenth century and the first years of the twentieth century saw the formation of the US economic dominance, which clearly manifested itself in the following years.

In that period, the perception of such a profound change in the world economic equilibria was, however, very limited. In those days, there were no synthetic economic indicators, such as GDP, and it was therefore very difficult to perceive and correctly assess the importance of world economic transformations. Moreover, the great Western European powers, the UK, France, and Germany had a vast colonial empire, so their economic strength was augmented by the important economic and financial links with their colonies.

There was, moreover, a remarkable ignorance of what was happening out of their national boundaries or out of their empires even in some of the prominent political leaders. Education at school was then, as it is today, strongly nationalistic, and in Europe, euro-centric, but its effects were not attenuated, as it now happens, by extensive travelling abroad, the massive diffusion of international media and the widespread use of internet.

In any case, the colonial empires, though vast and powerful, were giants with clay feet. They were destined, in the long run, to dissolve, as it happened in three-four decades after the Second World War. They were, in fact, undermined by four intrinsic weaknesses.

From the economic point of view, the European empires were substantially based on the principle *center-periphery*. The rapid growth of industry and of modern tertiary activities, and so a faster economic growth, was mainly concentrated in the center of the empire, while the periphery (the colonies) acted mainly as furnishers of raw materials and as a market for manufactured goods. It follows that there was a very unequal economic growth in the center and in the periphery of such empires and therefore large and growing tensions towards a social and economic resurgence of colonies.

Within colonial empires, there were, moreover, great ethnic, linguistic, and religious differences, which in the long-run contributed to undermine their existence.

The marked difference in citizenship status among the inhabitants of the center and of the periphery of the empires contributed to induce the discriminated or disadvantaged people of the colonies to rebellion and to a fierce search for independence.

Finally, there was a strong territorial discontinuity which made the movements of armies and security forces in all the empire's zones difficult, costly, and time-consuming. It is not by chance that in a few decades after the Second World War all colonial empires dissolved while the US, China, India, and Russia, which had a full or quasi-complete territorial continuity, could survive, although since 1947 India had suffered from the dramatic India-Pakistan partition, and in 1991 there had been the dissolution of the Soviet Union.

The prodigious economic ascent of the US in the years 1870–1913 is mainly due to three elements:

1. The existence of the *frontier* until the beginning of the twentieth century
2. The consequent rapid expansion of *population* and of *technical progress*, and therefore of real productivity and real GDP
3. The activation, when the advantages of the frontier began to gradually shrink, of the *fordist model of development* that contributed to prolong the possibility of the rapid economic growth of the US economy

1.2 The Economic Consequences of the Frontier

After reaching independence, and in particular during the nineteenth century, the US fully utilized a crucial and peculiar growth determinant: *the frontier*, namely, the possibility to move west to exploit new natural resources.[4]

In the west, there were abundant arable lands, pastures, mines for gold and other important minerals, coal and oil fields, forests, water resources, buffaloes, furs, fish-rich lakes, rivers, and the ocean.

The existence of the frontier had permitted the US to dispose of enough food and national resources to be able to rapidly expand its population. The rapid growth of the US population was due to the acquisition of vast, new territories, often at the cost of the extermination of a large part of the preexisting indigenous tribes, and to the positive demographic natural rate and to the continuous large net inflow of immigrants.

While even in the richest European countries, such as the UK and France, the population was growing very slowly, in the US it was growing very fast. As we can see in Table 1.1, in 1820 the total US population was less than half of the UK population and less than one third of France's, but in 1870 it had already surpassed the level of the two great European powers, and in 1913, it had more than doubled.

The rapid expansion of the population contributed to an increase in the demand for goods and services, stimulating a massive rise in the investment of enterprises and of public and private investment in infrastructures, such as railways, roads, ports, schools, and hospitals.

The existence of the frontier also led to a strong technological progress, as it is shown in Fig. 1.1. The mere possibility for specialized workers in the eastern coast or in Chicago to move to the West increased, ceteris paribus, the contractual strength of skilled workers vis-à-vis their entrepreneurs, and therefore the possibility of obtaining wage rises.

This, together with the pressure of the ascending labor unions in the last decades of the nineteenth century, pushed the enterprises to innovate and invest more in new *labor-saving* machines and in modern plants in order to be able to increase labor productivity and to maintain acceptable profit margins. These forms of *intensive investment* generally embodied

Table 1.1 Population in the US and other selected countries: 1820–1913 (in millions)[a]

Years	France	Germany	UK	Italy	US
1820	31.3	24.9	21.2	20.2[b]	10.0
1870	38.4	39.2	31.4	27.9	40.2
1913	41.5	65.0	45.6	37.2	97.6

Source: Maddison (2003), pp. 36–37, 81–82
[a]With the present borders
[b]Before unification, but assuming the present borders

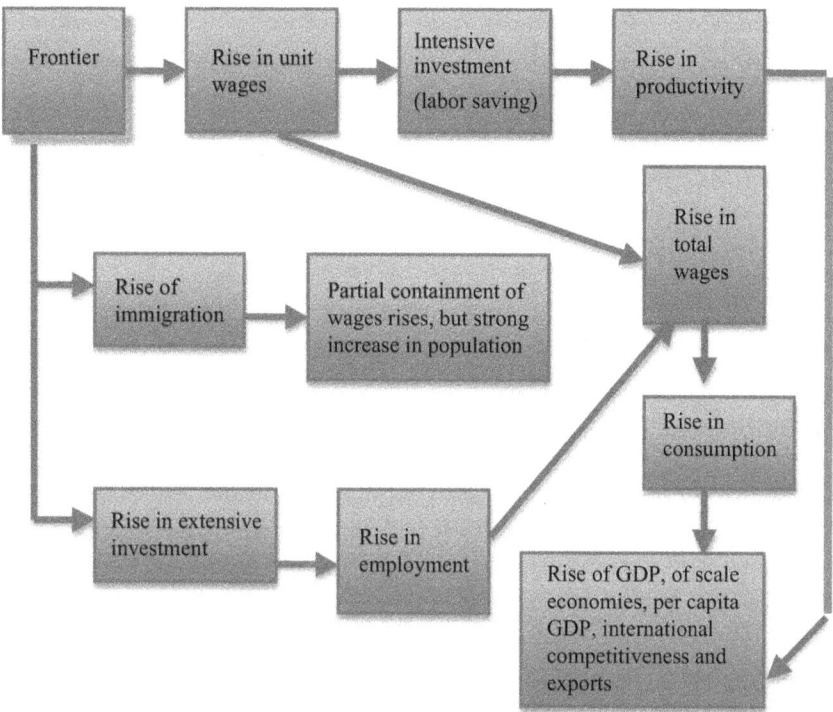

Fig. 1.1 The economic consequences of the frontier
Source: Our elaboration

new technologies, therefore leading to a general rise in the level of technological progress and of labor productivity.

In order to attenuate the rise in wages, there was also the growing recourse to a large mass of immigrants, made possible by the existence of the frontier. But at the same time, the frontier induced also to make *extensive investment* aimed at increasing productive capacity and employment. The rise in population and consumption required in fact new railway lines, new roads, bridges, houses, and shops. It was necessary to supply new-born and immigrants with food, clothes, and other goods and services. All this contributed to raise investment, production, and employment. The rise in unit wages and in employment led to a rapid increase in total wages and therefore the consumption, and this induced to make further extensive investment in order to adapt the level of production to the continuous rise in demand. The rise in productive capacity led, in certain sectors, to large-scale economies, which contributed to increase in productivity and therefore international competitiveness. Exports grew and their revenues contributed to finance imports and to sustain the value of the US dollar. The economies of scale also favored, in certain sectors, economic concentration, and thus the constitution of very large corporations. The presence of large numbers of workers in the vast plants of the major corporations favored, on the other hand, the birth of a *countervailing power*,[5] namely, the constitution of powerful labor unions and of liberal or leftist political parties. The massive rise of both intensive and extensive investment led to a rapid growth of GDP, per capita GDP, and labor productivity. The rate of change of total GDP is approximately equal to the sum of the rate of change of population and the rate of change of per capita GDP.[6] In the US, both the addenda grew very fast, so their sum grew even more rapidly. This permitted the US to reach and then surpass and rapidly distance the level of total GDP in PPP of the other major industrialized country, the UK. In 1872, the US had in fact surpassed the level of total GDP of the UK, which had been the largest industrial power at the time. About three decades later, in 1905, the US per capita GDP came to exceed that of the UK and then rapidly outdistanced it. The US labor productivity, measured by GDP divided by employment, which in 1870 was 88% of that of the UK, overtook it in the early twentieth century and in 1913 exceeded the UK's level by about 15%.[7]

In 1913, the US not only was the largest economy in the world, but also the most advanced in terms of the average level of technology, per capita GDP, and labor productivity. The existence of the frontier, the lack of a feudal heritage, and other historical and cultural elements were also able to inject significant amounts of democracy and freedom in American society as well as a considerable social mobility.[8] While in the nineteenth century, the latter worked almost exclusively for white Anglo-Saxon men and much less for women, blacks, Hispanics, and American Indians, nonetheless, it had allowed the emergence of the so-called *American Dream*, the ability of each man to be able to successfully forge his future counting on his skills and commitment to work.

However, in 1913, the advantages of the frontier, which were the highest in the nineteenth century, had largely vanished. Most of the western lands had already been sold or rented, many mines of gold and other minerals had already been discovered and exploited, the buffaloes exterminated, and large forests destroyed. A number of resources, such as large oil fields, then only partially discovered and put into production, still remained to be exploited. Moreover, lands in several western states and the Midwest were still largely publicly owned and could be rented at prices far lower than the average European price. This allowed to cultivate only the most fertile lands and to apply extensive cultivation, which was more profitable than the intensive one prevailing in many parts of Europe and Asia, which were much more densely populated.

Since 1908, however, the US could begin to replace some of the declining advantages associated to the frontier, with the benefits arising from the *Fordist model of development*. The introduction of this model can be traced back to the opening of the first large-scale automotive plant producing with large assembly lines a car much cheaper than previous models: the famous Ford Model T. This model was produced in over 17 million units from 1908 to 1927. It did cost at the beginning about $ 850, less than half the price of competing models. The price further diminished over time due to economies of scale and production improvements, reaching $285 for the basic version in 1926–1927. Cars, which previously were a luxury good for a few rich people, became a mass-product, accessible to middle- and upper-middleclass people and even to a growing share of workers in the car industry. This was the beginning of the *Fordist phase* of American economic development. It was similar in some aspects to the one prevailing in Western Europe and Japan about 40 years later, in the 1950s and 1960s, and in emerging countries like China in the years 1980s and 1990s and in the early twenty-first century.

The First World War, which the US entered alongside the allied forces against the German and Austrian troops, only partially interrupted the fordist phase in the US. The war, which led to a large number of casualties and a temporary reduction of civilian production in some areas, had, however, allowed the US to move its productive force and Fordist methods of production from the civil to the military sector and to transfer subsequently some technological military advancements to the civil sector. Overall, the First World War, although causing about 117,000 US casualties, left the US strengthened militarily, politically, and economically, significantly increasing its economic power in the world.

Notes

1. See Maddison (2001, 2003, 2007). Total GDP, though being a very rough and incomplete indicator, gives us an idea of the economic size of a country. The measures in PPP take into account the actual purchasing power of a currency in different countries and so they permit more reliable comparisons among countries than the ones based on official rates of exchange.
2. See Maddison (2001), p. 261.
3. See Maddison (2003), p. 263.
4. On the importance of the frontier in the US economic development, see for example, Turner (1920), Williams (1961), Habakkuk (1962). For more general views on the main aspects of American economic development since 1870, see Beard and Beard (1921), North (1961), Kuznets (1966), Denison (1974), Valli (1978), Vaudagna (1981), Pianta (1988), Landes et al. (1991), Mammarella (2003), Teodori (2008), Gordon (2016).
5. See Galbraith (1967).
6. The rate of change of GDP is equal to the rate of change of population plus the rate of change of per capita GDP, plus the product of the two rates of change. Since last term is very small, for approximate calculations it is usually omitted.
7. See Maddison (2001), p. 349. Total and per capita GDP and labor productivity are all calculated in PPP Geary Khamis (GK).
8. On the particular characters of American democracy, see the classical book by Alexis de Tocqueville (1835–1840).

References

Beard, C.A., and M.R. Beard. 1921. *History of the United States*. London: Macmillan.

Denison, E.F. 1974. *Accounting for U.S. Economic Growth*. Washington, DC: Brookings Institution.

de Toqueville, A. 1835–1840. *De la démocratie en Amerique*. Italian translated by G. Candeloro. *La democrazia in America*. Milano: BUR, 1999.
Galbraith, J.K. 1967. *The New Industrial State*. Princeton: Princeton University Press.
Gordon, R.J. 2016. *The Rise and Fall of American Growth: The U.S. Standard of Living Since the Civil War*. Princeton: Princeton University Press.
Habakkuk, H.J. 1962. *American and British Technology in the Nineteenth Century*. Cambridge: Cambridge University Press.
Kuznets, S. 1966. *Modern Economic Growth*. New Haven and London: Yale University Press.
Landes, D.S., P. Higgonet, and H. Rosovsky. 1991. *Favorites of Fortunes: Technology, Growth, and Economic Development since the Industrial Revolution*. Cambridge: Harvard University Press.
Maddison, A. 2001. *The World Economy: A Millenium Perspective*. Paris: OECD.
———. 2003. *The World Economy: Historical Statistics*. Paris: OECD.
———. 2007. *Contours of the World Economy, 1-2030 AD; Essays in Macroeconomic History*. Oxford: Oxford University Press.
Mammarella, G. 2003. *Storia degli Stati Uniti dal 1945 ad oggi*. Roma and Bari: Laterza.
North, D.C. 1961. *The Economic Growth of the United States, 1790–1860*. Upper Saddle River, NJ: Prentice-Hall.
Pianta, M. 1988. *New Technologies across the Atlantic: US Leadership or European Autonomy?* Hemel Hempstead: Wheatsheaf.
Teodori, M. 2008. *Storia degli Stati Uniti e il sistema politico americano*. Roma: Newton Compton.
Turner, F.J. 1920. *The Frontier in the American History*. New York: Henry Holt. Italian transl. *La frontiera nella storia americana*, Bologna, il Mulino, 1959, 1975.
Valli, V. 1978. *Il sistema economico americano: 1945–1977*. Milano: Etas libri.
Vaudagna, M. 1981. *Corporativismo e New Deal, Integrazione e conflitto sociale negli Stati Uniti (1933–1941)*. Torino: Rosenberg.
Williams, W.A. 1961. *The Contours of American History*. Cleveland: The World Publishing Company. Italian transl. *Storia degli Stati Uniti*, Bari, Laterza, 1964, 2 vols.

2

The Fordist Model of Economic Development

2.1 The Concept of Fordism

Antonio Gramsci, in *Americanism and Fordism*,[1] introduced the concept of *Fordism*, which was then taken up, with somewhat different meanings, by many other authors and schools of thought.

Gramsci laid special emphasis on the Taylorist organization of work and production in the large Fordist factory, accompanied by rising wages that facilitated the reluctant consent of workers to operate in worse working conditions. *Taylorism* entailed large mechanization in factories; specialization and fragmentation of the production process; ceaseless repetition and simplification of tasks, gestures, and movements of workers; increase of the intensity and pace of work; and increased coercion on workers and pressure on labor unions. The common factory worker was subject to higher alienation and largely lost the need to use much of her/his brain and particular skills in the job.

Anyone who, even temporarily, has experienced or observed work at the assembly line of an old Fordist factory knows that the fast and continuous mechanical repetition of a few gestures requires the use of a limited portion of the brain to avoid injury to the worker or the damage of handled pieces. This leads the mind to wander, and daydreaming contributes to a gradual intellectual impoverishment, if there is no corrective action of robust intellectual activities outside working time.

Gramsci, however, thought that this type of work in any case allowed the workers to think more than before, and this could lead to rebellion, so that entrepreneurs used to introduce various training activities for their workers, partly in order to counter this danger.

Gramsci argued, moreover, that *Fordism* increased production, productivity, and profits and therefore allowed for wage increases that diminished the resistance of workers. He believed that *Fordism* had been rooted first and most successfully in the US, while it had encountered serious obstacles in Italy and the rest of Europe in the 1920s and 1930s. This happened because in the US there were no residuals of the feudal regime, there was no opposition of parasite classes, there was a strong business and financial autonomy and a legal system that allowed industrial and financial concentration.

Gramsci, however, in his analysis underestimated the importance of the much larger size of the US market, compared with each individual European country, and of its faster rate of growth. So, in those years, in the US, the importance of economies of scale was much more sizable than in the smaller and less dynamic European productive systems. After 1914, most European economies were also heavily protected by a long series of tariffs and quotas, only partially removed after the First World War, but re-enforced in the 1930s.

If *Fordism* is associated with Henry Ford and his Model T, some aspects of the same, like *Taylorism* and the production chain, had already been introduced in the slaughterhouses of Chicago, while others, as the strong rise in wages and the reduction of working hours, were introduced in the Ford corporation later than 1908 and, although finally decided by Henry Ford, derived largely from a tough confrontation with the unions.

Another key-aspect of *Fordism* was, in fact, a substantial growth in wages and a large cut in working hours. In 1914, Henry Ford decided to raise the minimum wage to $5 per day, more than double the average of other companies, and reduce working hours from 9 to 8 per day using the facilities 24 hours a day on three shifts. It was, however, not a generous and spontaneous decision by Henry Ford, but the outcome of a hard struggle with the unions in the years 1908–1913, and it was made possible by the enormous productivity gains resulting from the new plants and production methods.

The chain of productive interdependencies was crucial to the generalization of the model to other sectors. The car is produced with raw materials and components of the steel industry and of many other sectors, which in turn get their supplies from firms in other sectors. Moreover, cars and other motor vehicles need gasoline, sale and repair shops, roads, bridges, and so on. Many of the companies providing these goods or services had large economies of scale and could also adopt Fordist methods.

Another more complex concept of *Fordism* is due to the French school of *regulation*, which flourished in the years 1970s and 1980s with authors such as Aglietta, Boyer, Mistral, Lipietz, and others. The *regulation school*, nourished by influences of Marxism and structuralism, was born with the 1976 book by Aglietta, *A Theory of Capitalist Regulation: The US Experience*. This approach is based on two fundamental concepts: "regimes of capital accumulation" and "modes of regulation".[2] The first concept involves a period of relative stability in the margins of profits and the rate of growth of capital accumulation. When the paradigm changes and the economy enters a structural crisis, the regulation mode changes, that is, there is a transformation of the entire series of socio-political and institutional elements that seek to restore profits and accumulation. The Fordist period is identified by these authors especially in the years 1945–1969. In this period, in several countries, there were mass production, mass consumption, Taylorism, macro-economic Keynesian policies, and all this led to high rates of growth of consumption, investment, and profits. Between the late 1960s and early 1970s that system went into crisis because of energy crises, inflation, labor disputes, and globalization, while Keynesism went into crisis in many countries as the main inspiration to macro-economic policy.

The approach of the *regulation school* has some attractiveness, but a major weakness consisted in the overly ambitious attempt at jointly explaining very complex economic, social, and political-institutional transformations. Since at present we lack a satisfactory integrated social science and an adequate approach to the relations between micro- and macroeconomics, it is probably wiser to focus the analysis mainly on its macro-economic aspects, as will be done in the next section with my concept of the *Fordist model of development*.

It is also important to stress the large time lag—about 40 years—passing between the beginning of the *First Fordist wave* in the US and *the Second Fordist wave* in Western Europe and Japan, starting in the 1950s. There was another substantial time lag—about 30–40 years—passing between the second and the *Third Fordist wave*, mixed with some Toyotist elements, operating in China and then in India and in several other emerging countries since the 1980s.[3]

2.2 The Fordist Model of Economic Development

If we do not consider the crucial microeconomic aspects, such as the working conditions in factories, and the more general political and institutional aspects, and try only to isolate the macro-economic fundamental relations of Fordism, we can outline what I have called the *Fordist model of Economic development*, that is represented in a stylized way in Fig. 2.1.

The essential elements of the model are the *economies of scale, of network*, and *of scope* and the rise in unit wages. Around 1908, the US had a large and rapidly increasing market. Large manufacturing firms such as Ford corporation, could obtain strong *economies of scale* (a rise in scale, i.e. the size of production, could reduce unit production costs) and *economies of network* (e.g., a large network of sales and assistance for very few automobiles is very expensive, but, if it regards a lot of cars, the unit costs are drastically reduced).

In the automobile and truck industry or in interrelated fields, like oil, one can also obtain *economies of scope (scope economies)*, that is, lower costs achieved through the joint production of different products or by achieving several objectives with the same inputs (same equipment, same resources, and same know-how).

The various types of economies (scale, network, and scope economies) can sharply increase labor productivity and thereby reduce the unit costs of production. The benefits of strong productivity growth can be redistributed in

The Fordist Model of Economic Development   15

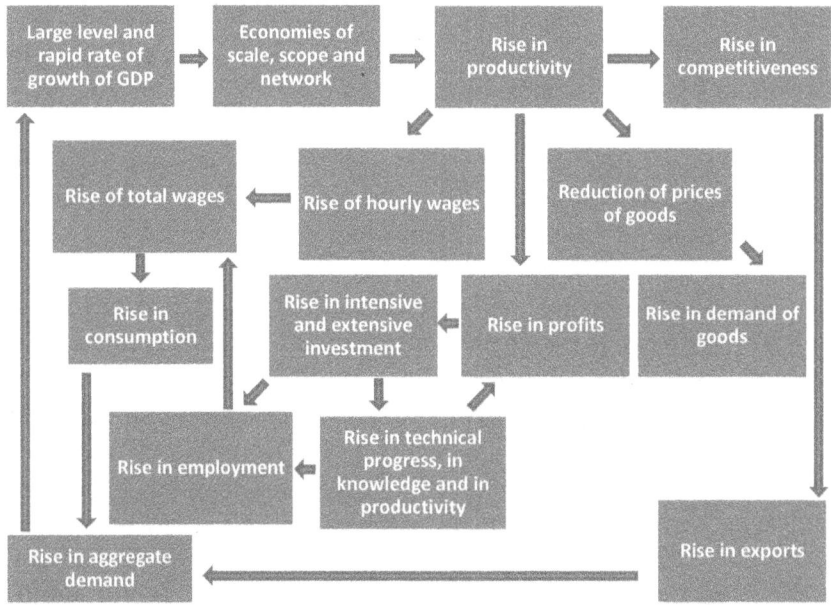

Fig. 2.1 The Fordist model of development in the US

three ways: (a) increasing wages for employees, (b) reducing the prices of goods produced (in our case the car) and then stimulating a strong growth in the demand for cars, (c) increasing, if possible, profit margins and even more, given the strong rise in sales, total profits. High profits and high expectations of increased sales lead to larger *extensive investment* (new plants, new machines, etc.).[4] This will undoubtedly determine further increases in productive capacity and output. There will also be a rise in *intensive investment* aimed at reducing labor costs through new labor saving technologies. Total investment can contribute to increase technical progress and knowledge, determining so a further rise in productivity.[5] A strong growth in both intensive and extensive investment leads to an increase in employment, which, in tandem with the increase in wages per employee, causes a rise in total wages.

This promotes a rise in consumption which, joined to the expansion of investment, leads to increased domestic demand. In turn, increased productivity conducts to greater international competitiveness and hence to more exports (in the case of the Ford T, this occurred mainly in Canada and the UK) and this helps to increase aggregate demand. The latter carries with it a further increase in GDP, in the size of the market, then in economies of scale, productivity, and so on. All this creates a development that feeds on itself, creating a sort of *virtuous circle of development*.

This virtuous circle was in no way restricted, in the years 1910 and 1920, only to the production of cars, but, by the chains of productive interdependence, it extended to many other sectors of industry and services. More cars meant more roads; more bridges; more tunnels; more sales agents and car rentals; and more service stations, garage for repairs, and car insurances. It meant more raw materials and components, thus more steel, more tires, more electric batteries, more leather or fabric for the interior, more petrol and gasoline. In turn, the large Fordist firms of steel, tire, or oil industries could trigger similar virtuous circles, through economies of scale, productivity gains, wage increases, and so on.

Besides the automobile industry and the interrelated sectors, other manufacturing sectors had similar effects on the US economy, although inferior in size. There was a rapid development in the production of tractors, trucks, motorcycles, airplanes, electrical household appliances, electricity; in banking and insurance services; and so on. The Fordist model became dominant in the US in the years 1910 and 1920 since it was generated by *a variety of economic sectors* with significant economies of scale or network economies. There was, however, an original sin in this rapid growth, namely the strict interrelation of the Fordist model with oligopolistic industry and of the latter with big banks and finance and with the rapid rise in stock market values. It thus prepared the violent crisis which culminated in the collapse of Wall Street in 1929 and in the *great depression* of the 1930s.

Notes

1. See Gramsci (1978).
2. See, for example, Aglietta (1976), Boyer (1990).
3. See Valli (2015) for the application of the Fordist-Toyotist model of development in China and India and Valli (2017) for Japan, Indonesia, and South Korea.
4. Capital formation can be conventionally divided into *extensive investment* and *intensive investment*. Traditionally, *extensive investments* are the ones

which increase output and employment (new plants or new machines added to the older ones and which require additional workers). *Intensive investments* can increase instead labor productivity, but not output and employment, and thus they can even reduce employment. This happens when there is the substitution of old machines with new ones that need less workers for the production of a given output. Actually, in practice, there is often a combination of extensive and intensive investment and in recent decades is more and more frequent, the introduction of new machines or new techniques that are able to extend output without a parallel increase of employment. There is thus an increase of both output and labor productivity (product/employment). Yet, the stagnation of employment can contribute to raise unemployment and depress the growth rate of internal demand, especially if wages rise less than labor productivity.

5. See, on the relations between capital accumulation, technical progress, and knowledge, Chap. 5.

References

Aglietta, M. 1976. *A Theory of Capitalist Regulation: The US Experience*. Brookings and London: Verso books.
Boyer, R. 1990. *The Regulation School: A Critical Introduction*. New York: Columbia University Press.
Gramsci, A. 1978. *Americanismo e fordismo*. Torino: Einaudi.
Valli, V. 2015. *The Economic Rise of China and India*. Torino: Accademia University Press.
———. 2017. *The Economic Rise of Asia: Japan, India and South Korea*. Torino: Accademia University Press.

3

The Great Depression and the New Deal

3.1 The Wall Street Crash

In October 1929, there was a dramatic fall in stock exchange prices. For several years, the values of shares had been pushed up by heavy waves of speculation in a poorly regulated financial system. A period of overly expansionary monetary policy had contributed to lead to the outbreak of a *financial bubble*. Stock prices increased, generating widespread expectations of further growth, and many traders bought shares committing to sell the same shares at a certain future date, hoping that the market price would continue to increase. This led to an excess of demand of shares over supply and hence to a rise in their prices, inducing many investors and speculators to buy new shares, and thus creating the bubble. This could not go on endlessly. When the monetary authorities stiffened the money supply a little, the bubble burst, like a big soap bubble punctured by a needle. Thus, there were two very violent falls in stock prices, on October 24 and 29, 1929 (*Black Thursday*). In the two following years, the New York Stock Exchange and the American financial and banking system deteriorated in a dramatically cumulative way. The Dow Jones index fell again during 1931 by 52.7%, the worst annual result ever.

© The Author(s) 2018
V. Valli, *The American Economy from Roosevelt to Trump*,
https://Doi.org/10.1007/978-3-319-96953-4_3

Those who had made purchases of shares or other securities by obtaining bank loans pledging their shares, suffered from the collapse of collateral values. Soon they were asked to return the loans obtained by the banks and were forced to sell their assets, losing money or failing. Banks, fearful of growing losses and the falling value of the guarantees obtained from customers, reduced loans and credit lines, creating difficulties even to the most solid clients and forcing them to sell shares or other securities in the portfolio, or housing properties, in order to obtain liquidity. The excess supply of shares and houses led to further price falls determining a vicious circle. Many small and medium-size banks began to fail, because some of their clients had failed or because the rising panic induced depositors to withdraw their deposits (*bank run*). All this damaged even the larger and more solid banks, which reduced the interbank lending. Several financiers and speculators, economically ruined, committed suicide, increasing the collective panic.

The financial crisis became a crisis in real variables, like GDP, investment, and consumption, through seven different *transmission mechanisms*.[1]

The first mechanism consisted in the already mentioned strong reduction in banks' loans to industrial or service sectors. This contributed, along with the worsening of expectations on aggregate demand, to greatly reduce real investment, self-realizing the expectations of the fall in demand, since investment is an important component of aggregate demand.

The second mechanism was associated to the close relationship that existed between some investment banks and industrial companies: the former gave large loans to the latter and controlled a substantial part of their shares. When the economy was expanding all went well. When the crisis became very severe and several non-financial companies failed or reached the verge of bankruptcy, most banks began to suffer. For some time, banks were forced to increase their loans to companies in difficulty to avoid their bankruptcy, but this generally worsened the situation until the failure became inevitable. This led to heavy losses for the banks themselves, some of which finally went into bankruptcy.

The third mechanism was a *wealth effect*. Holders of shares or property, registering a sharp fall in the prices of their assets, felt less rich or more poor, and so reduced consumption, which diminished the propensity of the firms to invest. By consequence, aggregate internal demand (consumption + investment) collapsed.

The fourth mechanism consisted in the feedback between the labor market, income distribution, and aggregate demand. Firms in difficulty reduced unit wages and employment, so also total wages and consumption, and in this way they were further worsening their situation, because of the fall in their sales. Lower profits or corporate losses led to lower investment, but also to reduced consumption on the part of the capitalists and entrepreneurs whose businesses had suffered from the crisis. Aggregate demand collapsed because of the fall of both consumption and investment.

The fifth mechanism involved economies of scale, or of network, or of scope, for the sectors where they were important. The contraction of consumption and sales led to lower economies of scale, lower productivity, lower wages and profits, lower investment and employment, and so on. *The mechanism of the Fordist model of development was thus going backward way*, leading to serious business losses.

The sixth mechanism was associated to international economic relations. The crisis, once started, led to fewer imports and to a series of protectionist measures imposed by the Roosevelt administration, which triggered protectionist retaliations by other countries, higher tariffs, and therefore a reduction in US exports. Exports also lowered further due to the crisis of European economies, which were infected in greater or lesser extent from the consequences of the American great depression. Finally, the suspension of the US aid to Germany, which had to pay large war reparations to Britain and France, reduced the possibility of exports from the US to all three countries and worsened the German financial and economic situation contributing to open the way to the advent of Nazism.

The last transmission mechanism acted through the international monetary system. The crisis led, in fact, the American authorities to drop the strict linkage of the US dollar to the gold, thereby weakening the already precarious equilibria in the international monetary system and in the international movements of capitals, goods, and services.

3.2 The Great Depression

The Wall Street stock market crash had very serious and lasting repercussions on the real economy of the US.

As it can be seen in Fig. 3.1 and in Table 3.1, gross national product (GNP) in real terms fell by over 30% from 1929 to 1933. The economy began to recover slowly and painfully from 1933 onwards, but GNP reached the precrisis level of 1929 only ten years later, in 1939. Investment reached the 1929 level only in 1941, unemployment rate in 1943, exports in 1946. Table 3.1 also shows that the fall of real GNP was mainly due to the collapse of private investment (down 87% from 1929 to 1933); exports (−40%); and durable consumption goods, such as cars, electrical domestic appliances, or furniture (−49%). There was also a significant fall, but proportionally less accentuated, of the demand for non-durable consumer goods and services. Finally, there was a drop in the general level of prices, including those of agricultural products and foodstuffs, which heavily damaged agriculture for several years.

For over a decade, the Wall Street crash and the subsequent great depression had abruptly stopped the functioning of the Fordist model of development.

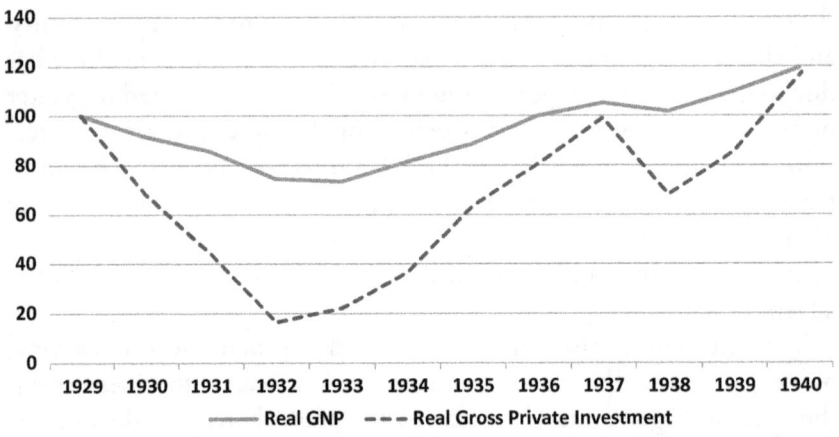

Fig. 3.1 The great depression in the US. Real GNP and Real gross private domestic investment at constant prices: 1929 = 100
Source: Department of Commerce-BEA (2017), our elaboration

Table 3.1 Indicators on the great depression in the US[a]

Year	GNP	Gross private investment	Personal consumption	Of which: durable consumption	Exports	Prices: GNP deflator	Rate of unemployment (%)
1929	203.6	40.4	139.6	16.3	11.8	100.0	3.2
1933	141.5	5.3	112.8	8.3	7.1	77.6	24.9
1939	209.4	24.7	148.2	14.5	10.0	85.4	17.2
1940	227.2	33.0	155.7	16.7	11.0	86.6	14.6

Source: CEA, *Economic Report of the President* (1975), pp. 250 et seq.
[a]Levels of the variables in billions of $1958 for columns 2–6; column 7: index with base 1929 = 100; column 8: unemployment as percentage of civilian labor force

The virtuous circle of development inherent in the Fordist model was thus turned into a vicious circle.

The lower demand for cars, steel, tires, and so on led Henry Ford and other industrialists to drastically cut production, employment, and unit wages. There was therefore a deep fall in total wages and consumption, in profits and investment. There was also a sharp reduction in the benefits of scale and network economies and hence a fall in productivity. The US crisis spread to Canada and Europe, prompting protectionist policies in the US and other countries. The consequences of the crisis and of increased protectionism severely reduced exports.

The great depression had also a dramatic effect on employment and unemployment. Civil employment fell from 1929 to 1933 from 47.6 million units to 38.8 million (−19%). Unemployment rose from 1.6 million people in 1929 to 12.8 million in 1933. The rate of unemployment rose from 3.2% in 1929 to 24.9% in 1933.

The magnitude of the crisis and the social devastation it produced, as well as some episodes of violent repression of social conflicts, contributed to the defeat of the outgoing President Hoover and the victory of the democratic candidate Franklin Delano Roosevelt in the presidential election of 1932. The latter came to power in March 1933 and soon tried to forcefully respond to the great depression introducing a new policy approach: the *New Deal*.

3.3 The New Deal

In 1929–1932, with the republican president Hoover in power, the public action had been very weak and uncertain, both because of ideological reasons (excessive faith in liberalism and in market mechanisms and the consequent principle of minimum interference of the state in the economy), and serious errors in the economic and financial policy. For example, according to neo-classical monetarist authors such as Milton Friedman and Anna J. Schwartz,[2] the policy of the US central bank, the *Federal Reserve*, was "passive, defensive, hesitant". Indeed, it allowed the fall of one third of the nominal money supply from August 1929 to March 1933 and to the closing of over 5000 banks and 85,000 enterprises.

With the rise to power of the democratic president Franklin D. Roosevelt in March 1933, public intervention in the economy became much broader and articulate. In the election campaign, Roosevelt had promised the program of the *Three R's (Relief, Recovery, and Reform)*. He had also proclaimed that he was committed to a new contract (deal) with the American people.

In the *first hundred days* of his presidency and the years immediately following, Roosevelt therefore attempted at addressing the crisis with an impressive array of measures (*New Deal*) and the opening of several important new institutions. New Deal interventions affected the banking and financial system (*Banking Act* and *the Federal Securities Act*), agriculture (*Agricultural Adjustment Act*), investment in a depressed area (*Tennessee Valley Authority*), industry (*National Industrial Recovery Act*, or *NRA*), industrial relations and social security (*Norris-LaGuardia Act, Wagner Act, Social Securities Act, Fair Labor Standards Act*).

The measures of the New Deal, as well as helping the country out of the economic depression, allowed the US to adopt a social security system quite advanced by then, though more limited than that of some North-European countries. They also helped to reduce the dangers of a major new financial crisis with a greater regulation of financial markets and the separation between commercial banks and investment banks, introduced with the 1933 *Glass-Steagall Banking Act*. The New Deal also contributed to initiate the so-called *great compression*,[3] reducing in the years 1933–1960 the great wages disparities and economic and social inequalities that had grown in previous decades.

3.4 The Debate on the Great Depression and the New Deal

A number of scholars have debated on the determinants of the great depression. Keynes, who dedicated several analyses and suggestions of economic policy to the great depression, had put the accent on *the decline of long-term investment* and then of industrial profits and on the too high interest rates maintained before the Wall Street crash of 1929. He also sustained the need of *massive interventions of public expenditure* (public works, etc.) financed with debt to fight the crisis.[4]

The remedies to overcome the economic depression that Keynes suggested to the US administration as well as to other countries overwhelmed by the crisis are the following: (a) means to "restore the confidence both of the persons providing loans and the ones who borrow money (b) the creation of new development programs under the direct auspices of the government or other public authorities..." (c) "the reduction of interest rates in the long term...."[5]

As the usual Keynesian analysis suggests, these tools could increase both public and private investment and thus boost profits, income, and employment.

We must remember that in that period there were no worries about inflation. It was indeed a period of strong deflation, that is, of reduction in prices, while in general Keynes was in favor of a moderate increase in prices in order to stimulate investment.

Some monetarist economists, like Milton Friedman and Anna J. Schwartz, have instead focused primarily on the financial and stock market slump of 1929 and the monetary and economic policy errors made by the Federal Reserve and the US government. In particular, the Federal Reserve had failed to inject enough liquidity in time of crisis.

While Keynes had put particular emphasis on the fall in investment to explain the crisis, some other authors, such as Charles P. Kindleberger and John Kenneth Galbraith,[6] analyzed the complex interrelationship between monetary, financial, and real factors to determine the origin and the aggravation of the crisis.

Joseph Schumpeter[7] interpreted the crisis as a phase of recession in his economy's *long-waves*, that is, the long and profound economic fluctuations, in which the period of expansion were mainly spurred by clusters of important technological innovations. These long waves, including the periods of expansion and recession, could last nearly 50 years and the phase of recession could last approximately a quarter of a century.

The Austrian economist Josef Steindl,[8] in *Maturity and Stagnation in the U.S. economy*, attributed, like Keynes, the great depression mainly to the fall in investment, but made the latter depend primarily on long-term structural changes in the American economy. In particular, according to Steindl, in the US there had been a gradual increase over time in the relative and absolute importance of large monopolistic or oligopolistic companies relatively to small competitive companies. In times of crisis, the latter had to reduce prices, and this brought to the exit of less efficient firms and so to a reduction in the excess capacity of the system. On the contrary, monopolistic or oligopolistic firms, having higher and more resilient profit margins, did not generally reduce prices, but the percentage of capacity utilization. Now, investments depend, according to Josef Steindl, mainly on internal savings of firms, their profit rate, and their capacity utilization. Therefore, during the crisis, large firms made very few investments, being able to cope with any possible increase in demand with a simple increase in the use of their existing productive capacity.

My own interpretation of the great depression is based on a mix of some of the elements introduced by the above-mentioned authors, such as the previous slow-down of investment and aggregate demand; the errors in monetary and fiscal policy; the lack in regulations of the financial market; technological changes; the effects of oligopolies on prices and investment; and so on. However, it integrates all these elements with other important ones: the cumulative effects of stock-flow relations, the backward functioning of the Fordist model of growth, and the heavy fall in knowledge and in technological formation.

When a major financial crisis occurs, the value of some stocks, such as financial and real wealth, plunges and the value of other stocks, such as corporate, household, and public debts, severely increases. As we will see in greater detail in Chap. 9, all this powerfully contributes to lead to a great and lasting economic depression, unless an immediate vigorous countercyclical monetary and fiscal policy is made by the government. When the financial and real crises are started, the effects of the Fordist model of development become negative, and they become more and more negative as long as the recession continues. There is a decrease in aggregate demand and so lower economies of scale, as less productive capacity is utilized. Therefore, unit labor costs increase while prices remain low because of the fall in aggregate demand, and therefore, in most firms, profits collapse and become losses. Wages and employment decrease as long as the firms in difficulty try to cut wages and reduce employees. Total wages diminish and so consumption falls. Both extensive and intensive investments fall. Finally, the propagation of the economic crisis to other countries reduces exports and induces more protectionism, which encourages trade wars and further diminishes export opportunities.

The great depression also led to a sharp reduction in investment in physical capital and in knowledge, thus depressing also the flow of innovation and technological progress. The interpretation of the great depression gave rise to an intense debate, but also the New Deal led to a significant number of different interpretations. The crux of the problem was the combination of various types of influences on Roosevelt and his advisers during the New Deal. Above all, there was a complex mix between the liberal tradition of Roosevelt and the introduction of Keynesian policies and of corporatist ideas. According to Maurizio Vaudagna,[9] during the Hoover administration, there had been a particular type of *dual corporatism* between the state and the representatives of business. The New Deal can be so interpreted as the classic neo-corporatism or democratic *triadic corporatism* of the European school, between the state, business representatives, and the trade unions. In the 1930s, the crisis led, in fact, to increased social tensions and conflicts, channeled in the New Deal by means of a vigorous support for the resumption of trade unions and their institutional legitimacy. Thus, the normal method of solving social conflicts through participation of both social sides and the state was introduced. During the New Deal, the state intervened in a democratic, not authoritarian, way, while in fascist corporatism, the state used the jail, repression, and violence to regulate social conflicts. In the US, the judiciary system maintained its autonomy and trade unions were free, while in Fascism and Nazism, the judges were restrained by the government and the free unions became corporate unions controlled by the regime (see Fig. 3.2).

To reduce social conflicts, the state granted measures to sustain employment and to substantially improve the welfare state, through laws such as the Norris-La Guardia Act, the Wagner Act, and the Social Securities Act.

Neo-corporatism, plus a gradual resumption of the positive feedbacks of the Fordist model of development during the recovery, strongly contributed to the economic expansion. However, only the additional

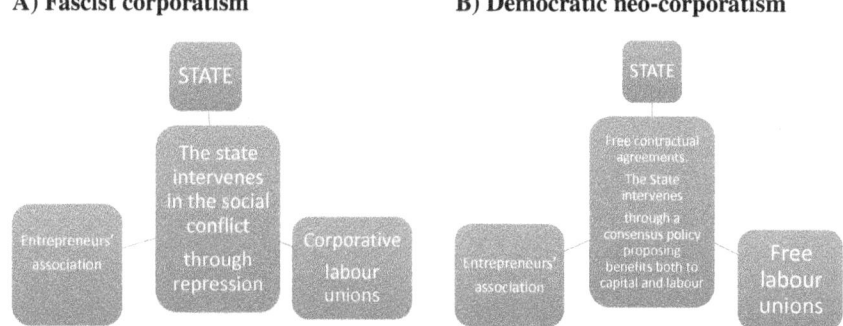

Fig. 3.2 Fascist corporatism versus democratic neo-corporatism

impulse given by the Second World War made it possible to complete and stabilize the economic expansion.

Yet, an important part of total production regarded the military effort, and this led to several difficulties for the reconversion to civilian production in the immediate post-war period.

During 1940s and 1950s, some of the achievements of unions and workers conquered during the New Deal were cancelled and there was an almost complete crisis of the neo-corporatist system. Yet, several improvements in the welfare system remained. Moreover, up to the Sixties, there was the continuation of the *great compression* of the inequalities in income, real wages, and wealth.

Notes

1. Further details on the mechanisms transforming financial crises into real crises are given in Chap. 9, when we will analyse *the great recession*.
2. See Friedman and Schwartz (1963).
3. See Goldin and Margo (1992).
4. See Keynes (1983).
5. See Keynes (1983), pp. 53–56.
6. See Kindleberger (1973) and Galbraith (1954).
7. See Schumpeter (1939).
8. See Steindl (1952).
9. See Vaudagna (1981a, b).

References

CEA (Council of Economic Advisers). 1975. *Economic Report of the President.* Washington, DC.
Friedman, M., and A.J. Schwartz. 1963. *The Great Contraction, 1929–1933.* Princeton: Princeton University Press.
Galbraith, J.F. 1954. *The Great Crash 1929.* Boston: Houghton Mifflin.
Goldin, C., and R. Margo. 1992. The Great Compression: The Wage Structure in the United States at Mid-Century. *Quarterly Journal of Economics* 107 (1): 1–34.
Keynes, J.M. 1983. *Come uscire dalla crisi.* Edited by P. Sabbatini. Roma and Bari: Laterza.
Kindleberger, C.P. 1973. *The World in Depression: 1929–1939.* Berkeley: University of California Press.
Schumpeter, J.A. 1939. *Business Cycles: A Theoretical, Historical and Statistical Analysis of the Capitalist Process.* New York and London: McGraw-Hill.
Steindl, J. 1952. *Maturity and Stagnation in American Capitalism.* Oxford: Basil Blackwell.
Vaudagna, M. 1981a. *Corporativismo e New Deal, Integrazione e conflitto sociale negli Stati Uniti (1933–1941).* Torino: Rosenberg.
———., ed. 1981b. *IL New Deal.* Bologna: Il Mulino.

4

Return and Crisis of the Fordist Model of Development

4.1 The War and Its Consequences

The Second World War led to large numbers of casualties, civilian and military, and extensive war destruction. The latter were, however, very limited in the territory of the US, which was only marginally touched by the war. The US emerged from the war plagued by a high rate of inflation and the difficulty to pass from military products to civilian ones, but stronger than ever in terms of economic, political, and military influence. The division of the world into two spheres of influence, the US in the West and the Soviet Union in the East, which had been decided in the Teheran and Yalta agreements, sanctioned a de facto situation. In the West, the US not only was the largest economy and the major technological and military power but it was also a great net creditor to the UK and France, which had emerged from the war weakened and heavily indebted. Not surprisingly, in the Bretton Woods agreements of 1944, that led to the establishment of the International Monetary Fund (IMF), the proposal of the US, advanced by White, prevailed over the much more far-sighted proposal by Keynes, the UK representative. Moreover, the US influence on major international economic organizations (IMF and World Bank) was predominant.

One aspect must be stressed. In the post-war years and in all the cold war period, the confrontation between the two super-powers, the US and the Soviet Union, was not, from the economic point of view, a confrontation between equals. In the whole 1918–1991 period, the Soviet Union never surpassed in terms of total GDP in PPP the 45% of the US level, and in terms of per capita GDP the gap was even greater.

So, in order to maintain a certain balance with the US in the military and strategic field, the Soviet Union had to badly compress civil production and household consumption, devoting a much higher proportion of its resources to military and strategic uses.

4.2 The Return to the Fordist Model: 1946–1969

With the conversion of the war economy to the civilian one, there was, in the US, a partial return to the Fordist model of development so that the American economy could participate to a certain extent also in the *second wave of the Fordist model of development* that mainly occurred in the 1950s and 1960s in Western Europe and Japan. In that period, the US automobile sector registered a recovery and then a sustained rise in output and sales. Other industrial sectors, such as those producing trucks, aircrafts, household electrical appliances, plastics, and chemicals, became increasingly important. However, since some of these sectors were, in the US, close to maturity, the growth impulse of the Fordist model was less important than in other industrialized countries, such as Japan, Western Europe, and Canada.

Cars, air travel, household appliances, and television drew along industries such as steel, plastic, petroleum, tires, electricity, advertising, and so on. Television also helped large companies to impose, through advertising, their branded products, sweeping away the competition of several small, marginal firms. There was therefore a rise in the industrial and financial concentration. The Fordist model of development contributed to the growth of labor productivity in real terms (see Fig. 4.1), which allowed the resumption and then the continuation of the increase in unit real wages up to the 1970s. Rising real wages were accompanied by a

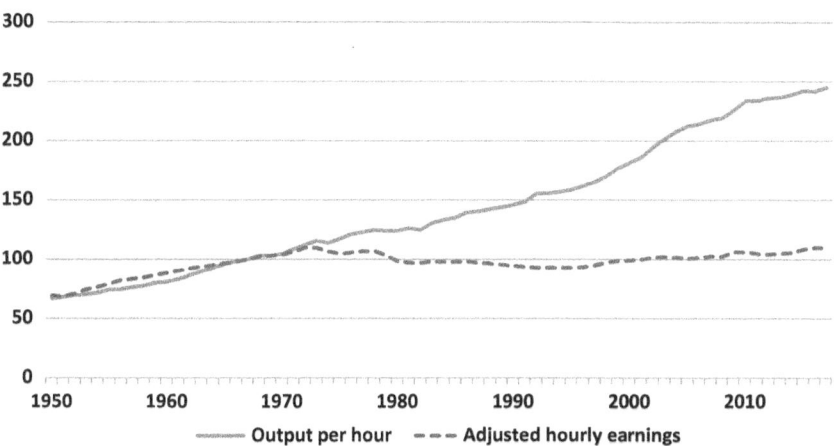

Fig. 4.1 US real output per hour and real adjusted hourly earnings: 1950–2017 (1967 = 100) (preliminary estimates for 2017). Total private nonagricultural sector
Source: Economic Report of the President (1980, 2018), our elaboration

consolidation of some aspects of the welfare state and by progressive taxation, so that there was a continuation of the *great compression* of economic and social inequalities until the end of the 1960s.

International conditions were, however, very different from those prevailing in the years 1910s and 1920s during the first wave of the Fordist model of development. In those decades, only the US was able, given its great size and the strong dynamics of the economy, to fully realize economies of scale and of network and therefore to have strong increases in productivity and wages. In the years 1950s and 1960s, other economies, such as France, Germany, Italy, Japan, Canada, Australia, and later on, Taiwan, South Korea, Spain, Portugal, were able to achieve their Fordist phase of development, that is, *the second wave of the Fordist model of development*. Other countries, like the Netherlands, Belgium, Canada, and then Ireland and Sweden, could also benefit from some aspects of the Fordist model. In these countries, the increasing liberalization of trade and the process of European economic integration made possible for large companies to easily sell their products on the largest EEC market or to establish subsidiaries in other member countries.

The UK could only tardily and very partially enjoy the benefits of the Fordist model. In fact, in the 1950s and 1960s, while the domestic market grew rather slowly, exports to the former colonies of the British

Empire shrank rapidly as these countries attained their independence and were therefore diversifying the sources of their imports. The UK had also delayed its entrance into the European Economic Community (EEC) until 1973, and the effects of the lack of participation in the EEC up to that year could not be fully offset by the participation to the much smaller European Free Trade Association (EFTA), founded in 1960 by the UK, Ireland, Austria, Iceland, Liechtenstein, Norway, and Switzerland.

The Soviet Union and the other Eastern European countries could enjoy but a very limited portion of the benefits of the Fordist model of development. In fact, central planners decided not to focus on producing mass-consumption goods like automobiles or some electric domestic appliances. Moreover, they did not substantially increase real unit wages and they did not take full advantage from the benefits of the diffusion of technological progress in the production for civilian use. In the 1950s and 1960s, the USSR and the Eastern European countries realized in any case a moderate pace of *extensive development*, based mainly on the growth of labor and capital inputs, but much less on the growth of productivity and technical progress. There were relatively few economic exchanges outside the protected CMEA area and Eastern Europe, and the Soviet Union did not constitute a strong competitor to the US firms in other markets, apart from the sale of weapons or of oil to several developing countries.

However, the US, which in the early 1950s had dominated many sectors of manufacturing and international services, was faced over the years with a growing and increasingly robust competition by enterprises of Western Europe and Japan, stimulated by the entrance in their Fordist phase of development. In 1950 and 1960, there was a period of exceptional growth, a veritable *golden age* of economic development in most Western European countries, and even more so in Japan. This rapid growth continued but with increasing difficulties until the first great energy crisis of 1973. As can be seen in Table 4.1, from 1950 to 1973, for several countries, there was *a relative economic ascent*, that is, a growth faster than the world average, and also a substantial catching up towards the level of the US. These countries included Japan and the four Eastern Asian tigers (South Korea, Taiwan, Hong Kong and Singapore), Germany, France, Italy, Spain, Canada, Australia, Mexico, and so on. By contrast, the UK had a relative economic decline and did not recover at all vis-à-vis the US, mainly because of the economic consequences of the progressive loss of its empire.

Various reasons, summarized in Table 4.2, are the basis of the extraordinary economic performance of some countries in Western Europe and Eastern Asia in the years 1950–1973.

One of the main reasons for these positive economic trends is, as we already know, the *second wave of the Fordist model of development*, which in the years 1950 and 1960 extensively involved Japan, Germany, Italy, France, the Netherlands, Belgium, Luxemburg, and so on and, later on, South Korea, Taiwan, and Singapore.

Table 4.1 Rates of change of GDP and per capita GDP in selected economies (1950–1973)

Country	GDP	Per capita GDP
Japan	9.3	8.1
South Korea	8.0	5.8
Germany	5.7	5.0
Italy	5.6	5.0
France	5.1	4.0
USSR	4.8	3.4
US	3.9	2.5
UK	2.9	2.4
World	4.9	2.9

Average annual compound rates of change on the data in PPP GK
Source: Maddison (2003), pp. 260, 263, 298, 304

Table 4.2 Main reasons for the rapid growth of selected economies in the years 1950–1973

Countries	Fordist model of development	Advantages of relative economic backwardness	European economic integration	Advantages from growing economic openness	Low cost of oil and other raw materials
US	X			X	X
Japan	X	X		X	X
South Korea	X	X		X	X
Germany	X	X	X	X	X
Italy	X		X	X	X
France	X		X	X	X

A second reason, partly interconnected with the first one, is due to the *advantages of relative economic backwardness*.[1] These advantages were enjoyed, but at a gradually decreasing pace, principally by Japan, Italy, South Korea, and Taiwan. The first main advantage consists in the possibility of moving labor from low productivity sectors such as agriculture, to sectors where productivity is higher, such as industry and modern services. A second advantage is associated to the possibility of acquiring, through purchase or imitation, the most advanced technology from more industrialized countries, such as the US, Germany, and France. In 1950, these countries were already economically and technologically advanced and could enjoy this benefit to a more limited extent than latecomer countries, such as Japan, Italy, South Korea and Taiwan.

The third reason is due, for Germany, Italy, France, the Netherlands and Belgium, to the positive effects of European economic integration. This process gradually reduced the tariff barriers between EEC countries, allowing several companies in competitive sectors to better exploit their productive specialization. Large firms in oligopolistic industries could increase production to face both domestic demand and rapidly rising exports, thus taking advantage from greater economies of scale.

The fourth reason is due to the benefits that several countries could enjoy, thanks to a gradual rise in economic openness, facilitated by liberalization of trade and by international GATT agreements.

Finally, there was a long period of declining prices for oil and other raw materials. In fact, the price of oil, after the up-surge following the Suez crisis in 1956, had a downward trend until the end of 1960 if compared to the price of manufactured goods exported by developed countries. The same happened to prices of several commodities exported by developing countries to Western industrialized ones.

We can, therefore, understand how the more rapid growth of various economies of Western Europe and East Asia and their increasing competitiveness has gradually tarnished the US dominance in the international trade of goods. While in 1950, the value of US exports of goods was nearly twice that of the UK, more than three times that of France, more than five times that of Germany, and almost nine times greater than that of Italy, by 1973 the situation had radically changed. Germany had almost reached the US level and had more than doubled the level of the

UK, while Japan, France, and Italy had sharply reduced the gap with the US, though also the latter had registered a significant increase in the value of its exports.

4.3 The Crisis of the Second Wave of the Fordist Model

Many analyses have attempted to understand the reasons of the crisis of Fordism and of *the second wave of the Fordist model of development*. This crisis, which occurred first in the US, in Western Europe and Japan between the late 1960s and the early 1970s, has convinced some authors to introduce the concept of *post-Fordism*. Other authors maintain that Fordism has been wholly or partly replaced by models of *flexible production*, or by the *fragmentation of production* on a global scale.

In fact, in today's world, there are countries with a complex mix of Fordist and post-Fordist aspects, flexible production, and international fragmentation of production. However, other countries, such as China since the 1980s, and partly India since 1992, are passing through their Fordist phase that we have called *the third wave of the Fordist model*, although accounting also for some pre-Fordist and post-Fordist aspects, including Toyotist elements.

But before discussing all these complicated issues, let us return to the main determinants of the crisis of the second wave of the Fordist model of development.

A first problem is associated with the possibility of using important scale, network, and scope economies. This crucially depends on the presence in the economy of an adequate number of important sectors with economies of scale, network, or scope. If, at a certain time, an economy has only one or two sectors with these characteristics, it is obvious that the productive system is mainly dominated by the trends in other sectors, which will in general have lower rates of productivity growth and hence, most likely, lower rates of unit wage growth. This will reduce, ceteris paribus, the dynamics of consumption, investment, and GDP.

Moreover, the economies of scale, or network, or scope, have to be easily exploitable. This is possible only up to certain levels of production. If, for example, for technical reasons, a plant reaches its maximum in economies of scale when it produces 300,000 units of goods, the unit costs of production will decrease until the plant reaches a level of output and sales of 300,000 units. If the units to produce and sell were, for example, 310,000, you have various possibilities. One possibility is to produce in the first plant 300,000 units with lower unit costs and another 10,000 units in another plant with less economies of scale and higher unit costs. A better solution is to use a combination of the two plants' production in order to have an output of 310,000 units that would minimize the overall average unit cost. In any case, the average unit cost will still be somewhat higher than the one you would have with a production limited to 300,000 units produced in one plant. This simple example shows that economies of scale fully function only up to a certain level of production, unless you find a way of breaking down the process of production in several sections or components. For example an automobile corporation can decentralize the production of a component to another firm, which furnishes the component to several auto-makers, and so can have greater volumes of production and greater economies of scale.

A second problem is *the income elasticity of demand* and the *maturity* of a market. For durable consumer goods, like cars or refrigerators, demand grows very fast when only few families possess these goods and many people are eager to buy their first car or their first refrigerator. As income rises, the demand for such goods thus grows rapidly. Yet, this happens only to the point where markets are saturated or become *mature*, that is, until the point where virtually all households have a unit of those goods. From that point on, the domestic demand for those goods is significantly weaker, remaining more or less stable or growing very slowly. It will in fact consist almost solely in the demand for replacement of goods that are worn out, or in the additional demand coming from relatively few families who need more units of that product, or want a better quality, and have income high enough to buy the new product. Now, in the 1950s and in the 1960s, the US economy had some sectors that continued to have consistent scale economies, but other ones that had already reached *maturity*, so that in the whole economy the Fordist model of development was operating only partially.

On the contrary, France, Germany, Italy, Japan, and so on, which at the beginning of the 1950s had started from a lower per capita income than the US, had simultaneously several productive sectors with significant scale or network economies, so that the Fordist model of development could almost fully operate. But in the second half of the 1960s, in Western Europe and Japan the situation began to change significantly. In fact, even in those countries the benefits of economies of scale for goods such as automobiles, motorcycles, TV sets, refrigerators, washing machines, and so on were almost completely exhausted and almost all markets of industrialized countries were now mature. There was, therefore, between the end of the 1960s and the early 1970s, a slower rate of productivity growth for those goods. There was also an increase in absolute prices, and, in some cases, also in the relative prices of the goods in question, a lower rate of growth for the demand of such goods, a lower real unit wage growth and more severe social conflicts in the sectors producing these goods. The Fordist model was gradually withering first in the US and then in Western Europe and in Japan.

Meanwhile, some other important events were taking place and contributed to the crisis of the Fordist model: (a) a gradual deindustrialization and the rapid rise of the service sector; (b) the massive introduction of flexible forms of production, thanks to new computer-aided technologies; (c) new forms of production organization, often associated to the diffusion of Japanese models (*just in time*, *Toyotism*, etc.); (d) the growing use of subcontracting, both internal and from abroad; (e) the good performance, in a few years and in some countries, of small firms operating in traditional sectors and organized in industrial districts and in areas of local development; (f) the end of the phase of cheap energy, with a modest rise in oil prices at the end of 1960 and the dramatic rise in prices due to the great energy crises in 1973–1974 and 1979–1980; (g) the slowing down, or the stagnation, since the 1980s in real wages growth in the US and West European countries and the sharp rise in wages and income inequalities.

Deindustrialization can be measured by the number of employed people in industry and by the percentage of industrial employment and value added on total employment and value added. As we will see in detail in Chap. 5, after the Second World War in the US employment in industry continued to increase up to 1979 before severely declining. The percentage of employment in industry on total employment continued to decline. The added value in real terms in industry as a percentage of total value added began to decline even earlier, since 1973. Meanwhile, the percentage of agriculture on total employment and value added continued to decline, while the percentage of services continued to rise. The latter had come to surpass, at the end of the 1920s for employment and in the 1930s for value added, the percentages of industry, sharply outdistancing them in the successive years. The overtaking of the services over industry as regards the percentage of employment on total employment and, decades later, the decline in absolute values of the number of industrial jobs marked the transition to the post-industrial phase in the US economy, which like in the UK, preceded by several years similar trends in France, Germany, Japan, and Italy. But several services, except in telecommunication and partly in banks, finance, insurance, and sea and air transportation, did not have large scale or network economies, so that the rise of the service sector heavily contributed to the crisis of Fordism. It should however be borne in mind that a substantial part of the rise of the service sector was a mere statistical phenomenon, being due to the increasing decentralization of tertiary functions outsourced by manufacturing companies to independent service companies. Moreover, the rapid fall in industrial employees in the US was, for a growing part, due to delocalization of industrial activities by US multinationals into foreign countries.

Technological advances and organizational changes had also facilitated the spread of flexible forms of production, as well as an extensive use of subcontracting and of methods of Japanese derivation, such as *just in time* practices. The increasing use of computers in the control and management of productive processes at first allowed small and medium-size enterprises to increase productivity, becoming highly competitive against the large corporations, thanks to their greater flexibility, and so developing a model of *flexible specialization*.[2] However, later on, ICT technologies also helped in increasing the production flexibility of several large corporations, who could, for example, easily change the color or other characteristics of their products following changes in consumer tastes. It was much less costly to change the colour of the cars and so it was no longer necessary to produce, as did the Ford corporation in the late 1910s and the 1920s, "only car model T in any color provided they were black." The growing use of subcontracting and the phase of rapid increase in the productivity of small and medium-size enterprises contributed to the expansion of small production units, increasing their relative weight in the second half of 1960 and, for several industrial sectors, also in the 1970s.[3]

There was indeed, in several countries and also in the US, a phase of substantial growth of *industrial districts*,[4] which were defined in 1975 by Giacomo Becattini as the "socio-territorial entities characterized by the active copresence in a limited area, naturalistically and historically determined, of a community of people and a number of industrial enterprises".[5] In these districts, many small and medium-size enterprises produce goods of the same type (e.g. furniture, ceramics, shoes, wine) and often also the specialized machines necessary to produce such goods These productions are based on traditions and material culture developed in the area, and with enterprises acting both "in competition and in cooperation".

This phenomenon, which has been studied in the US more in terms of *industrial clusters*[6] than in terms of industrial districts was, however, less widespread in the US than in other countries such as Italy or Spain.

It had, however, some very important examples, such as the wine-country of Napa Valley or Sonoma Valley in California, the cluster of rubber-plastic-ceramic industry in Chicago and, later on, the information technology-telecommunications in Silicon Valley in its early stage of development.

Another important determinant of the crisis of the Fordist model of development has been the sudden growth of social tensions in the mid-1960s.

Student movements initially developed on campuses and in urban America since 1964, then spread to workers and other social groups in the whole country and in Western Europe (the French May 1968 leftist student movement; the students' turmoil and protests in Germany and Italy; the Italian 1969 "hot autumn" in industrial relations, etc.).

In the US, social tensions were fuelled mainly by the issues of civil rights and by the draft for the Vietnam War, which was menacing the lives and the future of so many young people. In Europe, social tensions had complex anti-system motivations. In any case, they contributed to break the pattern "mass production-mass consumption, strong hierarchy in large factories, strong social hierarchy" that had marked the previous Fordist period.

Another element contributing to the crisis of the Fordist model was the strong rise in energy price and the consequent slowing down of economic growth due to the two great energy crises in 1973–1974 and in 1979–1980.

A final, but crucial, point regards real wages. Neo-liberalist policies like the ones followed by Reagan and Thatcher in the 1980s, the weakening of labor unions, and some of the effects of globalization brought about a semi-stagnation of the real wages of manual and middle-class workers in the US and in Western industrialized countries and an almost general rise in wages, income, and wealth differentials.

Has the crisis of the Fordist model of development in the US, Japan, and Western Europe led, as some authors believe, to a worldwide post-Fordist society since the year 1970? In reality, the situation is far more complex. The key elements of the Fordist model were economies of scale, network and scope, plus the rapid increases in wages and consumption. These elements entered into crisis in the years 1970s and 1980s in the US, Japan, and Western Europe, but they began to function in a growing part of the Chinese economy since the 1980s, and in a more limited segment of the Indian economy since 1992. Moreover, in countries such as Ireland, Spain, Portugal, Finland, Taiwan, Singapore, South Korea, Thailand, Indonesia, Malaysia, Brazil and Turkey, they have affected, in combination with Toyotist elements, a growing part of the economy for most of the years 1980–2016. Since the late 1990s, aspects of the *Fordist-Toyotist* model of development have also concerned, after the great transition crisis of the 1990s, Poland, the Czech and Slovak Republics, Hungary, Slovenia, Romania, Bulgaria, and Russia.

Globally, the Fordist model is therefore far from dead, but coexists with various combinations of *Toyotism*, production fragmentation, and global value chains. In addition, the 1990s and 2000s saw a new mini-Fordist phase linked to the explosion of internet and mobile telecommunications networks in the US and in many European and Asian countries. For example, in the 1990s and 2000s, the production of mobile phones was very important in the US, Finland, Sweden, Germany, South Korea, Japan, China, and so on. The ICT expansion has allowed companies such as Microsoft, Google, Amazon, Apple, HP, SAP, Siemens, Samsung, LG, Toshiba, Acer, Infosys, Lenovo, Huawei, Alibaba, and, for a more limited period, Motorola, Ericson, and Nokia, to rapidly expand output and productivity with significant effects on many other sectors of industry and services. E-commerce and internet services, such as those provided by Amazon, Google, and Facebook, had an impressive boom, both in the US and in a vast part of the world.

During the last decades, there has been a gradual reduction in the excessive standardization of manufacturing production. In addition, some repetitive, boring, dirty, or dangerous jobs have diminished in many modern factories with the introduction of robots and advanced automation, but there are still in the world a large number of traditional Fordist-Toyotist plants, though in some cases they have been decentralized to poorer low-wage countries.

Notes

1. See, for the introduction of this concept, Gerschenkron (1962).
2. See Piore and Sabel (1984).
3. See Contini and Revelli (1992), p. 19.
4. See Marshall (1890) for the introduction of the concept of industrial districts.
5. See Becattini (1975). See also Pyke et al. (1990).
6. See Porter (1990).

References

Becattini, G. 1975. *Lo sviluppo economico della Toscana*. Firenze: Irpet.
CEA (Council of Economic Advisers). 1980. *Economic Report of the President*. Washington, DC.
———. 2018. *Economic Report of the President*. Washington, DC.
Contini, B., and R. Revelli. 1992. *Imprese, occupazione e retribuzioni al microscopio*. Bologna: Il Mulino.
Gerschenkron, A. 1962. *Economic Backwardness in Historical Perspective*. Cambridge, MA: Harvard University Press.
Maddison, A. 2003. *The World Economy: Historical Statistics*. Paris: OECD.
Marshall, A. 1890. *Principles of Economics*. London: Macmillan.
Piore, M.J., and C.F. Sabel. 1984. *The Second Industrial Divide: Possibilities for Prosperity*. New York: Basic Books.
Porter, M.E. 1990. *The Competitive Advantage of Nations*. New York: Free Press.
Pyke, F., G. Becattini, and W. Sengerberger. 1990. *Industrial Districts and Inter-Firm Co-operation in Italy*. Geneve: ILO.

5

Capital Accumulation, Technological Progress, and Knowledge

5.1 The Main Determinants of Economic Development

Discussing the long-run determinants of the US economic growth, many authors have greatly emphasized the role of technological progress. From the last decades of the nineteenth century up to now, the US economy has proved to be, from the technological point of view, a very dynamic productive system. In the last part of the nineteenth century and in several decades in the twentieth century, the US has been indeed the most innovative system in the world so that now its overall technological level is definitely the largest in the world. Yet, in the 1970s and in the 1980s, Japan, and in the last three decades, China, have made an impressive, albeit partial, technological catching up, while in some industrial and financial sectors also, a few European and Asian countries have reached or maintained a fairly competitive position.

Yet, technological progress, though very important, is not the only factor which can explain economic development, nor is it a purely exogenous one. Other factors are essential, and some of them are intrinsically associated to technological advancement, and they work in a complex feedback with it.

Long-lasting economic development is determined by many cultural, social, and economic factors. You need an open, constructive culture; a society not too rigidly crystalized in groups, tribes, social strata, and conflicting religions; a sufficiently open economy; a developmental state or at least a state which can provide relatively good, "nonextractive" economic institutions;[1] an adequate rate of growth of capital, technology, employment, and knowledge; and the capacity to make important structural changes without creating too large economic and social inequalities.

A figure, the *pyramid of economic development*,[2] can give a simplified idea of the main economic factors that can determine a long-lasting economic development. In this representation, technical progress maintains a very important role, but it is considered largely dependent on other crucial, mostly endogenous, variables (Fig. 5.1).

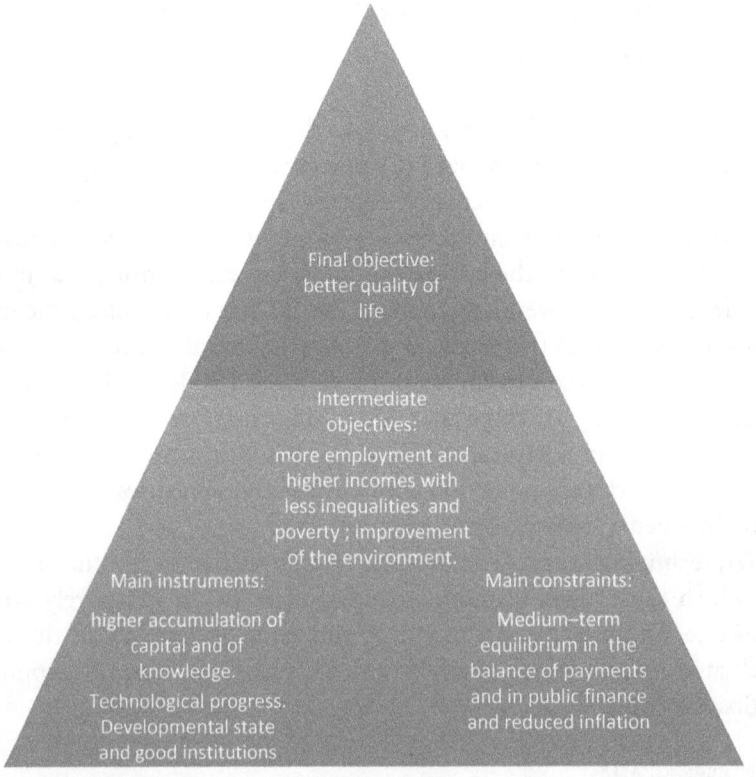

Fig. 5.1 The pyramid of economic development

5.2 Capital Accumulation

Capital accumulation is one of the most important economic factors. In the years 1870–1950, the rate of growth of gross capital formation in the US economy was considerably higher than that of other major economies despite the dramatic fall of real investment in the period of the *great depression*. This can be in large part explained by the virtuous circles associated to *the frontier* and then to *the Fordist model of growth*, with the great exception of *the lost decade* 1929–1939.

Yet, from 1950 to 1973, the US rate of growth of real capital formation became much lower than that of major catching-up countries, which could more fully exploit the advantages of the Fordist model. In particular, Japan had a real rate of growth of capital formation about three times higher than that of the US, and also most major Western European countries, such as Germany, France, and Italy, had a rate that was almost the double of the US. Since the 1960s, the US rate of growth of capital formation became much inferior also to that of *the four Asian tigers*, South Korea, Taiwan, Hong Kong, and Singapore. From the great energy crisis in the autumn of 1973 up to 2007, the US returned to rates of growth of capital formation close or even higher than those of major European countries, though inferior to those of Japan up to 1990, of South Korea, Taiwan, Singapore, Thailand, Indonesia, and Malaysia during the whole period, of China since 1978, of India since 1992, and so on.

In the years 2007–2017, during *the great recession*, the US had a great fall in real investment and then a difficult recovery. The US could return to the 2006 level only in 2014 and then it was able to expand capital formation at a relatively modest rate.

In the decades of rapid growth, the US had been able to introduce a large amount of both *extensive* and *intensive* investments, increasing at the same time output, employment, and productivity. In the 2000s, the US had, however, an average rate of growth of investment, employment, and productivity lower than that of the preceding decades and close to the modest performance of the European Union but much inferior to that of large emerging countries such as China, India, and Indonesia.

There is a rather strict association between *capital formation* and *technological progress*. In 1957 and 1962, Nicholas Kaldor had already anticipated that the introduction of new capital goods generally embodies technical progress. Kenneth Arrow had then argued that extensive investment determines also processes of *learning by doing* for the labor force, which can widely increase labor productivity.[3] These results have been reinforced by the seminal contribution of Paul Romer and several other authors who gave rise to different versions of the endogenous models of growth.[4]

On the other hand, economic innovations can greatly contribute to a rise in productivity and total product, and this can further stimulate growth in productivity, profits, and capital accumulation.

Yet, there is a third protagonist in this story: *knowledge*. The level and the rate of growth of knowledge incorporated in the labor force and in society at large give an essential contribution to economic development and are closely interlinked with capital accumulation and with technological progress, as we will see in paragraph 5.4.

5.3 The Role of Technological Progress

In the first half of the twentieth century, the great contributions of Schumpeter[5] and many other authors have emphasized the role of innovations and technological progress in economic development.

In the second half of the twentieth century and at the beginning of the twenty-first century, there has been an extensive use of Solow's neoclassical model of economic growth with technical progress and of his concept of technical progress as *a residual*.[6]

The rate of growth of GDP minus the rates of growth of capital and labor multiplied by their respective weights, that is, the shares of profits and of wages on income, gives the contribution of technical progress on the rate of economic growth as *a residual*. Several other authors, such as Denison, Maddison, and Barro, have partly modified and extended Solow's approach, trying to empirically estimate the contribution of technical progress in the long-run US growth and to compare its value with that of other countries.

The main weaknesses of this approach are the particular type of aggregate production function and the fragility of the theory of capital and of distribution underlying Solow's model.[7] Moreover, capital, labor, and technical progress are considered as single variables, overlooking the strict linkages and complex feedbacks existing among the three variables.

Most endogenous growth models have, more realistically, taken account of endogenous determinants of economic growth, such as saving and capital formation and their impact on the rise of knowledge in the economy, or of the rise in human capital, or of specialized learning by doing processes, or of R&D activities, and so on.[8] Most of these works, as the first Romer's endogenous model, have also assumed increasing returns to scale, rather than the constant returns to scale assumed in Solow's approach.

Starting from less aggregate approaches, Paul A. David and other authors have explored the path-dependent impact of great inventions, such as electricity, nuclear energy, railways, and the postal service, in the US economic development, or the positive impact on growth of good government spending and solid economic and legal institutions.[9]

Alfred D. Chandler Jr., in *The Visible Hand: the Managerial Revolution in American Business*[10] and in other influential works, has analyzed the profound innovations made not only in technology but also in organizational and managerial practices. In the Second Industrial Revolution, steam power, electricity, and the railways system favored the integration of mass distribution and mass production and thus the advent of giant corporations. Managerial and organizational changes in these firms largely contributed to shape the process of the US economic growth and to spread technological and managerial techniques also to small and middle-sized firms.

Also John Kenneth Galbraith, in *the New Industrial State* and in other books[11], gave great importance to the role of large corporations in the US economic growth and to their role in technological advancement, but he did so from a much more critical perspective. He stressed that in most cases only large business organizations could dispose of enough financial means to acquire costly machines, advanced technologies, and a technically sophisticated labor force. Large corporations could also heavily influence the choices of consumers through advertising and other promotional strategies and thus more easily reach their production and sales objectives. Finally, they could induce the state to heavily finance research and higher education and to regulate aggregate demand.

In recent decades, several big traditional manufacturing corporations have downsized their research laboratories preferring to buy patents or small innovative firms. However, in the internet world and in e-commerce, some former start-ups, such as Google, Facebook, and Amazon, have been able to grow very rapidly and become giant corporations devoting large budgets to R&D activities and frequently recurring to the acquisition of smaller innovative firms.

Most recently, Robert J. Gordon, in his 2016 celebrated book, *The Rise and fall of American Growth* and in some previous works,[12] has given a fascinating account of the impact of the great waves of major inventions on the US economic development. He distinguishes three main industrial revolutions. *The first industrial revolution* occurred between 1770 and 1820. It was mainly fuelled by coal energy and based on major inventions such as the steam engine, the cotton gin, more advanced techniques in the cotton industry, the steamship, the railways, and so on. Yet, Gordon gives even greater importance to *the Second Industrial Revolution* that mainly occurred between 1870 and 1900. The *great inventions* of the nineteenth century were electricity; urban sanitation; internal combustion engine; major technical advancements in chemicals, pharmaceutical, oil, and steel industries; modern communication; and so on. Together with their numerous extensions and applications (electric machines, urban and domestic lighting, refrigerators, washing machines, air conditioning, radio, television, W.C. and internal plumbing, automobiles, trucks, airplanes, plastics, antibiotics, telegraph, telephone, etc.), they gave abundant benefits to the process of US economic growth at least until 1972. These great inventions and their applications utilized, as main primary sources of energy, oil and gas, and then also nuclear power, gradually reducing the previously dominating role of coal. The great inventions could enormously improve the general standard of life, highly increasing labor productivity, domestic comfort, and health conditions; reducing the burden of domestic work; and greatly bettering transports and communications.

Gordon also gives greater importance to the benefits of the *second industrial revolution* over those of the *third industrial revolution*, the so-called *digital revolution*, based on computer-aided machines, PCs, internet, tablets, smart phones, robots, 3D printing, big data, and so on and operating through the period 1972–2018.[13]

The author disagrees with "techno optimists" such as Brynjolfsson and McAfee,[14] who sustain that we have entered an epoch of accelerating technological progress and that this will likely lead to an acceleration in the growth of productivity, though also to possible dangers for employment and social equity.

Gordon affirms that, in reality, productivity long-run growth has fallen since 1972 and will probably continue to be rather low. This is basically due to three factors: the consequences of the *great recession*; the fact that the great inventions of the *Second Industrial revolution* "eclipse" the set of innovations of the *Third Industrial Revolution*; and the six harmful *headwinds*, which have strongly contributed to the slowing down of US economic growth. These headwinds are essentially based on adverse demographic trends, worsened by the absence of a universal health system; the semi-stagnation of educational levels, partly associated to the very high cost of universities and the enormous rise in student borrowing; the rapid increase in economic inequalities, which have hit the large majority of the population; the heavy burden of a very large public debt; the price of globalization in terms, for example, of offshoring and plant-closures; and, finally, large energy and environmental problems.[15]

Gordon's thesis is rather convincing and well founded, although it is very difficult and somewhat risky to make long-term forecasts for the future as he attempts to do. However, he partly overlooks the fact that many of the great inventions and the pace of their extensions and applications have largely depended on a set of endogenous domestic and foreign decisions.

The consequences on the US economy of the deep crisis of the Fordist model of growth in the 1970s and of the two great energy crises had indeed an important part in the story, slowing down the rate of capital accumulation. Moreover, it is crucial not only to focus on what occurred in those years in the US, but also what governments, households, banks, and firms decided in other countries, such as China, Japan, or Germany, harshly competing with the US in the global market.

5.4 The Importance of Knowledge

The knowledge economics[16] and, for some aspects, also the economics of innovation and the endogenous theory of growth, have greatly emphasized the importance of *knowledge* in the process of economic development.

An economy can sustain a long period of economic development only if, together with good economic institutions, the rapid accumulation of physical capital, an abundant labor force, and a continuous flow of technological advancements, there is a rapid and pervasive increase in knowledge both in the productive system and in the entire society.

Knowledge cannot be easily measured. However, some partial and indirect indicators can give a general idea of the level and rate of growth of knowledge in an economy.

First of all, there is the quantity and quality of education. Secondly, there is the growth of the labor force and of its exposure to processes of learning by doing and of on-the-job training. Third, there is the quantity and quality of R&D activities carried on in firms, universities, and public and private research centers. Finally, there is the capability to rapidly diffuse the results of new ideas, of R&D, and of capital goods incorporating new technologies and new organizational models in the productive system.

It is also important to take into account the size of the economy and the stock of total and per capita knowledge existing at a given moment, as also the rate of growth of knowledge, which, in the medium-long run, can drastically change the initial situation.

There is no doubt that, at the beginning of the 1950s, the US was the major country with the highest stock of knowledge. The US had then the highest average level of education; the largest pool of workers with access to learning by doing in modern economic activities; the largest total and relative expenditure in R&D activities; the largest number of researchers; the highest number and value of patents; the largest stock of physical capital; the highest capability to transfer knowledge from public agencies, university research centers, and start-uppers to the productive sphere, thanks also to the aid of the State and of the financial institutions. Moreover, the large defense budget permitted to lavishly finance public and private institutions and the major universities in order to obtain military and strategic inventions and innovations, which later were often utilized in the civilian production of technologically advanced goods and services.

While the quality of several colleges was comparatively modest, the major US private and public universities could maintain a very high teaching and research level thanks to their good organization, but above all to their enormous budgets due to public financing, high university fees, and a number of private donations. In this way, thanks to the excellence of their faculties and their facilities and the large amount of scholarships and research grants, they could also attract a great number of brilliant foreign students and researchers, who often decided to remain in the US as professors, professionals, researchers, entrepreneurs, managers, or cadres. This colossal *brain-drain* in favor of the US, mainly coming from Indian and Chinese immigrants and also from Europe and several other zones, was one of the main factors that contributed to the high scientific and economic performance of the US, and that Trump's immigration policy risks damaging or even reversing.

In the following decades, gradually the US world leadership in knowledge has been, in large part, eroded. In the 1950–1973 period, some European countries and Eastern Asian countries, such as Japan, South Korea, Taiwan, and Singapore and since the 1980s, China, began to economically grow more briskly than the US. Thus, these countries were able to increase more rapidly their investment in education and R&D than the US, partially closing the gap, or even surpassing the US level in relative terms, that is, according to per capita indicators or in percent of GDP (see Table 5.1). For example, in 2015, the US had been marginally surpassed only by Switzerland and the UK in terms of mean years of education of the population over 25 years of age, but by 17 countries in terms of expected years of education.[17] Moreover, the quality of education of the students in the US aged 15–16 years, as measured by the OECD Pisa test, had given relatively modest results. In 2015, the US ranked 40th

Table 5.1 Knowledge indicators in the US and other selected countries

Country	Spending in R&D as % of GDP (2016)	Mean years of schooling (2015)	Expected years of schooling (2015)	Employment in % of working age population (2017)
US	2.7	13.2	16.5	70.1
China	2.1	7.6	13.5	–
Japan	3.1	12.5	15.3	75.3
Germany	2.9	13.2	17.1	75.3
France	2.2	11.6	16.3	64.8
UK	1.7	13.3	16.3	74.1
South Korea	4.2	12.2	16.6	66.6
Italy	1.3	10.9	16.3	58.0
Spain	1.2	9.8	17.7	61.1

Sources: UNDP (2016) and OECD (2018a, b)

out of 72 countries in Math, 25th in Science, and 24th in reading. The results had been badly worsening in Math in the years 2012–2015, and also in science and reading, the US results had worsened.

As regards *the expenditure in R&D in percent of GDP*, in 2016, the US (2.7%) had been surpassed by Israel, South Korea, Japan, Sweden, Taipei, Austria, Denmark, Germany, while China (2.1%) is rapidly closing the gap. Since the 1950s, as regards this indicator, all these countries have shown a much more rapid rate of growth than the US.

If we consider, instead, the *total value of spending in R&D* in PPP, the US remains at the top in the world, but China is catching up very rapidly.

In absolute terms, the US has maintained its leadership in most knowledge indicators owing to its large demographic and economic size and its high technological standard, but its advantage has considerably diminished when compared with several countries. However, China has recently surpassed the US level in terms of capital formation; in terms of the total number of university graduates, engineers, and researchers; and, in some big cities, also in terms of the average quality of education. The US maintains an advantage in learning by doing processes in high-tech industries, in the spillover from defense research to civilian uses, and in the capability to diffuse innovations in the economy, but China is vigorously catching up in all these fields.

5.5 Structural Changes in the US Economy

Capital accumulation, technological progress, the rise in knowledge and, in the last half century, the deep consequences of the globalization process, have led to great structural changes in the economy of the US.

In particular, from 1950 onwards, the US economy has undergone fundamental economic transformations.

We can start from the *law of the three sectors* due to Colin Clark and then used by Simon Kuznets, Hollis B. Chenery, Moshe Syrquin, and many other authors.[18]

This law says that, in the long run, growing economies tend to reduce the percentage of employment in agriculture on total employment[19] and increase the percentages of employment in industry and services. After some decades, there is usually also the decrease of the percentage of employment in industry and at the same time a great rise in the percentage of services.

As we can see in Table 5.2, by 1950, in the US, the percentage of employment in industry had already abundantly surpassed the one in agriculture, but it had been, in turn, significantly exceeded by that of services.

In 2017, employment in agriculture, forestry, fishing, and hunting had been about 1.6% of total employment, while the percentage in industry (inclusive also of mines, public utilities, and construction) had gone down to 17.5% and the percentage of services had gone up to 80.9%.

Table 5.2 Employment by sector of economic activity in the US (%): 1870–2017

	1870	1950	1973	1987	2007	2017
Agriculture	50.0	13.0	4.1	3.0	1.4	1.6
Industry	24.4	33.3	32.3	26.6	19.8	17.5
Services	25.6	53.7	63.6	70.4	78.8	80.9
Total	100.0	100.0	100.0	100.0	100.0	100.0

Sources: Maddison (1991), p. 248; OECD (2018c) for the years 2007–2017

But beyond these important and well-known secular trends, there was also a much less studied phenomenon, that is, a significant change in the internal composition of both industry and services. For industry, there was a consistent reduction in the percentage of people employed in traditional sectors such as textiles, clothing, food, and so on and a growth in the percentage of people employed in modern sectors, the average labor productivity of which was usually higher.

It should also be noted that employment in manufacturing in the US reached its peak in 1979. Since then, there was a slow long-term decline. This was principally due to one large cyclical event (the great recession) and three structural factors: the outsourcing of some functions previously made within the manufacturing firms to external furnishers of specialized services; technical changes, such as the entry of computers and robots in the plants and in the offices; globalization (offshoring, etc.). So, from 1979 to 2010, manufacturing employment had declined by about 8.4 million people, then regaining about 1.4 million units up to 2017 mainly as a result of the economic recovery following the great recession.[20]

In 2016, manufacturing pay-roll employees (wage and salary workers) were about 12.4 million units and had therefore been largely exceeded by the number of employees in leisure and hospitality (15.6); health and social assistance (19.1 million), professional and business services (20.1 million), wholesale and retail trade (21.7 million), and Public Administration (22.2 million).

By contrast, the number of employees in the construction industry had continued to grow until 2006, reaching 7.7 million units—that is, more than half the workers in the manufacturing sector—only to suffer a sharp decline during the *great recession*. The employees in construction fell to 5.5 million units in 2011 and then recovered up to about 7 million people in 2017.[21]

In the 2000s, in the services sector, there has been an increase in the percentage of employment in some relatively more modern sectors of activity having a higher average productivity, and often higher wages, such as professional and technical services to businesses, education, health care, and so on, while more traditional sectors such as wholesale and retail trade, utilities, and other services were relatively stagnant. There was, moreover, the growth of menial and poorly paid jobs, such as personnel at fast food, custodians, agricultural laborers, messengers, shop assistants, non-professional attendants in health care, and so on. Several people were in fact *working poor*. They had found employment, but only for *low-paying jobs* that offered very low wages.

For banking and financial services, there was a rise in employment and wages until 2006 and a drop in employment since 2008 due to the consequences of the great financial crisis of 2007–2008, triggered by the sub-prime financial crisis. There was, then, a recovery and a small expansion in the years 2011–2017.

It should be observed that, contrary to what is commonly thought in Europe, the Public Administration of the US is costly and numerous. Moreover, it has registered a progressive increase in employment over time, more or less in line with the rate of growth of total employment. Indeed, from 1950 to 2016, employment in the US Public Administration had increased from about 8.8 to 22.2 million units. While in recent years, the US has succeeded, with difficulty, in containing the increase in employment of federal government, at state and local level there has been a continuous ascent in employment, which rose from 17.1 million in 1998 to 19.2 million in 2007 and 19.4 million in 2016.

By 2017, the US employment in Public Administration in proportion to total employment or total population, excluding the armed forces, was larger than in most European countries, although it did not provide public coverage of health services to a great part of the population.

Since 1950, structural employment changes in the US have been very large, and also in terms of value added changes have been substantial.

From 1950 to 2015, agriculture had gradually reduced its relative share in GDP to about 1.1%, while industry had reached 18.9% and services had risen to almost 80%.[22]

5.6 Robots and the E-Economy

The future might reserve an even worse scenario to employment. The use of robots and artificial intelligence is gradually penetrating more and more sectors of industry and the services, replacing the work of millions of human beings. Moreover, web and ICT giants such as Google, Amazon,

Facebook, Apple; the Chinese giant Ali Baba and Baidu; and smaller but rapidly growing groups, such as Trivago, Booking, Uber, Airbnb, Foodora, car sharing organizations, and so on are gradually disrupting, or heavily reducing, the work of wholesale and retail trade, travel agencies, hotels, taxi drivers, car sellers, bookshops, and publishers and will progressively menace various financial activities of banks, insurance, and credit card companies. Crypto-currencies, such as Bitcoin, can influence the global financial market and the activity of governments and tax collectors. A rapid diffusion of online learning might reduce employment in schools, universities, and training institutions. Massive online activities with zero (or very low) marginal costs can disrupt the business of several firms that have to sustain heavy costs for their facilities and labor force. Useful innovations, such as socials, clouds, big data, and the internet of things, will not only badly reduce individuals' privacy, but they will also cut down the need for newspapers, marketing analyses, local sellers, and furnishers. The giant e-commerce or sharing economy corporations, such as Amazon or Uber, will amplify the need for wide logistic services. Most of the profits will, however, go to the giant e-corporations, while the physical providers of the logistic services will continue to be poorly paid.

However, new technologies might also increase productivity and increase the demand of selected new workers.

Technological, demographic, economic, and policy changes might lead to very different outcomes for future trends of employment and wages in the US. Any forecast on these matters is therefore subject to large margins of error.

A 2017 McKinsey study[23] tried to evaluate how many jobs will be lost and gained from 2016 to 2030 in "the time of automation". In the midpoint automation scenario, in which 23% of current work activity is supposed to be automated, 39 million jobs would be displaced, and about 33% of the labor force would be obliged to switch to other occupational categories. In the most favorable scenario about labor demand (step-up scenario), care providers (surgeons, nurses, etc.) will increase by 4.9 million units, builders by 2.7 million, professionals by 1.7 million, and also managers and executives, web and IT experts, educators, and so on will increase. On the contrary, retail sales employees, and especially office support employees (−4.5 million), machinists, cooks, and so on (−6.8 millions) will substantially decrease. Only in this very optimistic hypothesis (step-up scenario) will the number of jobs created be enough to face both the number of jobs displaced by automation and the rise in labor force.[24]

However, the McKinsey figures are based on the rather optimistic assumptions of an annual rate of growth of per capita GDP of 1.3%, a consistent rise in labor force and a relatively low automation trend. Robert J. Gordon imagined a very different scenario for the future, with a lower rate of growth both for per capita GDP and the labor force and a particularly low rate of growth in the real income of the bottom 99% of the income distribution.[25]

In any case, both the analyses anticipate a further reduction in the manufacturing jobs and this can have heavy consequences on employment and the US trade balance. Moreover, these trends will probably favor the increasing divide between well-paid jobs and a mass of second-rate and low-paying jobs, contributing to an increase in social and economic inequalities.

Yet, in the internet services, the US and the other giant economy, China, might greatly benefit from the enormous size of their domestic market and the large financial means that ICT and e-companies can collect. The very large domestic market can lead to huge economies of scale that, together with the easiness to find large private and public funds, can facilitate a very rapid expansion into the world markets, where smaller national companies are unable to compete with US and China's giants. So Google, Facebook, Amazon, Alibaba, Baidu, and so on have succeeded in dominating the internet world market. They have become semi-monopolistic giants and have been favored by poor regulations in many of the countries in which they operate. So, they have scarcely respected the individuals' privacy and have massively evaded taxation, skillfully using the existence of several fiscal paradises.

5.7 Summing Up

Have great inventions and new technologies been important in the US long-run economic development?

The answer is definitively yes, but, in the last 150 years, technological progress has been in large part endogenous, mainly depending on the decisions of the State, the firms, and the households regarding infrastructures, physical investment, education, research, and economic institutions. It has also been strongly influenced by the different economic phases: the frontier, the Fordist model of development, and the third wave of globalization.

Technological progress and its impact on economic development have also been deeply affected by epochal historical events, such as the two world wars, the decolonization period, the dissolution of the Soviet Union and China's radical economic reforms.

As we shall see more in detail in Chaps. 7, 8, and 9, in the third wave of globalization, the US economy and Western Europe have initially greatly profited from the possibility of making huge outflows of international direct investment into less advanced economies. They could thus exploit the combination of their technological advantage and of the higher productivity of their multinationals with the lower wages, the weaker labor, and environmental regulations and the more dynamic markets existing in several emerging economies. But, in the 1990s and in the 2000s, China, India, and some other emerging countries could use the ingoing FDI and other financial flows to rapidly, though partially, catch up in technology, capital accumulation, and knowledge. In the 2000s, some of these countries, and in particular China, were also able to make growing FDI into the rest of the world, to buy a lot of modern technology from the US and other advanced economies and to become fierce competitors in many sectors of the world markets, following the earlier examples of Japan, South Korea, Taiwan, Singapore, and Hong Kong.

There has been thus a powerful *backlash*. The US has invested much in emerging countries to get high profits for its multinationals and has exported there many technologically advanced capital goods, but by doing so it has helped China and a few other emerging countries to rapidly reduce their technological gap and to accelerate the US deindustrialization process through a huge rise in their exports to the American market.

Notes

1. See, for the useful distinction between extractive and inclusive institutions, Acemoglu and Robinson (2012).
2. This is a modified and extended version of the chart presented in Valli (2015), p. 111.
3. See Kaldor (1957), Kaldor and Mirllees (1962), Arrow (1962).
4. See Romer (1986). See also Lucas (1988), Grossman and Helpman (1994).
5. See Schumpeter (1911, 1939).
6. See Solow (1956, 1957, 1970).
7. See Valli (2005), p. 74.
8. See the already cited works by Romer, Lucas, Grossman and Helpman. See also Romer (1990) and Barro (1990).
9. See, for example, David (1975), Aghion et al. (2009), and Acemoglu and Robinson (2012).
10. See Chandler (1977).
11. See Galbraith (1952, 1958, 1967).
12. See Gordon (2012, 2014, 2016).
13. Several authors, such as Klaus Schwab (2016), prefer to distinguish between the *Third Industrial Revolution* and the *Fourth industrial revolution* or *Industry 4.0*. The former, occurring from the 1970s to the first decade of the 2000s, was principally based on the first wave of the digital revolution, while the latter is characterized by extensive use of clouds, big data, and blockchain; the ascent of internet giants, such as Google, Amazon and Alibaba; 3-D printing, the internet of things, robots and androids, nanotechnology, artificial intelligence, green energy and, in the very near future, self-driving cars and trucks, quantum computers, and possible great improvements in the medical, biological, and genetic fields. Some of these problems will be further examined in paragraph 5.6.
14. See Brynjolfsson and McAfee (2014).
15. See Gordon (2014), pp. 8–19 and Gordon (2016).
16. See, for example, Foray (2004), Arena et al. (2012).
17. See UNDP (2016). Expected years of education are the number of years of schooling that a child of school entrance age can expect to receive if prevailing patterns of age-specific enrolment rates persist throughout the child's life.

18. See, for example, Kuznets (1965, 1966), Chenery (1960), Chenery and Syrquin (1975), and the more complex structural approach of Pasinetti (1977, 1993).
19. It is interesting to note that from 2014 to 2017, the percentage of employment in agriculture has begun to slightly grow after the preceding secular decline. There has also been a rising interest of several young people in organic agriculture and the gradual expansion of farmers' markets.
20. See Bureau of Labour Statistics (2018).
21. See OECD (2018b).
22. See Bureau of Labour Statistics (2018).
23. See, for example, McKinsey (2017).
24. McKinsey (2017), pp. 102–103. In the rapid automation scenario, the loss of employment and the need to shift to other occupational categories would be much larger.
25. See Gordon (2014, 2016).

References

Acemoglu, D., and J. Robinson. 2012. *Why Nations Fail: The Origins of Power, Prosperity and Poverty*. New York: Crown Publishers.

Aghion, P., P.D. David, and D. Foray. 2009. Science, Technology and Innovation for Economic Growth: Linking Policy Research and Practice in 'STIG Systems'. *Research Policy* 38 (4): 681–693.

Arena, R., A. Festré, and N. Lazaric, eds. 2012. *The Handbook of Knowledge and Economics*. Cheltenham: Edward Elgar.

Arrow, K. 1962. The Economic Implications of Learning by Doing. *Review of Economic Studies* 29 (June): 155–173.

Barro, R. 1990. Government Spending in a Simple Model of Endogenous Growth. *Journal of Political Economy* 98 (5): 103–126.

Brynjolfsson, E., and A. McAfee. 2014. *The Second Machine Age*. New York: Norton.

Bureau of Labour Statistics. 2018. https://www.bls.gov/mobile/.

Chandler, A.D., Jr. 1977. *The Visible Hand: the Managerial Revolution in American Business*. Cambridge, MA and London: The Belknap Press of Harvard University Press.

Chenery, H. 1960. Patterns of Industrial Growth. *The American Economic Review* 50 (4): 624–654.
Chenery, H., and M. Syrquin. 1975. *Patterns of Development 1950–1970*. Oxford: Oxford University Press.
David, P. 1975. *Technical Choice Innovation and Economic Growth: Essays on American and British Experience in the Nineteenth Century*. Cambridge: Cambridge University Press.
Foray, D. 2004. *The Economics of Knowledge*. Cambridge, MA: MIT Press.
Galbraith, J.K. 1952. *American Capitalism: The Concept of Countervailing Power*. Boston: Houghton Mifflin Company.
———. 1958. *The Affluent Society*. Boston: Houghton Mifflin Company.
———. 1967. *The New Industrial State*. Princeton: Princeton University Press.
Gordon, R.J. 2012. Is U.S. Economic Growth Over? Faltering Innovation Confronts the Six Headwinds. *NBER Working Paper No. 18315*.
———. 2014. The Demise of U.S. Economic Growth: Restatement, Rebuttal, and Reflections. *NBER Working Paper No. 19895*.
———. 2016. *The Rise and Fall of American Growth: The U.S. Standard of Living Since the Civil War*. Princeton: Princeton University Press.
Grossman, G.M., and E. Helpman. 1994. Endogenous Innovation in the Theory of Growth. *Journal of Economic Perspectives* 8 (1): 23–44.
Kaldor, N. 1957. A Model of Economic Growth. *The Economic Journal* 67 (268): 591–624.
Kaldor, N., and J. Mirllees. 1962. A New Model of Economic Growth. *Review of Economic Studies* 29 (3): 174–192.
Kuznets, S. 1965. *Economic Growth and Structure*. Portsmouth: Heinemann.
———. 1966. *Modern Economic Growth*. New Haven and London: Yale University Press.
Lucas, R. 1988. On the Mechanics of Economic Development. *Journal of Monetary Economics* 22 (1): 3–42.
Maddison, A. 1991. *Dynamic Forces in Capitalist Development, A Long-run Comparative View*. Oxford: Oxford University Press.
McKinsey. 2017. *Job-Lost Jobs Gained*. McKinsey Global Institute.
OECD. 2018a. Gross Domestic Spending on R&D (Indicator). Accessed May 29, 2018. https://doi.org/10.1787/d8b068b4-en.
———. 2018b. Employment Rate (Indicator). Accessed May 29, 2018. https://doi.org/10.1787/1de68a9b-en.
———. 2018c. Employment by Activity (Indicator). Accessed May 29, 2018. https://doi.org/10.1787/a258bb52-en

Pasinetti, L. 1977. *Lectures on the Theory of Production.* New York: Columbia University Press.
———. 1993. *Structural Economic Dynamics.* Cambridge: Cambridge University Press.
Romer, P.M. 1986. Increasing Returns and Long-Run Growth. *Journal of Political Economy* 94 (5): 1002–1037.
Romer, P. 1990. Endogenous Technological Change. *Journal of Political Economy* 98 (5): 71–102.
Schumpeter, J.A. 1911. *The Theory of Economic Development.* Cambridge, MA: Harvard University Press.
———. 1939. *Business Cycles: A Theoretical, Historical and Statistical Analysis of the Capitalist Process.* New York and London: McGraw-Hill.
Schwab, K. 2016. *The Fourth Industrial Revolution.* Geneva: Global Economic Forum.
Solow, R. 1956. A Contribution to the Theory of Economic Growth. *The Quarterly Journal of Economics* 70 (1): 65–94.
———. 1957. Technical Change and the Aggregate Production Function. *The Review of Economics and Statistics* 39 (3): 312–320.
———. 1970. *Growth Theory—An Exposition.* Oxford: Oxford University Press.
UNDP. 2016. http://hdr.undp.org/en.
Valli, V. 2005. *Politica economica. Introduzione all'economia dello sviluppo.* Roma: Carocci.
———. 2015. *The Economic Rise of China and India.* Torino: Accademia University Press.

6

The Global Power of the US

6.1 After Teheran and Yalta

In Teheran (November 1943) and Yalta (February 1945), two crucial agreements between Roosevelt, Stalin, and Churchill took place. The Soviet Red Army entered Berlin and occupied a great part of Eastern Europe, while Anglo-American troops occupied Italy and part of Germany and Greece. In April 1945, Mussolini and Hitler died and on May 8, 1945, Germany surrendered. Finally, on August 6 and 9, 1945, two deadly and devastating US atomic bombs were dropped on Hiroshima and Nagasaki, leading to the conclusion of the Second World War.

Great part of the world was thus divided into two major spheres of influence. There was the US' sphere of influence in the West and Japan and the Soviet Union's sphere in Eastern Europe.

Different was the situation of China, where the Chinese Communist Party came into power in 1949, and of Tito's Yugoslavia, which had been able to regain its freedom without the decisive intervention of the Red Army or of the allied forces. All this led to the creation of a bi-polar world, in large part dominated by two major superpowers: the US and the Soviet Union, and to a long period of perilous *cold war* between the two great antagonists since 1947. From the economic point of view,

Table 6.1 Population, GDP, and per capita GDP in the US, Soviet Union and Russia: 1950–1991

Indicators	US 1950	USSR 1950	US 1970	USSR 1970	US 1991	USSR 1991	Russia 1991
Population (million)	152.3	179.6	202.7	240.2	253.5	290.7	148.5
Population (US = 100)	100.0	117.9	100.0	118.5	100.0	114.7	58.6
GDP (US = 100)	100.0	35.0	100.0	43.9	100.0	32.2	18.9
Per capita GDP (US = 100)	100.0	29.7	100.0	37.1	100.0	28.1	32.3

Notes: Estimates for the Russian Federation after the dissolution of the USSR
Our elaborations on data from Maddison (2003) in PPP GK international 1990 US $

however, there was not a perfect bi-polar confrontation, a balance between equals, but an *asymmetric bi-polar world*, because the US economy had more than twice the size of the Soviet Union.

In fact, in 1950, the Soviet economy, which had just completed its recovery from the severe destruction of the war, had a total GDP in PPP GK of only 35% of that of the US (see Table 6.1). Since the Soviet Union's population was slightly higher than that of the US, the percentage of GDP per capita was even lower, that is, below 30%. The economic gap between the two superpowers had been slightly reduced up to 1975, and then it increased sharply in the subsequent years until the dissolution of the Soviet Union in 1991. The total GDP of the Soviet Union as percentage of that of the US had been constantly below the level of 44.4% reached in 1975. In 1991, just in the time of the dissolution of the USSR, it was back to 32.2% of the US, that is, to a level even lower than the one in 1950. With a size of the economy which varied between one third and less than 45% than one of the US, the Soviet Union had to make enormous efforts to maintain a relative balance in the military sector and in strategic technology with the US, and had to impose the severe compression of civil consumption. It had also to use the world influence of Marxist ideology in order to maintain some sort of equilibrium in the political sphere. The military-strategic balance was obtained by using a very large share of national resources in military industries, more than twice the proportion of the US, thereby greatly penalizing the level and the rate of growth of consumption for civilian use.

The French defeat in Vietnam in 1954, the coming into power of Castro in Cuba and the subsequent entry of Cuba (July 1960) as well as of several African countries in the socialist camp, considerably increased the Soviet influence in the world. However, the breaks between the USSR and Tito's Yugoslavia in 1948 and between the Soviet Union and China in 1959–1960 greatly narrowed the perimeter of Soviet's sphere of influence. The building of the Berlin Wall in August 1961 showed East Germany's economic weakness, since the country was unable to prevent a severe hemorrhage of people seeking to move to West Germany by any means. The outcome of the Berlin blockade (1948–1949), with the US air corridor to supply West Berlin; the 1950–1953 Korean War, which sanctioned the division between North and South Korea; the Cuban missile crisis of October 1962, all these events showed that neither of the two superpowers intended to unleash a nuclear war, which would have led to a planetary catastrophe. From 1947 up to the late 1980s, the balance of terror froze the two opposing blocs during the *Cold War*. There were, however, bloody indirect confrontations with conventional weapons, such as in Korea and then in the Vietnam War. From the point of view of science and technology, the Soviet Union was not far below the US in the strategic and military sector, with temporary moments of leadership in the space industry, such as the first human space flight in April 1961. However, the Soviet Union had a much lower average technological level in the production for civilian purposes, not only if compared with the US, but also if compared to most Western industrialized countries. This was mainly due both to the difficulty in fully using the Fordist model of development in an economy which compressed both consumption and wages, and to some important features of the planned economy.[1] Planning was very rigid; it was almost totally lacking in incentives for efficiency and quality and for the dissemination of innovations into the production of consumer goods for civilian use; it was too obsessed by military secrecy which hindered the transfer of technological innovations from the military to civilian use, transfer that instead had been so important for the US economy.

The US had thus a considerable advantage over the Soviet Union not only because of the larger economic size, but also for the greater product diversification, the better average quality of products, the more advanced technological level and the much higher average labor productivity. On the other hand, the Soviet Union maintained a higher employment rate and a lower unemployment rate than the US. Moreover, it could count on abundant reserves of natural resources, including oil and natural gas, in which it was a large net exporter, while the US had become a net oil importer since 1947.

The US was, however, a huge net exporter of wheat and other cereals, while in the post-Second World War period the Soviet Union had sometimes been a net importer of cereals.

After the dissolution of the Soviet Union in 1991, the Russian Federation, which had just over half the population and total GDP of the entire Soviet Union, saw the gap vis-à-vis the US dramatically widen both for population and economic size. As can be seen in Table 6.1, in 1991 the GDP of Russia accounted for only 18.9% of the US level. From 1989 to 1999, the severe transition crisis further greatly increased the gap for GDP, GDP per capita, and productivity of the Russian Federation vis-à-vis the US. The gap had instead diminished in the years 2000–2007 because of the robust Russian economic recovery. During the succeeding great recession, the gap decreased in the years 2008–2010, but then rose again.

After 1991, there no longer was a bi-polar world, albeit asymmetric, but there was a dominant economic, military, and political power, the US, while China was starting to become the rival economic giant. However, the Russian Federation maintained two important instruments of power: the very large exports of petroleum and natural gas and the strong military complex with its huge nuclear arsenal disposing of a variety of medium and long-range carriers.

However, in the last three decades, the rapid economic rise of China, India, and other emerging countries are deeply changing the world equilibrium.

6.2 The Main Points of Strength of the US Economy

What were the major strengths of the American economy after 1950?

They were numerous, although some had been fading over time—disappearing completely or gradually weakening.

In 1950, the US was the largest, richest, more complex, and technologically advanced economy in the world. It still had abundant reserves of a large number of raw materials; it housed the headquarters of the major international organizations (UN, IMF, the World Bank), where statutorily, the US held a decisive role. Moreover, the US were net creditors to most other major countries to which they also supplied raw materials, capital goods, and essential consumer goods. The US had also the key currency of the international monetary system (the dollar), which was prominent as a reserve currency, as means of international payment and as denominator of international financial assets. Finally, the US possessed the largest stock and commodity exchanges in the world, exceeding in breadth and financial sophistication the historic London financial market and also the Tokyo, Hong Kong, Paris, Frankfurt large stock exchange markets. These factors were associated with the huge military US machine, the political and ideological influence of the "country of freedom" and "the American myth", the gratitude owed by those Western countries which had benefited both from the decisive contribution of US troops in the two world wars and from the Marshall Plan. Moreover, there were many important cultural influences from the US (Hollywood cinema, pop music and jazz, vertical skyscrapers, great literature, mass advertising, the renowned universities, etc.).

It is therefore easily understandable how, in the second half of the twentieth Century, the US could exercise not only a great *hard power* but also an extensive *soft power*.[2] For a large part of Western public opinion, all this kept in the shade many illiberal aspects of the American model (the McCarthyism of the 1950s, the racial problem, the frequent military interventions abroad), and several major weaknesses in the American economic mechanism, which will be extensively dealt with in Chap. 7.

6.3 The Economic Consequences of the Wars

In the years before the First World War, if anybody asked both the man in the street and most political leaders which the largest economy in the world then was, the answer would have been the UK or one of the other major European powers. In reality, as we already know, the US was by far the largest economy in the world. However, in those years, the military and political force of the US was much lower than its economic strength. On the eve of the First World War, the armed forces of the US were less numerous than those of several other countries. The technological level of weapons, ships, and vehicles was, however, rather high and the production system for civilian use was huge. Thus, in a few months after entering the war, the US was able to recruit, arm, and equip growing masses of men and produce a large number of new warships, guns, machine guns, rifles, aircrafts, vehicles, uniforms, and supplies, for which the US contribution proved decisive to the outcome of the conflict.

In that period, there was a great and revolutionary change in military technology. The advent of machine guns, motor vehicles, rudimentary tanks, and aircrafts had radically changed the war on land. The increasing speed and autonomy of warships and the rapid growth of the power and range of cannons made the fleets an essential tool in the domain of the seas and of maritime communications and a formidable instrument for attacks on coastal cities and commercial convoys.

The relationship between economic size, technological capabilities of a country, and military power had become much closer. In the long run, the country with a larger economy and more advanced technological capabilities could have the upper hand over a country with more armed men and capable generals, when the former succeeded in prolonging the conflict over time.

In the Second World War, the association between economic size, advanced technology, and military strength was even more evident. The number and quality of tanks, aircrafts, ships, and motor vehicles and the use of radar and of massive bombing became decisive elements for the destiny of the war.

In the Second World War, the large economic, demographic military, and natural resources of the US and the Soviet Union, together with the enormous sacrifices of the UK and other countries, in the long run allowed the allied forces to defeat Germany, Japan, and Italy. Added together, the economies of these three countries did not attain the size of the US, and they were even more distant from the sum of the economies of the US, the Soviet Union, the UK and its empire.

In the US, during the Second World War, many Fordist corporations had to increase their investments and their size to cope with the enormous military effort and had to convert a large part of their production to military uses. The war was also a giant accelerator for new technologies and new products, often conceived or improved for military use and then transferred, in the post-war years, to civilian production. Jet airplanes, nuclear energy, the use of radar and nylon, rudimentary forms of computers and TV, and so on were mostly prewar inventions, but their development and mass production were strongly accelerated during the war by military usages and vast state financing.

Finally, the Second World War dramatically weakened the financial position of the UK and of most other European countries and Japan so that the US became a huge international net creditor country and could consolidate its leadership in world finance and the role of the dollar as key currency in the international market. The generous financial aids given to several European countries through the Marshall plan in the post-war years greatly enhanced the US economic, financial, and political leadership in the Western world, while the constitution and expansion of NATO contributed to the US dominance in military and strategic issues of the Western bloc.

Regional bloody wars, such as those in Korea, Vietnam, Iraq I and II, Afghanistan, Syria, Libya, and so on contributed to sustain the size and influence of the US military-industrial complex in the post-Second World War period and to extend the war arsenal and military technologies.[3] Yet, these wars caused enormous expenditures, and above all a great number of victims and human costs. In some cases, they determined hate and resentment toward the American imperial policy in a part of the US and world population, and in particular in the Islamic countries, reducing the global appeal of American soft power.

6.4 Economic, Military, and Political Powers

For the reasons presented in paragraph 6.3, in the long term, a large and growing economic power may determine, after considerable delay, an increased military power. As it is represented in Fig. 6.1, a growing mili-

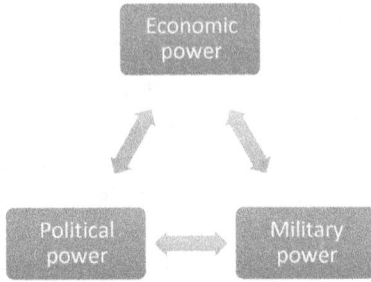

Fig. 6.1 Economic, political, and military powers

tary power, together with a large economic power, can lead, with further delays, to a greater political power, which in turn can help maintain or increase the economic power in a complex feedback between the three kinds of power.

At the end of the nineteenth Century, the US had already become the largest economic power. After the First World War, the US had also become the top military power and so it could enhance, despite the negative phase of the great depression, its financial and political power, becoming the top world power after the Second World War (Fig. 6.1).

6.5 The US and the Turin Index of Economic Power

A research group at the University of Turin has built a composite index of economic power, which we have called *Turin Index of Economic Power (TIEP)*. Since economic power depends on the interweaving and overlapping of internal and international elements, putting them together in a synthetic index allows us to build an economic power ranking and monitor its changes over time.

As with most composite quantitative indicators, the index has several limitations. They mainly depend on the choice, reasoned, but in any case discretionary, of the indicators which are at the basis of the synthetic index and on the difficulty of giving proper weights to the various indicators.

Favoring simplicity over methodological sophistication, we used a methodology widely employed in the construction of composite indexes. First, we chose six simple indicators: three associated to internal variables (total GDP in PPP, labor productivity, the Gini coefficient of income distribution), two indicators for external economic relations (the volume of exports, the stock of outbound FDI) and finally, a simple indicator for science and technology (the number of R&D employed persons).

Each indicator can provide a ranking of countries for each period—in our case a year. The exercise was restricted to ten major countries and repeated for several years, but here we report only the comparison between the years 1952, 2008, and 2017. Putting 1 for the country which ranks first for an indicator, 2 for the second place in the ranking, 3 for the third place, and so on, we came to build the composite index for economic power.

Tables 6.2 and 6.3 show the rankings of 10 selected countries for economic power in the years 1952, 2008, and 2017 for each of the six indicators used to build the composite TIEP index.

Table 6.2 Selected internal indicators in selected countries

Country	Total GDP in PPP EKS			Labor productivity			Gini index		
	R. 1952	R. 2008	R. 2017	R. 1952	R. 2008	R. 2017	R. 1952	R. 2008	R. 2017
China	10	2	1	10	9	9	1	9	8
US	1	1	2	1	1	1	6	8	9
India	7	4	3	9	10	10	9	6	6
Japan	8	3	4	8	6	6	3	1	4
Germany	3	6	5	4	4	3	4	3	1
USSR-Russia	2	5	6	7	7	7	2	7	7
Brazil	9	7	7	6	8	8	10	10	10
UK	4	9	8	2	5	5	8	5	5
France	5	8	9	3	2	2	5	2	2
Italy	6	10	10	5	3	4	7	4	3

R = Rank. Labor productivity = GDP/employment. USSR in 1952, Russian federation in 2008 and 2017. The data refer to the present borders except for Russia (2008 and 2017) and the USSR (1952). For the Gini index, closest available data to the years 1952 and 2017. Our elaborations on data extracted by Maddison (2003), Conference Board (2018), World Bank (2018), and national sources

Table 6.3 Exports, stock of outward FDI, and persons employed in R&D

Countries	Exports of goods			Stock of outward FDI			R&D employed persons		
	R. 1952	R. 2008	R. 2017	R. 1952	R. 2008	R. 2017	R. 1952	R. 2008	R. 2017
China	10	2	1	10	9	4	10	1	1
US	1	3	2	1	1	1	1	2	2
India	8	10	8	9	10	10	8	8	8
Japan	9	4	4	8	5	2	6	3	3
Germany	4	1	3	3	3	5	4	5	5
USSR-Russia	5	7	9	6	7	8	2	4	4
Brazil	6	9	10	5	8	9	9	9	9
UK	2	8	7	2	2	3	3	6	6
France	3	5	5	4	4	6	5	7	7
Italy	7	6	6	7	6	7	7	10	10

Note: Our elaborations from data extracted from OECD (2018), UNTCAD (2018), UNESCO (2018) and estimates from various national and international sources for 1952. Number of R&D employed persons from UNESCO and OECD sources and from various national sources in the years closest to 1952 and 2017

The final result for the index of economic power in the three years is shown in Table 6.4. In 2017, the US was first, followed by Japan and China, while in 1952, the US had preceded the UK, Germany, and the Soviet Union.

The indicators used to construct the TIEP were chosen for the following reasons.

1. Total GDP in purchasing power parity (PPP) is an indicator, albeit crude and for many aspects controversial, of the economic size of the country.
2. The index of labor productivity (GDP/employment) was chosen as a proxy of the efficiency and technological capability of the country.
3. The Gini coefficient on income distribution helps explain the degree of social cohesion of the country, assuming that the smaller the economic disparities are the greater, other things being equal, is social cohesion.

So, in our ranking, a lower Gini index is considered better than a higher one.

Table 6.4 The TIEP: 1952, 2008, and 2017[a]

Country	1952 Score	1952 TIEP rank	2008 Score	2008 TIEP rank	2017 Score	2017 TIEP rank
US	12	1	16	1	17	1
Japan	42	7	22	2	23	2
China	51	10	32	5	24	3
Germany	22	3	22	2	27	4
France	25	4	28	4	32	5
UK	21	2	35	6	34	6
Italy	29	6	39	8	40	7
USSR-Russia[b]	25	4	37	7	41	8
India	50	9	48	9	45	9
Brazil	45	8	51	10	49	10

[a]The scores are given by the sum of the position of a country in the rankings of the six indicators
[b]USSR for 1952, Russia for the other years

4. Exports of goods represent an indicator of the country's ability to penetrate foreign markets.
5. The stock of outward FDI is an indicator of the active presence abroad of multinationals which originate in the country.
6. The total number of people employed in Research and Development activities is a crude measure of the research capacity and the innovation drive of a country, since the people involved in research and development activities not only help in producing inventions and innovations but also convey the knowledge of other people's contribution in research and innovations to the domestic productive system. We have preferred to use the total number of people employed in R&D rather than total spending in R&D since the unit pay for these people greatly varies among countries according to the level of development and the cost of living prevailing in the various economies.

In 2017, as can be expected, the US was at the top of the ranking for productivity and the stock of outward FDI, but it was preceded by China for total GDP in PPP and for the number of persons employed in R&D. It was also surpassed by several other countries as regards the Gini coefficient and again by China with regard to the value of exports of goods. The US was then the world's leading country for the overall economic power (TIEP), but with a much less dominant position than in 1952 and in 2008 when the US headed the ranking for the majority of the indicators.

Although in 2017 China ranked third in World TIEP, after the US and Japan, the Asian giant is rapidly advancing in the world ranking and will soon exceed Japan, and in the future also the US Its present main weaknesses consist in the relatively high Gini index, the low labor productivity, and the limited FDI presence in the world, but for the latter two indicators, China is growing much more rapidly than most other countries and so will fairly soon close the gap with Japan, and in the long run, it will probably exceed also the US.

As regards economic inequality, as measured by the Gini index, China is at present very close to the vastly unsatisfactory US situation. However, in China, the rapid increasing inequality trend seems to have been checked and slightly reversed during recent years.

The USSR was in the fourth place in the 1952 TIEP index, after the US, the UK—which then was still at the head of a mighty colonial empire—and Germany. In 2017, the Russian Federation was in eighth place, after the dissolution of the Soviet Union and the severe transition crisis in the 1990s, and the recovery occurred during 2000s.

The international great economic recession starting in 2007–2008 and badly hitting, with different intensity and duration, the US and several other economies has led to some relevant changes in the TIEP positions of our selected countries. It must be noticed that the position of the two great Asian emerging powers, China and India, have remarkably improved in some of the six indicators and, for China, also in the overall TIEP index.

Notes

1. See, for this aspect also Valli (2002), pp. 40–41.
2. See Nye (2004).

3. Vietnam War and Islamic terrorism have, however, indicated that traditional forms of conventional warfare encounter great difficulties against guerrilla tactics or terrorist actions.

References

Conference Board. 2018. Accessed June 9, 2018. https://www.conference-board.org/data/economydatabase/.
Maddison, A. 2003. *The World Economy: Historical Statistics*. Paris: OECD.
Nye, J.S., Jr. 2004. *Soft Power: The Means to Success in World Politics*. New York: Public Affairs/Perseus Books.
OECD. 2018. http://www.oecd.org.
UNESCO. 2018. https://en.unesco.org.
UNTCAD. 2018. www.untcad.org.
Valli, V. 2002. *L'Europa e l'economia mondiale*. Roma: Carocci.
World Bank. 2018. www.worldbank.org.

7

Main Weaknesses in the American Economic Power

7.1 The Dependence on Foreign Oil and Other Raw Materials

In the 1950s, though being the most powerful economy in the world, the US had some creeping and insidious structural weaknesses.

The first weakness is associated to the dependence on net imports of oil and other strategically important raw materials.

Up to 1946, the US was still a net exporter of oil and oil products, but since 1947 it has become a net importer and, later on, for a long period, its dependence from abroad has significantly increased. Up to the beginning of the 1970s, the foreign dependence mainly increased because the rise in consumption was faster than the rise in domestic production, but later on also because the US was experiencing a large and continuous decline in crude oil production. While in 1950 net imports of crude oil were still very low (about 0.5 million barrel per day), up to 2005 they rapidly increased, reaching over 12.5 million barrel per day (see Fig. 7.1). In the following years, net oil imports progressively fell, reaching 3.7 million barrel per day in 2017 mainly because of the large growth in shale oil production.[1]

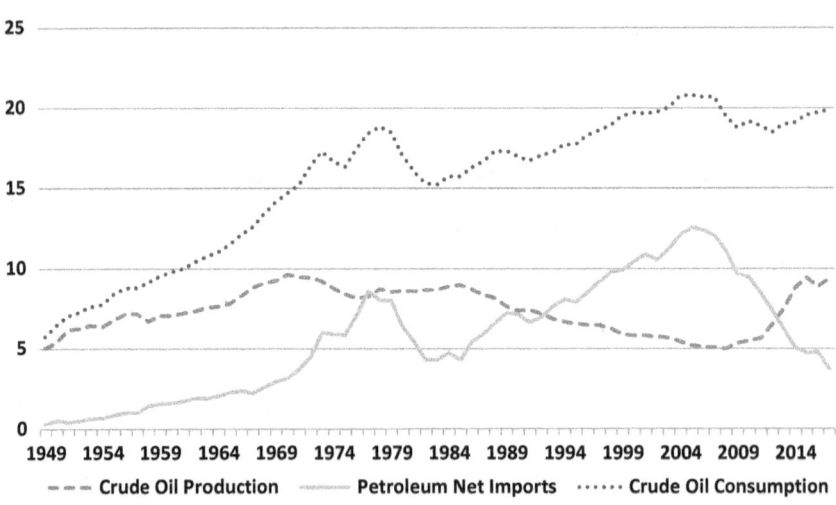

Fig. 7.1 US oil dependence from abroad: 1949–2017 (million barrels/day)
Source: EIA (2018), our elaboration

In the 2000s, the US has, in fact, experienced *the shale oil and shale gas revolution*, which has strongly reduced US dependence on foreign crude oil and has cancelled the dependence on natural gas. If, as regards oil, the US has greatly reduced its net imports from foreign sources, as regards gas the US has become self-sufficient and even a net exporter since the beginning of 2017. This revolution has consisted in the exploitation, through innovative fracking techniques and other means, of oil and gas trapped in shale or present in sandstone and carbonate formations (tight oil or gas).

After the end of the Second World War, US crude oil production rose to a peak of 9.6 million barrels per day in 1970, then diminished to 5 million barrels per day in 2008 and went back to 9.3 million in 2017. The recovery was essentially due to shale oil that, in 2016, represented about 48% of total production, while it had been marginal up to the 1990s. The production of natural gas had a rapid growth from 2005 on, mainly due to the boom in shale and tight gas, which in 2016 went up to about half of the total dry natural gas production.[2]

The shale revolution has profoundly changed the energy situation in the US. Not only is the country much less energy dependent from abroad but in the US also the cost of unconventional natural gas (shale and tight gas) has become much lower than the international price fixed in long-term contracts for gas supplies between EU countries, Japan, and the main producers (Russia, Algeria, Indonesia for liquefied gas, etc.). This has induced the US to utilize gas instead of coal and oil products for several purposes (electrical power stations, domestic heating, etc.), somewhat reducing CO_2 emissions. The lower price of energy has, moreover, contributed to increase the US competitiveness in world markets vis-à-vis Japan and European competitors which have to pay much higher rates for imported natural gas.

However, the shale revolution has also produced severe negative effects on the environment. Fracking techniques require vast lands, deep multiple drilling, and the use of great amounts of pressurized water and solvents. In this way, deep water reserves are wasted and polluted, the stability and fertility of the soil can be damaged, and large rural areas are seriously spoilt.

The shale revolution has contributed to sustain oil and gas world production and world reserves, postponing for a few decades the peak in world production that had been foreseen by several authors for the beginning of the twenty-first century. At the same time, *the great recession* that commenced in 2007 in the US has contributed to reduce the growth in world demand for energy, while the increased production of energy from renewables has diminished the utilization of oil in electricity production and other usages. All this, together with the erratic oil policy of Saudi Arabia and other OPEC countries and the consequences of the wars in Middle East on oil output, have contributed to the compression of oil prices. The prices went down from the historical maximum of about 156$ a barrel reached in June 2008 to a level of 30–65$ from the second half of 2015 to the first quarter of 2018. Very low oil prices, under 30$ a barrel, led to several failures of shale oil and gas producers or to sharp reductions in their investment, but such abnormally low oil prices lasted only for a few months in the first half of 2016.

Besides oil and gas, other strategically important raw materials, such as manganese, rare earths, iron, bauxite, zinc, nickel, titanium, lithium, and silicon carbide, have been imported in huge and growing proportions by US firms from China, Canada, and other countries.[3] Some of these imports are aimed at maintaining strategic domestic reserves or at benefiting from lower foreign prices, but many are due to the exhaustion of domestic mines or the incapacity to face the rapid rise in demand for these goods.

7.2 The Environmental Problem in the US

Since the 1950s, the growing utilization of oil and natural gas has been accompanied by a severe worsening of the natural environment, which has not been faced by adequate environmental policies for several decades.

As regards environment, the US has benefited from privileged conditions if compared with many overpopulated zones of Europe, Asia, Africa, and Latin America, which have more intensively exploited their natural resources. The far-sighted creation of large national and State natural parks and the US lower population density had maintained some of these advantages.

However, since the end of the Second World War, there has been a vast population growth; a great enlargement of big metropolitan areas; the expansion of voracious energy-consuming steel and cement industries; the rapid increase of many polluting and land-consuming industrial and services activities; the enormous growth in cars and trucks circulation; the too limited recourse to public transportation (with the partial exception of cities such as New York, Chicago, New Orleans, and San Francisco); the massive usage of coal, oil, and gas; the mounting recourse to air conditioning and to electricity in the whole country.

All this, in the absence of an adequate anti-pollution policy, has led to the production of an enormous level of total emissions and wastes, which have polluted air, water, and soil in a large part of the country and have heavily reduced the extension of green, clean zones.

For several decades, as regards total CO_2 emissions, the US has been the largest polluter in the world,[4] and it has been surpassed only by the much more populous China since 2005. Total US CO_2 emissions have somewhat diminished since 2007, mainly because of the reduction in the use of coal in electric power plants and the increase of less polluting gas powered units and of solar, wind, and other renewable sources. However, per capita CO_2 emissions in the US are still among the highest in the world, only surpassed by Australia and smaller oil-rich countries, such as Qatar, Kuwait, United Arab Emirates, and Oman.

CO_2, nitrous oxide, and methane emissions coming from human activities powerfully contribute to *greenhouse gas* effects and to *global warming*.[5] Several international agreements, such as those decided in

Kyoto (1997) and Paris (2015) international conferences on climate change, have therefore tried to limit and control these emissions.

As regards environment, the US policy has been weak and erratic, partly because of the enormous influence of the major oil, coal, and electricity corporations on US politics, and in particular on the Republican party. For example, the US did not ratify the Kyoto protocol and, although in 2016 President Obama had signed the Paris Agreement, in 2017, President Trump announced that the US will withdraw from that international agreement.[6]

7.3 Phases of Ascent and Decline of the US Economy

If we define *relative economic ascent* a period of about two-three decades in which the per capita GDP of a country grows substantially more than the world economy, and *relative economic decline* a period in which it grows substantially less than the world economy, we can see that the US has passed through alternate phases.

In the 1870–1950 period, as Table 7.1 shows, notwithstanding the severe *great depression* of the 1930s, the US had a period *of relative economic ascent* and registered an average rate of growth of per capita GDP considerably higher than the world economy.

Table 7.1 Phases of ascent and decline of the US economy (1870–2017)

Country or area	1870–1913	1913–1950	1950–1973	1973–2003	2003–2017
US	1.8	1.6	2.5	1.9	0.9
Western Europe	1.3	0.8	4.0	1.9	0.9
Russia-USSR-Russia	1.1	1.8	3.4	−0.4	3.0
Japan	1.5	0.9	8.1	2.1	0.9
China	0.1	−0.6	2.8	6.0	8.8
India	0.5	−0.2	1.4	3.1	6.2
World	1.3	0.9	2.9	1.6	2.7

Average compound rate of change of per capita GDP in PPP
PPP GK until 2003; PPP EKS after 2003
Sources: Maddison (2007), p. 383. Conference Board (2018): our elaborations for the years 2003–2017

In the years 1950–1973, the US, though improving a little their rate of growth, had a phase of *relative economic decline*, mainly due to the partial, but impetuous, *catching up* of Japan, the four Asian tigers, and several European and non-European countries.

As we shall see in detail in the next chapter, after the first great energy crisis, the US tried to react to the preceding phase of relative economic decline with a strong push in favor of international trade liberalization and then of an extensive *economic and financial globalization* in an attempt to create a *global economic empire*.

In the years 1973–2003, the US thus managed to grow a little more rapidly than the world economy, in a period characterized by the great economic advancement of large emerging economies such as China since 1978 and India since 1992. On the other hand, especially in the 1980s and in the 1990s, many African, West Asian, and Latin American countries had to face severe economic difficulties.

The US results were, however, uncertain and partially contradictory. The rapid deindustrialization, the growing importance of services, and the loss in competitiveness of some US industrial sectors led to a weakening of the trend rate of growth of labor productivity and to a structural worsening of the balance of current accounts.

Finally, in the years 2003–2007, the US continued to nurture the preconditions for the great financial crisis of 2007–2008 and the consequent *great recession*. Despite the following recovery and expansion, in the whole 2003–2017 period, the US economy grew slowly, like the European Union, but more weakly than the world economy and, in particular, than those of China, India, Indonesia, and several other emerging economies. In those years, therefore, the US had another phase of *relative economic decline*.

7.4 From Surplus to Structural Deficit in the US Balance of Current Accounts

In the second half of the 1940s and in the 1950s, the US had benefited from three great advantages in international markets.

First of all, the US was the largest producer and net exporter of many goods, including cereals and most manufactured products, mainly because of the enormous size and strength of the American economy and the fact that war destructions had only marginally touched the American soil, while in most other industrialized countries, they had been devastating. Moreover, in the US the difficult reconversion phase from military to civilian production had been completed quite rapidly. This was partly due to the Marshall plan, which had allowed several European countries to be able to buy American goods with American money, favoring the US economic recovery in exports and aggregate demand.

Secondly, many great American corporations had bigger scale economies and more advanced technologies than European or Japanese competitors and so they could offset their higher labor costs thanks to a higher level of labor productivity.

Thirdly, the American economy could count on the strength of the US dollar, which, after Bretton Woods, had become the key currency in the international monetary system.

Finally, the gradual dissolution of the great European colonial empires in the second half of the 1940s and in the two following decades could open new markets to US exports and FDI in the former British, French, German and Dutch colonies.

It is therefore not surprising that in a large part of the years 1946–1968, the US could reach a conspicuous surplus in their balance of current accounts, registering small deficits only in a few years, and in particular when the US was engaged in severe military conflicts, such as the 1950–1953 Korean War.

However, at the end of the 1960s and at the beginning of the 1970s, the escalation of the Vietnam War strongly contributed to the deterioration of the US balance of current accounts.

Moreover, many other long-term economic factors, such as a growth in productivity lower than in other major industrialized countries and an anticipated deindustrialization process, were cooperating to deteriorate the balance of current accounts.

Within the current accounts, the merchandise balance remained positive until 1970, but then it became structurally negative in most of the following years.

From 1971 to 2017 the balance of current accounts was marginally positive only for 7 out of the 46 years. From 1992 to 2006 the deficit in the balance of current account in percentage of GDP rapidly increased from −0.8 in 1995 to −5.1 in 2004.

This was partly due to the rapid rise of the imports from China and the consequences of the wars in Afghanistan and Iraq. In the following years, the percentage remained negative, but diminished to −2.4 in 2016, also because of the consequences of the *great recession* and of the decreasing value of energy imports.

All this led to a progressive rise in the stock of foreign debt, which in 1987 surpassed the level of the stock of US credits toward foreign countries. Since 1987, the US has thus become a *net debtor country* toward the rest of the world and the stock of net external debt has progressively increased to almost $8000 billion in 2017,[7] the highest level in the world. This enormous stock of net external debt is sustainable only as long as the dollar remains the key currency in the world monetary system and the rest of the world continues to have confidence in the solidity of the American currency (Fig. 7.2).

For about half a century, the US has, therefore, benefited from the great power, as well as the responsibility, associated to its *international monetary seigniorage*. The US could continue to buy goods and services from other countries well in excess of the value of its exports as long as the US dollar was willingly accepted by the international community.

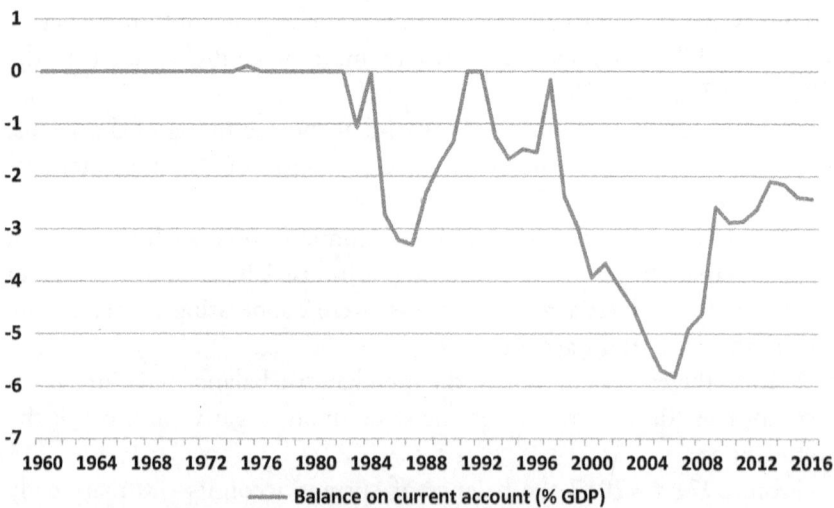

Fig. 7.2 Balance of current accounts in the US economy in percent of GDP (1960–2016)
Source: OECD (2018a), our elaboration

7.5 The Weakening of the Dollar

The economic events we have highlighted in the previous sections had important consequences on the trends of the rate of exchange of the US dollar.

In 1944, the dominant economic, political, and military power of the US greatly influenced the final results of the Bretton Woods Conference and led to the acceptance of White's plan instead of the more far-sighted and articulated plan proposed by the great British economist John Maynard Keynes. Bretton Woods built an international monetary system based on the US dollar, which at that time was convertible into gold. Two crucially important international financial organizations were created: the IMF and the World Bank, and their statute gave a prominent role to the US and to a few large European countries. The Bretton Woods system was founded on substantially *fixed exchange rates* among participating countries.[8] Exchange rates were anchored to the US dollar and indirectly to gold because of the fixed $-gold conversion rate. The US dollar, becoming the key currency in the international monetary system, has been detained in the reserves of many central banks in huge quantities, has been used in most international trade and financial transactions and has served as denominator of a number of international financial assets.

In the 1950s and in a great part of the 1960s, the balance of current accounts of the US was in surplus and so the main problem in the international monetary system was the *dollar shortage*, that is, the difficulty of obtaining a sufficient volume of dollars to face the continuous expansion of international monetary and financial transactions and the demand from central banks eager to replenish their international reserves with a strong currency such as the US dollar. However, as we have seen, the mounting foreign expenditures associated with the escalation in the Vietnam War and the structural worsening in the US balance of current accounts led to a severe crisis of the US dollar at the beginning of the 1970s.

In 1971, the Nixon administration was forced to declare the inconvertibility of the dollar into gold and a first official devaluation of the US dollar, followed by a second devaluation in January 1973. In that year, the passage of the US and of a number of other countries to a system of *flexible exchange rates* decreed the end of the Bretton Woods system as it was originally conceived.

After the 1973 great energy crisis and up to 1979, the exchange rate of the dollar worsened against strong currencies, such as the German mark[9] and the Japanese yen, but appreciated vis-à-vis the weaker currencies of most other countries.

In the first half of the 1980s, the dollar appreciated against most other world currencies, due to the particular mix of economic policies, which had been called *Reaganomics*. A highly restrictive monetary policy had led to relatively high interest rates, which had attracted large inflows of foreign portfolio capitals and had sustained the value of the dollar. A mixed fiscal policy (reduction of taxes and a sharp increase in defense expenditures, with heavy cuts in social expenditures) completed Reagan's macroeconomic package. All this brought about a consistent revaluation of the US dollar, which lasted till mid-1985, but was followed by a long period of depreciation vis-à-vis strong currencies such as the German mark and the Japanese yen (see Fig. 7.3).

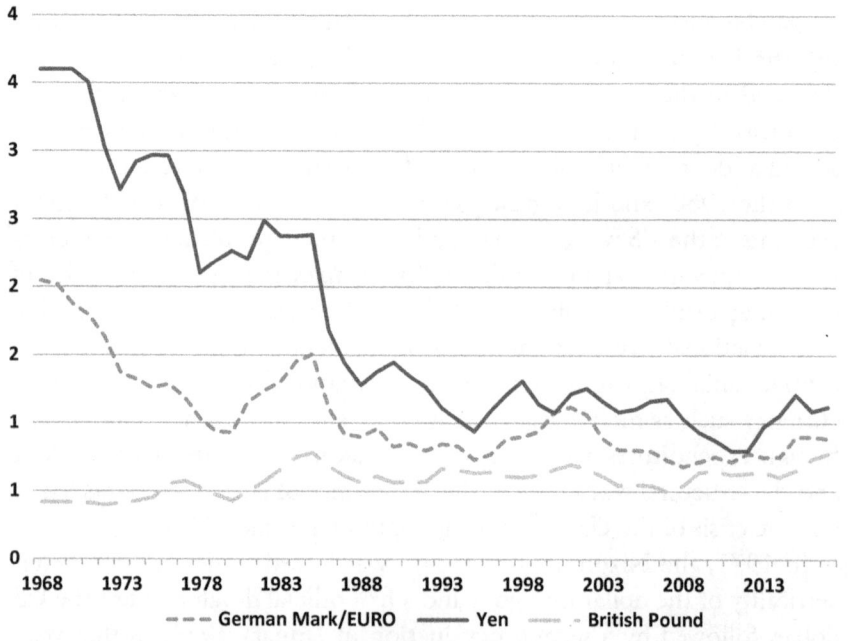

Fig. 7.3 US dollar rates of exchange: 1968–2017. Total, National currency units/ US dollar (a). Note: (a) For the Japanese yen 100 yen/dollar
Source: OECD (2017b), our elaboration

After the January 1, 1999, institution of the euro, the dollar found a new strong competitor in the international monetary market. The rate of exchange, that is, the number of euros necessary to get one dollar, was about 0.94 when the euro started; went up to over 1.1 in 2001; but, after several swings and a sharp fall, partly due to the sub-prime crisis, it went down to about 0.68 in 2008, then rose to over 0.90 in 2015–2016, finally reaching about 0.89 in 2017, relatively close to the level of 1999.

The very large fluctuations in the Euro/USD exchange rates in the last decade are mainly due to the *great recession*, which first struck the US and then, with a certain delay, spread to the European Union, hitting with particular violence Greece and the other most vulnerable EU economies.

Also the economic relations with China have had a rapidly growing importance for the American economy and the US dollar.

While from the beginning of the 1980s up to January 1994, the Chinese currency (Yuan) had a strong depreciation vis-à-vis the US dollar, from that time to January 2014 there was a 30% revaluation of the Chinese currency, followed by a new period of relatively modest depreciation. In the 1990s and 2000s the very rapid expansion of Chinese exports had contributed to lead to a huge surplus in China's balance of current account and to large positive trade balances toward the US and several other countries. The recent slowing down of the rate of growth of the Chinese economy and of its exports has somewhat reduced China's trade surplus toward the US and other countries, inducing Chinese authorities to decide a limited devaluation of the currency since 2014. On the other hand, since the 2000s, China has contributed to sustain the value of the dollar, buying a huge stock of US financial assets, and in particular US Treasury bonds, so that a substantial part of China's trade surplus has been reinvested in the US economy. Presently, China, having recently surpassed Japan, is the top country as owner of US financial assets, and in January 2018, it owned about $1.17 trillion of US debt versus the $1.07 trillion of Japan. Though being a huge sum, China owns only about 5.7% of the enormous US debt.

Until 2008, the euro seemed to be the rising competitor of the dollar, but the badly managed Greek crisis in 2010–2011, the errors of EU economic policies, the fragility of EU institutions, and the consequences of the *Brexit* have greatly weakened the world appeal in the European currency. On the other hand, the economic and financial ascent of China might give the Yuan, if made fully convertible, the opportunity to become the future great competitor of the dollar in the international monetary system.

7.6 Rising Inequalities in Wages, Income, and Wealth

Social cohesion in a country largely depends on low inequalities in wages, income, and wealth, on ample employment opportunities, and on an adequate welfare system.

During the *New Deal*, in the Second World War and in the post-war period, the US attained a large reduction in economic inequalities until the late 1960s.

Inequalities in wages were very high before and during a part of the *great depression*, but in the 1940s there was *the great compression* in wage disparities.[10]

While in the 1950s and 1960s there was only a minor increase in wage differentials, in the succeeding decades *wage differentials* exploded, reaching the 1948 level around mid-1980s and then continuing to grow, in particular favoring top wage earners (CEO or other top managers) versus the rank-and-file workers.[11] Generous bonuses, fringe benefits, and stock options in favor of top managers heavily contributed to enlarge the gap. While in the 1950s the compensations of US top managers (wages + all benefits) were 30–50 times the average wages of blue-collar workers, in the 2000s several CEOs earned (including stock options) 400–500 times the pay of common workers in their firms. For example, in 2008, Rick Wagoner, the CEO of the giant automobile corporation General Motors, obtained total compensations of $14.9 million, although the firm had lost $30.9 billion, risked failure, and was saved only by a massive public intervention. The same happened for top managers in several investment banks in 2007, though most of them were largely responsible for the incoming great financial crisis.

Several authors justify the present enormous compensations of top managers of big financial and industrial firms as due to their high contribution to the productivity of the firm, to their generally high human capital and to the burden of the risks and responsibilities associated with their jobs.

Other authors emphasize the role played by the contracts with shareholders that provide top managers with rich incentives in order to induce them to maximize the total shareholders' revenues in form of dividends and capital gains. However, it is probably true that, as Bebchuk and Fried[12] have sustained, the very high compensations of top managers are mainly due to their *managerial power*, that is, to the fact that they control or have a heavy influence on the board of directors and are able to maximize their compensations, with the limit of a sort of *outrage constraint*.

Our opinion is that, in general, the problem is due to a complex feedback between power and economy. Let us imagine a very large bank or a non-financial corporation which obtains great profits, that has branches and relations in several parts of the world, that, maybe, keeps black funds in fiscal paradises to use for incentives or corruption, that has a huge advertising budget and can influence mass media, political parties, and political leaders. Consequently, the power of the bank or corporation and the power of their top managers will be very strong and the latter might also heavily influence the board and the compensation committee of their firm. Moreover, since the beginning of the 1970s, the growing globalization has greatly widened the size, and therefore the financial and economic power of several giant banks or multinational corporations and of their leaders.

High and growing wages differentials, together with the rising profit margins associated to the faster growth of productivity with respect to wages occurred since the end of the 1970s, strongly contributed to determine rising income and wealth inequalities.

In the US, high paid workers and rich people could save more than rank-and file workers and of people living on a meager and sometimes precarious pay. Annual savings accumulated over time and the growing stock of savings of rich individuals or households generated rising yields in the form of interests on bonds, or dividends and capital gains on shares, or rents from the location of apartments, or large capital gains in housing and in financial assets. Therefore, old wealth or growing and persistent wage differentials could lead to rising income and wealth differentials. Besides, entrepreneurs or other independent workers with big earnings could save much more than other autonomous workers, so that in this field there were growing income and wealth disparities as well.

Moreover, the sharp rise of neo-liberalist economic policies in part of the 1970s and even more during Reagan's and George W. Bush's administrations, led to large tax reductions for rich people, and this has heavily contributed to the rapid increase in income inequalities. A work by Piketty, Saez, and Zucman shows that, while the tax rate of the top 1% pre-tax income group fell from about 44% in 1974 down to about 37% in 2014, the tax rate of the bottom 50% rose from 27% to almost 30%.[13]

In his second book, *The Audacity of Hope*, Barack Obama wrote of an encounter with one of the richest men in the world, the US billionaire Warren Buffett, who rather surprisingly told him that he considered deeply unjust that he, without any attempt to evade taxes, could pay an effective tax rate lower than the one paid by his receptionist.[14] Obama explained that this mainly depended on the fact that a great part of the billionaire's income derived from dividends and capital gains, which, since 2003 were paying only a 15% tax rate versus the almost double tax rate paid by Buffett's employee on her wages. When elected president, Barack Obama unsuccessfully tried to pass the so-called *Buffet rule* stating that "no household making over $1 million a year should pay a smaller share of its income in taxes than middle-class families pay".

Emmanuel Saez, Thomas Piketty, Gabriel Zucman, Anthony B. Atkinson, and several other authors have demonstrated the great rise in income inequalities in the US at the end of the 1970s and in the following decades.

In 1980, the share of national income going to the top 1% was about 10.6% and it almost doubled in 2016 exceeding 20%. In the same period, the share going to the bottom 50% diminished from 20.3% to about 13%. Moreover, the US trends were much more divergent than the Western European one. In Western Europe, from 1980 to 2016, the share of top 1% rose from 10% to 12% while the share of bottom 50% fell from a little less than 24% to less than 22%.[15]

Also a synthetic indicator on income distribution among households, such as the Gini index, going from zero (no inequality) to 1 (perfect inequality), shows that, according to World Bank estimates in 2015, the US had the highest Gini index among the major industrialized countries and that its level had greatly increased since the 1980s.

7.7 Terrorism and Organized Crime

The US has also been plagued by international and local terrorism and by the widespread activity of large criminal organizations, such as the mafia, the Chinese triads, and the Latin American drugs cartels.

International terrorism, which previously had frequently hit American targets in foreign locations but had seldom operated on the American soil, on September 11, 2001, had struck the very heart of America with the devastating attacks on the Twin Towers and the Pentagon and then has been active in several other cases.

In the September 11, 2011, tragic attacks, 2996 people died and over 6000 were injured.

The reaction of the George Bush Administration led to the wars in Afghanistan and Iraq. The war in Afghanistan began in October 2001 and was directed against the Taliban regime, which had supported Osama Bin Laden and his organization (al Qaeda), the originators of the September 11 attacks. The Iraq war began in March 2003 and was made under the false assumptions that its ruler, Saddam Hussein, had favored the terrorist attacks and that he possessed and was ready to use mass-destruction weapons. The war, though introducing some forms of democracy in Iraq, had dreadful effects on the difficult political, social, and military equilibriums of the entire Middle-East and has heavily contributed to the Syrian crisis and the rise of fundamentalist Islamic movement ISIL (DAESH) in vast Iraq's and Syria's zones. ISIL was then fought and defeated by a heterogeneous coalition composed by the US, Russia, and Syrian armed forces, Kurds, Hezbollah, and so on whose objectives, as regards the future of Syria, were divergent. The Syrian unending civil war has also led to over 5 million refugees desperately trying to emigrate to neighboring countries, to Europe or to the US.

The George Bush administration and the fight against terrorism also led to cases of torture and severe violations of human rights in Cuba's Guantanamo and in Iraq's Abu Ghraib prisons. Although Obama's administration had put a brake to these practices, it had not closed Guantanamo, as Obama had promised in his 2008 electoral campaign, and the Trump administration has continued its use.

Domestic terrorism is mainly due to supremacist groups or violent individuals and is favored by the easy access to deadly war weapons sustained by right-wing groups, such as the National Rifle Association.

The most poisonous fruit of criminal organizations, the smuggling of heavy drugs, has contributed to produce, in a rapidly growing trend, over a million addicts and hundred thousand deaths a decade, like a major war. In 2015, drug overdoses killed over 52,000 people, more than car crashes or several minor wars. Overdose deaths have more than tripled from 1999 to 2015, are growing very rapidly, and are much more widespread in the US territory than at the end of the 1990s.[16]

A large part of these deaths are due to the illicit diffusion of drugs operated by the main criminal organizations with immense profits despite the great efforts made by US agencies, such as the Drug Enforcement Administration (DEA).

The lucrative, but highly corruptive, activities of the major criminal organizations in the US have regarded, besides drugs trafficking, racketing, extortion, the control of prostitution and gaming, usury, the recycling of dirty money, and so on. Moreover, big crime has massively and increasingly invested in restaurants, in constructions, and in a number of other legal economic ventures.

7.8 The Withering of the American Dream

Since the 1980s, the social and economic policy of Reagan and the two Bush and Trump administrations, only in part revised during Clinton's and Obama's presidency, has gradually modeled American society in order to protect the interests of the more affluent part of the population and to largely exclude from the benefits of economic growth a sizable and growing part of the population, that is, the very poor and part of the middle class.

Social mobility has also gradually but sharply diminished since the beginning of the 1980s. In 2007, the Nobel laureate Paul Krugman wrote that social mobility in the US is weaker than in France, Canada, and perhaps in Great Britain and much weaker than in Scandinavian countries.[17]

Social mobility had already deteriorated in the late 1980s. On this regard, Krugman has quoted an interesting result from a 1988 national survey, which had compared the results of the test taken by all students at the end of their final high school year and the rate of entrance to college. Only 29% of the best students coming from low-income families entered the university system, versus 74% of the best students coming from richer families. But, even more, the percentage of second-rate students coming from richer families entering colleges was 30%, therefore higher than the percentage of first-rate students coming from poor families.[18] Since, on the average, university degrees lead to better job opportunities and higher wages than high school degrees, the results show that social mobility was difficult for a large part of good students coming from low-income families. We must also take into account the very high cost of tertiary education in the US, the inadequate number of scholarships, the high financial burden of educational loans, and the fact that, in the 1990s and in the 2000s, social mobility has further decreased for high school graduates who could not continue their studies at university level.

In 2017, Davis and Mazumder[19] have also shown that, after the large rise in inequality started around 1980, there has been a sharp decline in the US intergenerational mobility.

One may think that the American dream remains high in a country where a black president such as Barack Obama can be elected, but we must remind that in 2006 senator Obama chose for his book, *Audacity of Hope*, the subtitle *Thoughts on Reclaiming the American Dream*, meaning that the American dream had almost vanished and had to be refreshed and fully restored. Moreover, writing about the effects of globalization, Barack Obama, pointed out that in the preceding decade the strong economic growth of the US economy had been accompanied by "an anemic growth of jobs, big leaps in productivity but flatlining wages, hefty corporate profits, but a shrinking share of those profits going to the workers...."[20]

7.9 The Erosion of Democracy

In the last decades, there has been a process of gradual *erosion of democracy* in the US and in several other democratic countries.

In 1859, John Stuart Mill reminded us that, in spite of its many limits, representative democracy is the form of state that can better reconcile political authority with individual freedom. A great success of modern representative democracy has been the universal suffrage, which has given the possibility of voting to every adult citizen, without regard to wealth, education, gender, religion, and race.

With the universal suffrage, every adult man or woman has one vote, and thus the possibility to determine in equal way the election of their representatives.

However, the political organization is so complex and so costly that soon it was necessary the constitution of many associations, movements, and parties that could powerfully influence the voting decisions.

There has also been the growing development of a great number of media: newspapers, books, reviews, radio, television, internet blogs, socials, and so on that can strongly influence the political parties and the electoral decisions of voters.

In recent decades, there has also been another crucial trend. The traditional forms of political process (meetings and debates in the sections of parties or in public forums, face-to face encounters, public speeches, etc.) have gradually been largely replaced by the growing and extensive, but very expensive, use of traditional media (TV debates, interviews to newspapers, electoral spots) and by the rapid and massive use of internet through specialized sites, blogs, socials, internet messages, twitter, and so on.

Political parties have been structurally weakened, while their political leaders have become stronger. In particular, the leaders who could have, for their function or for the vast amount of money they could collect, a large audience in popular media or internet, felt sufficiently strong and so they drastically reduced their direct human contacts with the sections of the party and their relations with the common citizens.

Using a rough, but useful neologism, we will call this phenomenon the *mediatization* of *politics*.

Parties have gradually lost the drive of their supporters that, for long time, had been sustained, for good or evil, by the triumph of ideologies. In many countries, ideologies are now in deep crisis and are in part supplanted by short-term electoral objectives and the power of money. Political movements and parties have often become half-empty shells, with very few statesmen, some decent representatives and a large number of people attached to titles and remunerations.

Several young people, full of hope and ideals, have started political activities, but have found growing difficulties in the dialogue with their leaders and the party machine. This has led to disappointment and discomfort, which has often determined either the exit from the party or the search for material compensations.

In general, exit or avidity can lead to an *adverse selection* in political cadres and this reduces the average quality of political activity. The contact with the basis can appear less important to the leaders than in the past because they think they are able to better influence the public opinion through an extensive recourse to the traditional media and to internet.

Yet, who controls the media in modern democracies?

It is necessary to distinguish between the direct control practiced by the owners of the media and the indirect control exercised by the firms providing big advertising budgets to the media, or by the banks financing the media's expansion or survival.

As regards the ownership of the media, in the US there are big publishers, such as Murdoch, large financial or industrial holdings, internet companies like Google, or the State or political parties. As regards public TV, in the US, the role of the State is rather limited, but the Government and the Congress can influence all the media through legislation, tax rebates, or financial incentives.

In democratic countries, the majority of mass media is usually controlled by private publishers, but also radios and State TV can be influenced by industrial or financial groups through their large advertising budgets. Even the publications of political parties, if they accept advertising or donations, can be, to some extent, influenced by private interests. Generally, in democratic countries, over half the revenues of public and private mass media comes from advertising.

Globalization has greatly amplified this phenomenon. For several consumption goods or services, the conquest of global markets requires an enormous effort in sales promotion and therefore a growing flow of advertising expenditures.

Yet, there are important differences among enterprises. So firms produce mass-production consumer goods or services, whose survival is critically dependent on advertising. Other firms, instead, produce capital goods, whose promotion is principally based on technical reviews and the participation to specialized fairs that, as they do not regard the general public, have a lower political impact. Finally, there are firms working in the military field, in the construction industry, in public services (telecommunication, electricity, gas, motorways, etc.), or in the financial world. All these firms need continuous and close relations with the political power in order to obtain higher sales, permits, concessions, financial deregulation measures, and so on. These corporations often try to directly influence political parties or political representatives with different sorts of financial donations and with lobbying activities, or they are able to influence the mass media that can have a heavy impact on general or local elections.

In some sectors, the expansion of large corporations has been more rapid than the expansion of local markets, so that there has been an increase in the market share of great oligopolistic producers, and thus of their political and financial power.

In addition, globalization has in general greatly diminished the influence on the national economies of each State, government, parliament, political party, and national labor union, while raising the power of big financial groups and large multinationals.

International organizations, regional unions, such as the European Union, the various international associations of firms, or the labors union, have not been able to effectively counter-balance the consequences of this trend.

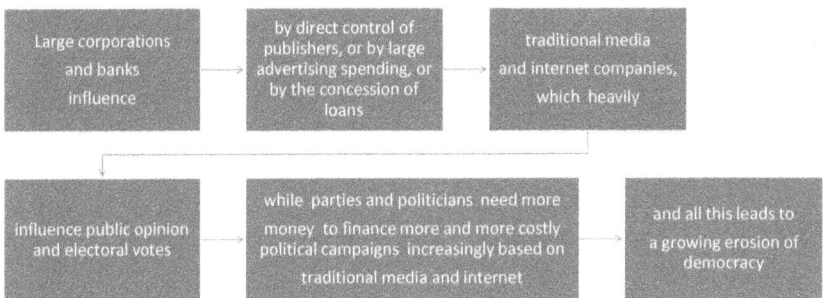

Fig. 7.4 The erosion of democracy

There is therefore a slow, but continuous *erosion of democracy*, which is described in a stylized way in Fig. 7.4.

The mediatization of politics strengthens the power of traditional media that in turn is associated to the economic power of large and middle-size corporations.

These firms, often active in the global markets, may grow in size and increase their advertising spending and also the direct or indirect financial contributions to political leaders and political parties. The latter have to face the rising costs of politics, partly due to the increasing and costly recourse to mass media and so politics, even in the absence of widespread corruption, can be partially "captured" by influential donors.

For some authors, the rapidly growing use of internet in political campaigns, as it happened for Obama, Hillary Clinton, and Trump, is deeply changing the state of affairs because of the lower costs and the more interactive role of internet with respect to traditional media. This is in large part true, but we must remember that the priority for diffusion of contents in internet through research engines, or the access to big data, require large payments. Moreover, the on-line presence of major traditional media (newspapers, TVs, books, etc.) is constantly growing.

The old media have been subject to a sharp reduction in the revenues from their traditional products, but some of them have been able to increase other revenues thanks to the public's direct or indirect online access to their contents. Also Google, YouTube, or Facebook have been in part nourished by the information, images, and videos coming from traditional media. Yet the giant internet corporations, thanks to their semi-monopolistic position and the control of an enormous mass of big data, have been able to gain a great autonomous political and economic power in deciding to whom, and at what price, to concede access to their services and to the use of their huge and rapidly growing stock of information.

Notes

1. See IEA (2018).
2. See IEA (2017).
3. See USGS (2017), p. 6.
4. See http://edgar.jrc.ec.europa.eu/news_docs/jrc-2016-trends-in-global-co2-emissions-2016-report-103425.pdf.
5. See http://ipcc.ch/pdf/assessment-report/ar5/syr/AR5_SYR_FINAL_SPM.pdf.
6. For environmental policies in the US in the last decades, see also Chaps. 10 and 11.
7. See BEA (2018), U.S. Bureau of Economic Analysis.
8. In reality, a small margin of oscillation of exchange rates around the central parity was tolerated, but for larger variations, the acceptance of a formal revaluation or devaluation due to structural basic imbalances was necessary.
9. The German mark had a previous revaluation vis-à-vis the US dollar in 1969–1970.
10. See, for the introduction of the concept, Goldin and Margo (1992). As regards wage inequality in the US and EU, see Bertola and Ichino (1995).
11. See also Chaps. 5 and 10 for some important determinants of this trend.
12. See Bebchuk and Fried (2004).
13. See Piketty et al. (2018).
14. See Obama (2006), p. 225 of the 2008 Vintage edition of the book.
15. See World Inequality Report (2018), Executive summary, pp. 6–8, figures E3 and E4. On economic inequalities in the US see also, for example, Stiglitz (2012), Atkinson (2015).
16. See CDC (2016).
17. Krugman (2007), p. 249.
18. See Krugman (2007), p. 248. The data come from National Center for Education Statistics. *The Conditions of Education 2003*, p. 47.

19. See, for example, Davis and Mazumder (2017), pp. 1–2.
20. See Obama (2006), p. 173.

References

Atkinson, A. 2015. *What Can Be Done About Inequality?* Harvard: Harvard University Press.
BEA. 2018. U.S. Bureau of Economic Analysis. https://www.bea.gov/.
Bebchuk, L.A., and J.M. Fried. 2004. *Pay without Performance: The Unfulfilled Promise of Executive Compensation.* Cambridge, MA: Harvard University Press.
Bertola, G., and A. Ichino. 1995. Wage Inequality and Unemployment: United States versus Europe. *NBER Macroeconomics Annual* 10: 13–66.
CDC. 2016. Rudd, R.A., P. Seth, F. David, and L. Scholl. *Increases in Drug and Opioid-Involved Overdose Deaths.* https://doi.org/10.15585/mmwr.mm6550e51e1.
Conference Board. 2018. https://www.conference-board.org/data/economydatabase/.
Davis, J., and B. Mazumder. 2017. The Decline in Intergenerational Mobility after 1980, No WP-2017-5. *Working Paper Series from Federal Reserve Bank of Chicago.*
EIA. 2018. www.eia.gov.
Goldin, C., and R.A. Margo. 1992. The Great Compression: The Wage Structure in the United States at Mid-Century. *The Quarterly Journal of Economics* 107 (1): 1–14.
IEA. 2017. https://www.iea.org/.
———. 2018. https://www.iea.org/.
Krugman, P. 2007. *The Conscience of a Liberal.* New York: W. W. Norton.
Maddison, A. 2007. *Contours of the World Economy, 1-2030 AD; Essays in Macroeconomic History.* Oxford: Oxford University Press.
Netherlands Environmental Assessment Agency The Hague. 2016. *Trends in Global CO2 Emissions: 2016 Report.* http://edgar.jrc.ec.europa.eu/news_docs/jrc-2016-trends-in-global-co2-emissions-2016-report-103425.pdf.
Obama, B. 2006. *The Audacity of Hope.* New York: Crown Publisher (First edition Vintage Books edition 2008, New York, from which are taken ours citations).

OECD. 2018a. Current Account Balance (Indicator). Accessed May 30, 2018. https://doi.org/10.1787/b2f74f3a-en.
———. 2018b. Exchange Rates (Indicator). Accessed May 30, 2018. https://doi.org/10.1787/037ed317-en.
Pikkety, E. Saez and Zucman G. 2018. Distributional National Accounts: Methods and Estimates for the United States. *Quarterly Journal of Economics* 133 (2): 553–609.
Stiglitz, J. 2012. *The Price of Inequality: How Today's Divided Society Endangers Our Future.* New York: W. W. Norton & Company.
USGS. 2017. *Mineral Commodities Summaries*, p. 6. http://minerals.usgs.gov/minerals.
World Inequality Lab. 2018. *World Inequality Report 2018.* http://wir2018.wid.world/files/download/wir2018-full-report-english.pdf.

8

Toward a Global Economic Empire

8.1 The Instruments

Some of the main structural weaknesses of the US economy and, since the late 1960s, the crisis of the Fordist model of growth, convinced the US and its major industrial and financial groups to react through the gradual construction of a global economic empire.

The main instruments used by the US in its attempt to create a global economic empire are the following:

1. The post-war aids and the Marshall plan
2. A strong push in favor of the liberalization of international trade
3. A rapid expansion in foreign direct investment
4. An important push toward the liberalization in capital movements and in international finance
5. Consequently, a decisive contribution to enhance the third wave of economic and financial globalization since the 1970s

6. A large and growing global influence of US media
7. A large diffusion of American ideology, mass consumption, and the US lifestyle
8. The recourse to several military interventions and to US diplomatic strength.

8.2 Post-war Aids and the Marshall Plan

After the conclusion of the Second World War, and even earlier in the territory subtracted to the German domination, the US conceded generous economic aids to the countries involved in the war. As the US was not only a great and rich country but also the one, among the major powers, less struck by war destructions, it was the only country that could provide large financial aids for the acquisition both of food and other primary goods and the investment goods needed for the reconstruction.

The aids policy made an important step in 1947, with the adoption of the *Marshall Plan* in favor of several European countries, including two of the former enemies, Germany and Italy. For a four-year period, the Marshall plan allocated about 17 million US dollars in favor of 17 European countries. The most consistent aids went to the UK (about 3.3 million USD), France (2.3 million), Western Germany (1.5 million), Italy (1.2 million), and the Netherlands (1.1 million). The Soviet Union, which at first seemed interested, decided not to participate and prohibited Eastern European countries from taking part in the program.

The Marshall Plan favored the reconstruction and the economic recovery of the European countries participating in the program, but also greatly extended American political and economic influence in Western Europe. Moreover, it helped the US economy to get out from the short, but severe, 1946–1947 reconversion crisis. The Plan also sustained recovery and economic expansion and strengthened the dollar as the key currency in the international monetary system.

8.3 The Path toward Trade Liberalization

The US government and the great international economic organizations, such as the International Monetary Fund (IMF), the World Bank, OECD, several UN agencies, and the General Agreement on Tariffs and Trade (GATT),[1] vigorously pushed toward a great and progressive trade liberalization. Also regional institutions such as the European Economic Union (EEC) and then the European Union, NAFTA, MERCOSUR, and ASEAN collaborated in this trend favoring the abolition or the gradual reduction of tariff barriers between their member-countries and trying to establish new trade agreements with other countries or regions. This trend has become more global after the fall of the Berlin wall, the dissolution of the Soviet Union, the passage from GATT to the World Trade Organization (WTO) in 1995, and the entrance of India in 1995 and of China in 2001 into the WTO.

In general, it can be affirmed that, up to the election of president Trump, the US has been the principal architect of the trade liberalization drive, directly or through its influence on international organizations.

This comes from two fundamental reasons: the neo-liberalist ideology and economic profitability. The neo-liberalist ideology has been triumphing since the 1980s in the US, in the UK, and progressively also in several other countries. Moreover, the US, the strongest economy in the world, had suffered, as we already know, from two great problems, maturity, the relatively slow expansion of several sectors of the domestic market and the high foreign dependence on energy sources and other raw materials. Finally, in the US, there were also many large and medium-size corporations with potential or effective global projection, eager to extend their sales and their direct investments abroad.

It was, therefore, necessary to strongly encourage multilateral agreements for a greater openness of international markets. Yet, in order to protect the domestic producers and some home market sections, the US also patiently arranged a very thick net of bilateral agreements. In any case, the general tendency was toward a gradual, but massive, reduction in the average tariff levels of the US and of several other countries, the removal of a great part of extra-tariff trade barriers and the rise in the liberalization of FDI and portfolio capital movements.

According to the 2017 UNCTAD data, from 1980 to 2016, the stock of world outward FDI rose from $559.0 billion to $26,159.7 billion, while it increased from $215.4 billion to $6383.8 billion for the US.

In this way, the US multinationals could more easily enter the Western European market that until the 1980s was more dynamic than the domestic one. They did so by means both of trade and FDI: exports of goods and services, the installation of new branches abroad, the purchase of European firms, or the fragmentation of their productive process into complex *global value chains* and the rapidly growing inter-firm trade.

Among the major industrialized countries in the American sphere of influence, Japan only was able to limit, by a variety of means, both the volume of its imports from the US and the penetration of US foreign direct investment into Japanese territory.

Unsurprisingly, the Soviet Union and CMEA countries up to the end of the 1980s, China up to 1978, India up to 1992, and a few other countries, rigidly limited the access of US goods, FDI, and portfolio capital movements. However, in the 1990s and 2000s, most of these countries opened their markets, in different degrees, partly in order to obtain an easier access into the huge American market and other rich Western countries. In 2001, the entrance of China into the World Trade Organization (WTO) was a decisive step in this direction.

In the years 1950–1973, the US could notably increase its exports, as we can see in Table 8.1. However, in these years also, US imports increased rapidly and this was mainly due to the rising value of imports for oil and

Table 8.1 Selected indicators on economic globalization: 1980–2016

	1980	1990	2003	2007	2016
World openness degree[a]	19.4	19.5	25.6	29.6	28.3
Stock of FDI as a % of world GDP[b]	6.2	9.8	24.3	31.2	34.8
External liberalization index[c]	51	58	95	96	96

Sources: World Bank (2018) for first line, UNCTAD (2018) for second line, WTO (2018)

[a](exports + imports of goods and services)/2 in the world as a % of world GDP
[b](stock of inbound FDI + stock of outbound FDI)/2 as a % of world GDP
[c]% of world population having significantly liberalized international economic relations (our estimates based on WTO data)

other raw materials and to the growing competitiveness of countries such as Germany, Japan, France, and Italy. In this period, these countries had entered *the second wave of the Fordist model of development*, reaching a labor productivity growth higher than the US, lower levels of wages and, in some years, a lower growth in unit costs of labor.

In addition, there were two bloody wars, the Korean War in 1950–1953 and the Vietnam War in the years 1964–1971, which greatly raised US imports of goods and services.

In the years 1970s and 1980s and in the following decades, there were, as we already know, two important additional factors: periods of strong increases in oil prices during the *energy crises* and the progressive *deindustrialization* of the American economy, with rapid increase in the services sector. The latter had a share of the value of exportable services on total services much lower than the share of exportable goods on total goods in the industrial sector and thus the deindustrialization process heavily contributed to determine a structural deficit in the US trade balance.

Finally, in the 1970s and 1980s, the US registered a loss in external competitiveness in various mature sectors for products such as automobiles, TV sets, and so on in front of the emerging drive of firms from Europe and from Japan, South Korea, and so on (Fig. 8.1).

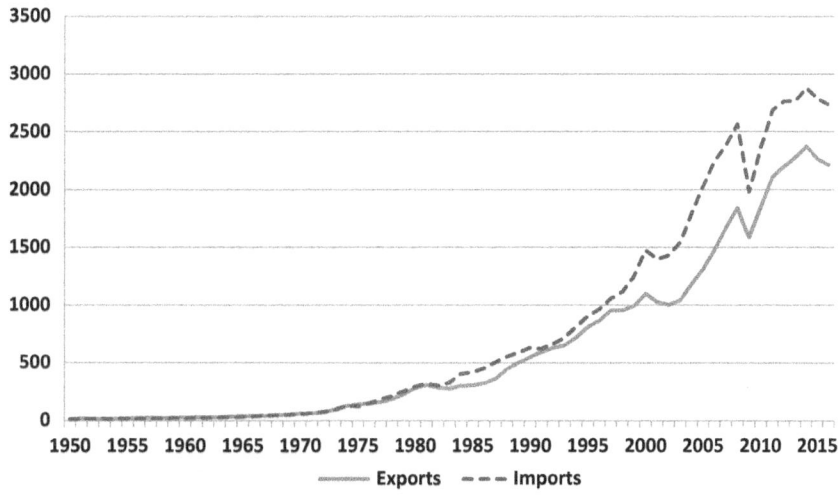

Fig. 8.1 US exports and imports of goods and services in the US: 1950–2016 (billion $)
Source: Department of Commerce-BEA (2017), our elaboration

At the beginning of the 1990s, the competitiveness of Japan, which had entered a long structural crisis, had become less aggressive. The following years saw the progressive advancement of South Korea, and later on, of China, in the production and export of ships, steel, domestic electric appliances, PCs, mobile phones, and many other products, and of India in software, steel, pharmaceutical products, and so on.

In this period, however, the US corporations could regain competitiveness in some ICT products, in the internet economy, and other high-tech sectors, partly because of the decentralization of a large part of their productive phases to low-cost countries and partly because of the enormous foreign financial inflows, coming mainly from Japan in the 1990s and from China in the 2000s. In particular, the US multinationals and some very successful start-up companies invested massively in aircrafts (Boeing, etc.), ICT hardware (Apple, HP, Intel, etc.), software (Microsoft, Oracle, etc.), and internet services (Google, Facebook, Amazon, etc.), maintaining or expanding their world leadership.

Yet, several manufacturing firms operating in industries such as steel, electric domestic appliances, textile, clothing, automobiles, PCs, mobile phones, and so on entered progressively into crises under the growing competition of firms from Japan, Germany, South Korea, China, Taiwan, and so on.

The wars in Iraq, Afghanistan, Syria, and Libya largely contributed to increase in US expenditures abroad, raising the structural deficit in the balance of current accounts.

8.4 Foreign Direct Investment and the Growth of the US Presence in the World

The theory of foreign direct investment explains FDI flows and stocks mainly on the basis of five reasons:

1. The attempt at securing the availability of strategic raw materials, such as oil and gas, copper, nickel, and so on.

2. The expansion of sales in foreign markets that grow more than the domestic one, and where exports would be difficult because of the protectionist policies of the local governments, the excessive transportation costs, or the high costs of commercialization and post-sales assistance.
3. The delocalization of a part of production, or of entire productive phases, to countries where the cost of labor, the cost of energy and other inputs, the cost of compliance with antipollution rules and the fiscal burden are considerably lower.
4. The research for local know-how, or high-quality labor force, or important global brands in foreign countries.
5. More in general, the recourse to a *fragmentation of production*, or the insertion into *global productive networks* among several firms or branches operating in many countries. This can be due to a complex mix of advantages such as economies of scale and scope, lower labor costs, knowledge and access to markets, technological transfer, lower taxation or higher incentives, good infrastructures, acceptable bureaucracy, quantity and quality of workers, and so on.

The US has made massive and growing outward FDI, following one or the other of these motivations, and has also been able to attract a rising stock of inward FDI (see Fig. 8.2).

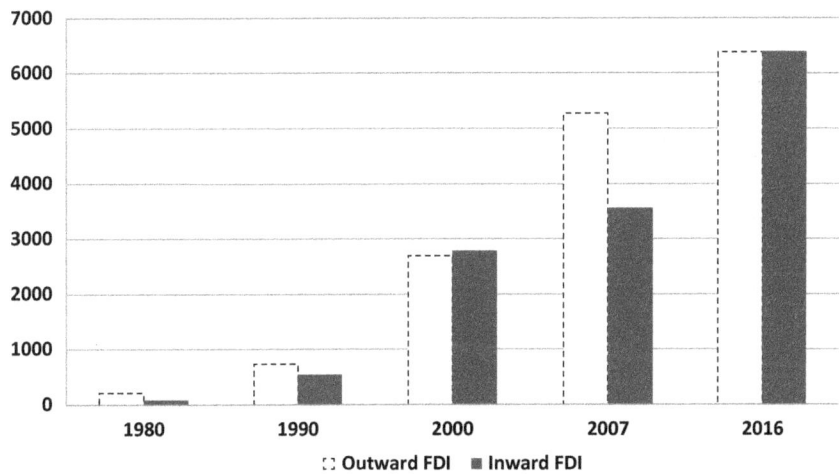

Fig. 8.2 US outward and inward FDI stocks in selected years: 1980–2016 (in $ billion)
Source: UNCTAD (2017), our elaboration

In the years 1950s and 1960s, the big American oil multinationals acquired a large number of concessions to exploit oil and gas resources in several oil-producing countries and built refineries and a large network for the commercial distribution of their products in many countries.

The institution of OPEC in 1960 and the expansion of state-controlled energy companies, such as ENI in Italy and Total in France, had partially changed the situation.

The foundation and growth in the oil-producing countries of many energy companies, such as Aramco in Saudi Arabia, Kuwait Petroleum Corporation, National Oil Corporation Libya, Petrobas in Brazil, Pemex in Mexico, Lukoil in Russia, Petrochina in China, together with the nationalization or repurchase of various oil resources in some of these countries, have progressively reduced the strong market power of the great American oil corporations and their share in the world market since the late 1960s.

Yet, American giants, such as Exxon-Mobil, Chevron, Conoco-Phillips, have maintained the rights for a relevant, though decreasing, share of world oil and gas reserves.

Various mining activities (gold, copper, molybdenum, phosphate, potash, etc.) have also attracted large outward FDI from US firms, such as Freeport-McMoRan Copper and Gold, Mosaic Co., Newmont Mining, and so on.

The expansion abroad of US multinationals has been even larger in the manufacturing sector and in some tertiary activities, especially in rapidly growing markets.

For example, before the *great recession* started in 2007, Ford Corporation and General Motors (GM), directly or by means of their European affiliates, Ford Europe and Opel, had conquered a consistent part of the European and Latin American markets. Moreover, they had also taken a sizable portion of major Asian markets through their branches, or their joint-ventures with Chinese and Indian firms, or the automobile division of South Korean Daewoo, bought by GM in 2001.[2]

However, in 2007–2010 the *great recession* violently struck the automobile sector, and in particular General Motors and Chrysler, which went very close to bankruptcy. A big financial State intervention decided by the Obama administration saved the two great corporations, but Chrysler passed under the control of the Fiat group, which in 2014 created FCA (the Fiat-Chrysler Automobiles group), while in 2017 General Motors had to sell Opel to the French group PSA.

Presently, a large part of the components of the ICT hardware of US multinationals, such as Apple, Dell or H. P.,[3] is produced or assembled in China or in other low-wages countries, and a substantial part of the software of many US groups (H.P., IBM, Cisco, Oracle, Dell, Intel, Accenture, Microsoft, etc.) is produced by research centers located in India or by sub-contracting Indian firms such as Infosys.[4]

A relevant part of garments, sneakers, leather articles, produced by American multinationals such as Gap or Nike are produced or assembled abroad, mainly in low-pay countries.[5]

However, since the 2000s, the FDI flows and the associated expanding *productive fragmentation*, the creation of *global value chains*, or of complex *productive networks* among firms of different countries, are increasingly going in both directions: from older industrialized countries such as the US to emerging countries such as China and India and the other way around.[6] The acquisition of the IBM PC division in 2004 and of Motorola mobility in 2014 made by the Chinese private group Lenovo has been an important signal of this new trend. Since 2013, Lenovo has thus become the top world producer in PCs, while in 2017 it already was the fifth world's largest producer of smartphones.

The globalization trend has also heavily involved several large US corporations of the services sector (banks, insurance companies, and other financial intermediaries; consulting groups, advertising, software, transport, telecommunication, internet, media, etc.).

However, a too rapid and poorly regulated economic and financial globalization process has led to increasing resistances and protests, like the no-global movement, and to populist responses, like those ridden by Donald Trump in his electoral campaign and during the first two years of his presidency.

8.5 The US and the Third Wave of Economic and Financial Globalization

As we have seen, the US has powerfully contributed to enhance the process of economic and financial globalization through its incessant drive toward the liberalization of international trade, FDI flows, and portfolio capital movements.

In modern and contemporary history, *economic globalization* has taken place in at least three major waves.

The *first wave of globalization* took place in the sixteenth to seventeenth centuries, when the Portuguese, Spanish, British, Dutch, and Venetian ships, packed with expensive goods, sailed the seas and the Flemish, Lombard, British, and Tuscan bankers financed the great European kingdoms and the expansion of world merchandise trade.

The *second wave of globalization* took place in the last decades of the nineteenth century and at the beginning of the twentieth century up to the outbreak of the First World War.

The *third wave of globalization wave* started at the beginning of the 1970s, rapidly progressed up to 2007, and is tiredly going on even now, although the *great recession* and Donald Trump's presidency have hindered its prosecution.

Economic and financial globalizations do not only consist in the large expansion of international trade in goods, services, and capitals, but are essentially associated to the process of growing real and financial *interconnections* between the world economies.

This process can be roughly measured for each country by means of a series of indicators:

1. The rise in the *degree of openness*, measured by the percent ratio between the sum of exports and imports of goods and services, divided by two, and the GDP of each country
2. The increase in the sum of inward FDI and outward FDI, divided by two, in percentage of GDP. The ratio can be estimated in terms of annual FDI flows or of the FDI stocks accumulated over time

3. The increase in flows and stocks of international portfolio capital movements
4. The rise in flows and stocks of international migrations
5. The reduction in transport and communication costs
6. The reduction in tariff and non-tariff protectionist barriers and in customs controls.

The third wave of globalization was profoundly different from the first one, but differed also significantly from the second one. The second wave mainly regarded the economic relations between Western countries (the US and European countries) and those between the center and the periphery of major colonial empires. However, the relations within the colonial empires were unequal, given the much stronger position of the centers of the empires when compared with the colonies.

After the decolonization period and the dissolution of the USSR, the present globalization wave has instead concerned fully independent states, though with very different levels of political and economic power. In fact, in their major economic decisions, the poorest or smallest countries are often deeply influenced by the great powers through the actions of their multinationals, widespread corruption, or financial and military pressure.

In any case, *the third globalization wave* has gradually involved emerged or emerging Asian countries, such as Japan, South Korea, Taiwan, Singapore, Hong Kong, and then China, India, Indonesia, Thailand, Malaysia, Vietnam, plus most Middle-Eastern countries, Russia and Eastern European countries, several Latin American and African countries, and so on.

Tables 8.1 and 8.2 give an idea of some aspects of the globalization process operating in the whole world and in the US.

It can be noticed that, from 1980 to 2016, while the world openness degree rose by about 46%, in the US it increased only by about 32%. After the outbreak of the great recession in the US, the openness degree diminished from 14% in 2007 to 13.3% in 2016.

As the US is a very large and diversified economy, it maintains an openness degree inferior to the world average, but the level of this indicator has considerably increased from 1990 up to 2007.

Table 8.2 Selected indicators of the US in the third globalization wave

	1980	1990	2003	2007	2016
US openness degree[a]	10.1	9.9	11.2	14.0	13.3
Exports of goods and services as a % of GDP	9.8	9.2	9.0	11.5	11.9
Imports of goods and services as a % of GDP	10.3	10.5	13.4	16.5	14.7
Stock of outward FDI as a % of GDP	7.8	12.2	23.7	36.4	34.4
Stock of inward FDI as a % of GDP	3.0	9.0	21.3	24.5	34.4

Sources: World Bank (2018) for the first three lines; UNCTAD (2018) for the last two lines

[a](Exports + imports of goods and services as a % of GDP)/2

Moreover, from 1980 to 2016, the stock of outward FDI of the US in % of GDP has grown by more than four times, even though it has decreased a little since 2013.

The average tariff rate of the US decreased from almost 4% in 1989 to 1.44% in 2007 and then has slightly risen to 1.64% in 2015, while in the world it fell from about 34% in 1996 to around 2.6% in 2015.[7]

Transportation and communication costs have also rapidly decreased.

The stock of immigrants to the US, mainly composed, since the 1950s, of Hispanic and Asian people, has continued to rise.

The globalization process has produced both positive and negative effects in the US as in many other countries.

The immigration flows and the rapid expansion of US imports of manufactured goods from emerging countries, such as China, India, or Mexico, have contributed to reduce mass-poverty in the world and have powerfully helped to diminish the price level of many goods and services in the American market, and thus the overall inflation rate in the US.

Yet, while the great flow of US outward FDI to other countries has helped to sustain the international competitiveness of US multinationals, it has in several cases favored an increase in the profits of these firms as well, and a rise in the compensations and bonuses paid to their top managers. The common people as consumers have profited from the lower prices of several goods, but as workers have heavily suffered from the potential or effective transfer of productive units to low-wages countries and, in some cases, also from the competition of immigrant workers in some segments of the labor market. Therefore, since the 1980s, the employment opportunities of the workers in the US manufacturing industry have worsened, their real wages have been almost stationary and the strength of labour unions has fallen. As we already know, the gap between the rank and file workers and the high paid managers of their firms and of the financial sector has continued to increase. Moreover, the people fired, or no longer absorbed, by the manufacturing sectors have put an increasing pressure on the labor market of the traditional services sector, causing a reduction in its real wages.

Another negative aspect is the powerful pressure that unregulated globalization has imposed on firms and workers, accelerating fast, and sometimes brutal, industrial redevelopment and restructuring decisions, or the offshoring of important parts of the productive process.

All this has led to employment problems for unskilled workers, but also to deep social and psychological costs for all employees. The sharp increase in geographical mobility associated to accelerated restructuring, redevelopment or delocalization processes, has contributed to break social and family links obliging many workers to move a long distance from family and community, or to make continuous business journeys to foreign countries.

Globalization has favored a rise in inequalities both *between* countries and *within* countries. There has been an increasing economic divide between rich countries, which could better exploit the opportunities of new markets and the access to raw materials and cheap labor, and the majority of poor countries. However, a few but very important and highly populated emerging countries, such as China, India, and Indonesia, were able to reduce the economic gap with respect to richer countries during the third globalization wave.

Yet, most rich countries and some emerging ones, including the US, China and to a lesser degree India and Indonesia, registered, as we already know, a large increase in their domestic economic and social inequalities. This was caused by a complex of internal and external reasons, but, also by the impact of economic and financial globalization.

In the 1980s and 1990s, there was a brisk acceleration of *financial globalization* in a great part of the world, followed by a gradual, albeit partial, financial opening of countries such as China and India, which had earlier been quite closed to international financial movements.

The acceleration of financial globalization in the 1980s and 1990s was mainly due to three reasons:

1. The great *financialization* of the world economy, which has been favored by the sharp reduction in many countries since the 1980s by the constraints on capital movements, by the ICT revolution, by the explosion of new financial tools such as derivatives, and by the *big bang* in world financial markets.[8]
2. The gradual financial liberalization proposed, and in some cases imposed, to several developing or emerging economies by international organizations, such as the IMF or the World Bank, on the basis of the so-called *Washington Consensus*.[9]
3. The rapid diffusion of the recourse of firms and households to investment funds, pension funds, hedge funds, mortgages, consumer credit, derivatives, and various banking and insurance financial tools. These practices, associated to extensive financial deregulation, led to a gradual reduction of the traditional propensity to invest primarily in low-risk domestic financial assets and to the progressive enlargement of financial investments to many lucrative, but often risky, world opportunities.

8.6 The Financial Supremacy

The expansion of US foreign direct investments and portfolio capital movements has been strongly favored by the central role of the US dollar and of American financial intermediaries in the world monetary and financial system.

In 2006–2007, before the *great recession*, American financial intermediaries (commercial banks and investment banks, investment funds and pension funds, hedge funds, insurance companies, etc.) seemed to be in good health.

Profits were fairly high, the capitalization in the US stock exchange markets was elevated, the expansion of financial services was good, both internally and in the international markets.

Many of the US financial institutions were operating from New York, or London, or Hong Kong, as wholesale furnishers of financial packages or derivatives, sold to local commercial banks and investment funds, or pension funds, which mainly functioned as retailers in a large number of domestic markets.

The financial leverage was heavily used in the US, sometimes in a highly risky way, thanks also to the very scarce regulation of the *shadow bank* system and the harmful abolition of the separation between commercial banks and investment banks made during the Clinton administration.

The prevalent usage of the US dollar highlighted the supremacy of the US on international financial markets, while the US, some of its allies, and the international organizations continuously pushed toward a progressive liberalization of capital movements. In the 1990s, a substantial freedom in capital movements was already extended to a large part of the world, with the partial exception, among the major economies, of China, India, and Russia, which, however, in the following decades have taken some steps in this direction.

The excessive recourse to financial leverage, the too easy concession of mortgages in the housing market, the explosive diffusion of complex and risky derivatives and the too expansionary monetary policy of the Federal Reserve in the years 2003–2005 had created the preconditions for the great 2007–2008 US financial crisis, which will be discussed in detail in Chap. 9.

8.7 Ideology and the American Lifestyle

The American ideology was founded on the ideas of a mobile and dynamic society (*the American dream*), on vast spaces and great opportunities (*the land of opportunity*), on *freedom* and *democracy*, on the *melting pot* between races, religions, and cultures, and on the vast diffusion of *mass-consumption goods*.

All these ideas had a great importance in the ascent of American power, even if, as we already know, some of the basic aspects of this vision had been partly imaginary or have badly deteriorated in recent decades.

Similarly, the American lifestyle, represented in a massive number of pictures, TV serials, short stories, novels and socials, has entered the collective imagination of a great number of people in the world and has exerted a powerful attraction, not always filtered by an adequate critical distance for some of its aspects.

8.8 The Influence of Media and Internet

The big US media and an important part of the European media that have often evoked and sometimes magnified the American model have powerfully contributed to expand the US influence in the world. TV networks, such as CNN and Fox, and important newspapers and weekly magazines, such as *The New York Times, The Wall Street Journal, Business Week, Times,* and *Newsweek*, have influenced the European public opinion and that of a large part of the world. Cultural and scientific journals, books, American TV programs, pictures, pop, folk and jazz, mass-advertising of American products or services, such as Coca Cola, Apple, McDonald, or Amazon, have projected important aspects of the American model in the world. Prestigious US universities have attracted a large mass of foreign students and researchers, who have strongly contributed to the US technological and economic development and to the worldwide diffusion of American culture.

Moreover, in a great part of the world, internet services are at present dominated by US giant e-corporations, which largely diffuse American culture and American goods and which have conquered a strong semi-monopolistic position in fields, such as big data, online advertising, and e-commerce.

8.9 The Power of Arms and Diplomacy

Wars and the arms sector have had a great influence in the formation of American global power, but also in shaping the structure of the US economy and adding weight to the US diplomatic efforts.

The Second World War has consolidated the financial and economic leadership of the US in the Western world. The Korean War has limited the communist expansion in East Asia. The Vietnam War, a poisoned fruit of the cold war and of the naive "domino theory", has shown that ideology, patriotism, guerrilla techniques, and the support of the Soviet Union could effectively contrast the powerful war machine of the US.

The first Iraq war had some good reasons. It preserved Kuwait's independence, putting a brake to the expansionary policy of Saddam's regime. The second Iraq war in 2003 has instead revealed how the decision of a president could provoke, using fake proofs on the mass-destruction arms of Saddam, a war which had not been previously approved by the United Nations and which has led to long-standing ruinous consequences.

The direct and indirect cost of the second Iraq war has been enormous, about 3000 billion US dollars, according to the estimates of Bilmes and Stiglitz.[10] Iraq has been partly destroyed during the war and then shattered by several political conflicts between the part of the population belonging to Shia Islam and the Sunni and Kurd groups. In addition, Iraq became one of the main incubators of the ISIL fundamentalist movement, which was escalating in size and power in 2015–2016, temporarily occupying various zones of Syria and Iraq during the long and bloody 2011–2018 Syrian civil war.

The cold war with the Soviet Union and all the wars of the post-Second World War period have contributed to deeply transform the American productive system.

The wars have required enormous public funds dedicated to the production of weapons (armed vectors, airplanes, tanks, military ships, nuclear submarines, etc.) or to the maintenance of troops and military bases, or to R&D expenditures in the strategic and military field. Several sectors of the economy and vast zones of the country, such as certain areas in Texas and in California, where military production is important, have greatly profited from the rise in military spending.

It is true that several inventions and military innovations have had large spillovers in civilian production, but it is likely that the same amount of resources, if directly applied to the civilian sector, would have led to extensive positive effects on medical research and health care, on renewable energy, on public education and research, on the war on poverty, and so on.

The recurring war effort has led to a very large, though strongly fluctuating, number of soldiers and to very high military expenditures.

The armed forces, which were about 11.4 million units in 1945, fell under 2 million units in the years 1947–1950, went up to 3–3.5 million units during the Korean war, and were then relatively stable, around 2.5–3 million units, until 1965. The escalation in the Vietnam War led to an increase in military forces to about 3.5 million units. After the war, the armed forces returned to around the level of 2–2.5 million units, but during the two Iraq wars, they went up again to around 2.5–3.5 million units.

In the post-Second World War period, US military spending had widely fluctuated, alternating between brief peaceful periods and the participation in a number of minor or large wars,[11] but has also registered a long-run rising trend.

In 2016, according to SIPRI estimates, US military spending was up to $611 billion, by far the highest in the world, while China and Russia, the second and third largest spenders, spent, respectively, about $215 billion and $69 billion.[12] In the same year, the share in world military spending of the US was 36%, while China's share was about 10%, and Russia's share was over 4%.

The global power of the US has been also accompanied by the strength of its diplomacy and by the activity of the US intelligence agencies.

The latter have often interfered in the internal affairs of several countries. In two major cases, in 1953 in Iran against Mohammad Mossadeq, and in 1973 in Chile against Salvador Allende, their intervention has contributed to overturn legitimate and democratically elected governments. For some years, these interventions have helped to preserve American influence in the two countries and to maintain the control of a large part of their oil or copper resources for a while, but they have deeply poisoned both Iran's and Chile's internal history and politics and severely damaged the US reputation in the world as regards democracy and the respect of human rights.

In another case, the *Bay of Pigs invasion* in Cuba, the military intervention had miserably failed.

The American diplomacy has frequently acted through bilateral relations, as it happened with the Soviet Union in the severe crises of the Berlin Blockade (1948–1949) and of the Cuban missile case (1962).

In the 1956 Suez-canal crisis, the US diplomatic intervention, backed by the UN and the Soviet Union, could prevent the enlargement and continuation of the conflict between Egypt and the armed forces of Israel, France, and the UK.

In many cases, US diplomacy has also operated through its great weight in international organizations. The US has in fact a great influence on the United Nations and its agencies and maintains, with its allies, a predominant power in the International Monetary Fund, the World Bank, and the World Trade Organization. This predominance is favored by the location of important sections of the United Nations in New York and of IMF and World Bank in Washington D.C.

In addition, the distribution of voting rights in IMF and World Bank are particularly favorable to the US and to Western European countries, partly because the statutes of these international organizations have been established in a period in which the hegemony of the US in the Western world was very strong. The succeeding reforms introduced in IMF and World Bank voting rights, which have somewhat increased, for example, the shares of Japan and China, have only partly reflected the radical changes that have occurred in world economic and financial equilibriums.

Notes

1. GATT went gradually expanding to the majority of world countries, and in 1995 was transformed into a new international organization, the World Trade Organization (WTO).
2. At first, GM renamed Daewoo motors as GM Daewoo and in 2011 as Daewoo Korea. In several countries, Daewoo cars are presented under the Chevrolet brand.
3. For example, several Apple products are assembled in the enormous Chinese plants of Foxconn and Pegatron. Foxconn, a Taiwanese firm, which also produces Amazon and Sony goods in China, has large profits but appalling labor conditions, which have led, especially in 2010–2015,

to a number of suicides. In 2016, it has bought the Japanese firm Sharp, while at present it is trying to buy the Toshiba semiconductors division and is opening a large factory in Wisconsin.
4. See De Prato et al. (2013).
5. Pietra Rivoli (2005) provides an interesting analysis of the complex global production process of a simple T- shirt, conceived by a US firm, manufactured in China with American cotton, and then re-exported to the US to be serigraphed and then sold in national and international markets.
6. See Andreff and Balcet (2013) for an explanation of rising FDI flows from emerging countries to older industrialized ones.
7. See World Bank (2017).
8. *Big bang* consists on the possibility to make stock exchange transaction for shares, bonds, currencies, and so on at any hour of the day, thanks to very fast ICT connections and the differences in opening hours of major stock exchange markets in the world.
9. *Washington consensus* is the consensus prevailing in the 1980s and 1990s between IMF, World Bank, and the US treasury, all located in Washington, on the main lines of economic policies to be followed by countries needing financial assistance. These policies required harsh restrictive macro-economic measures and structural reforms, including severe cuts in public debt and public deficits and privatization and liberalization moves.
10. See Bilmes and Stiglitz (2008).
11. The main US military interventions were: Korea (1950–1953), Vietnam (1964–1973), Lebanon, Panama, Bosnia, Somalia, Serbia, Iraq I (1990–1991), Afghanistan (2001–), Iraq II (2003–2011), Syria (2014–).
12. See SIPRI (2017), Trends in world military expenditure, 2016, available at: https://www.sipri.org/sites/default/files/Trends-world-military-expenditure-2016.pdf (accessed on September 28, 2017).

References

Andreff, W., and G. Balcet. 2013. Emerging Countries' Multinational Companies Investing in Developed Countries: At Odds with the HOS Paradigm? *European Journal of Comparative Economics* 10 (1): 3–26.

Bilmes, L., and J. Stiglitz. 2008. *The Three Trillion Dollar War: The True Cost of the Iraq Conflict*. New York: W.W. Norton & Company.

Department of Commerce-BEA. 2017. http://www.bea.gov.
De Prato, G., D. Nepelsky, and J. Simon. 2013. *Asia in the Global ICT Innovation Network, Dancing with the Tigers*. Sawston and Cambridge: Chandos Publishing.
Rivoli, P. 2005. *The Travels of a T-Shirt in the Global Economy: An Economist Examines the Markets, Power, and Politics of World Trade*. Hoboken, NJ: John Wiley and Sons.
SIPRI. 2017. *Trends in World Military Expenditure 2016*. Accessed September 28, 2017. https://www.sipri.org/sites/default/files/Trends-world-military-expenditure-2016.pdf.
UNCTAD. 2017. www.unctad.org.
———. 2018. www.unctad.org.
World Bank. 2017. www.worldbank.org.
———. 2018. www.worldbank.org.
WTO. 2018. www.wto.org.

9

The Great Recession

9.1 Why the Great Financial Crises?

Periodically, great financial crises plague the world economy. In 2008, Michele Fratianni, updating 1978 Charles P. Kindleberger's estimates, counted 68 great financial crises since the 1640s—one every 5.4 years on average.[1] Yet, he also observed that, after the beginning of the third globalization wave and in a period of growing openness of the financial markets, the frequency of the crises has more than doubled. From 1974 to 2008, the number of great financial crises had been 16, one every 2.1 years.

Many great financial crises have originated in the more advanced financial markets (17 in the UK and 14 in the US) and the 2007–2010 financial crisis, started in the US, has been the second worst crisis in over a century after the 1929 Wall Street crash.

There have been some major explanations of main financial crises: (a) *credit booms and busts*, (b) *monetarist*, (c) *self-fulfilling*, (d) *speculative bubbles*.[2]

The first one, originally proposed by Irving Fisher, Hyman Minsky, and Charles P. Kindleberger, with our addition of some important antecedents and of the impact of stock-flow vicious circles, can probably give a more complete explanation of what happened from 2007 to 2010 in the US.

In brief, some long-run trends, erroneous economic and monetary policies, and external events can determine a shock that reduces interest rates, increases the profit expectations, and leads to a *credit and monetary boom* with effects of leverage. All this can determine a phase of *euphoria* and of increasing self-feeding speculations with *assets inflation*, that is, an excessive rise in the prices of stocks (houses, shares, etc.). This trend cannot go on forever. Finally, there is the *explosion of the bubble*, hence rising interest rates, negative stock-flow feedbacks, bank failures, and a heavy fall in housing and stock exchange values. All this leads to a phase *of panic* and to a sharp reduction of leverage, a liquidity crunch, and a major financial crisis, usually followed by a severe real crisis.

9.2 The US Sub-prime Financial Crisis

To better understand the origins of the US *sub-prime financial crisis*, which had generated the *great recession* both in the US and in many other countries, it is necessary to recall some important antecedents, which we have partly anticipated in previous chapters.

1. To face the consequences of the e-economy and stock exchange crises and of the September 11, 2001, attack, in 2002 the US monetary authorities decided to enact a more expansionary monetary policy by reducing the interest rates. The low interest rates of the years 2002–2005 created *asset inflation*, greatly contributing to create *structural bubbles* in the price of housing and in the stock exchange market.
2. From 1971 to 2007, the US balance of current accounts had been negative in almost all the years and this generated the passage from the status of great net external creditor to that of huge net debtor, especially to Japanese and then Chinese investors. The necessity arose to reduce the balance of the current account enormous deficit, to diminish inflation, to attract portfolio capital inflows, and to sustain the

dollar influenced US monetary policy in 2005–2007. Thus, it was decided to shift to a restrictive monetary policy and to a rise in interest rates after years of cheap money, and this highly contributed to determine the sub-prime crisis of 2007–2008.
3. As we already know, in the 1990s and 2000s, in the US and in a great part of the world, there had been an enormous and extremely dangerous *financialization* of the economy. In 2007–2008, the value of financial assets in the US was about 4.5 times the GDP, 3.6 times in the European Union, and about 10 times the GDP in Switzerland. In 2008, the total value of derivatives was estimated at about 14 times the world gross domestic product.

Moreover, in 1999, the Clinton administration, had decided the final repeal of the 1933 Glass-Steagall Act, and so the abolition of the separation between the commercial banks and the investment banks, which had been introduced during the great depression to contrast future great financial and real crises. In addition, unlike the commercial banks, an important part of the financial sector (investment banks, hedge funds, some insurance companies, etc.) was very poorly regulated.
4. In the 2000s, the saving rate (saving/GDP) of the US households was very low and in some years even negative. As Jacques Attali has observed,[3] this was a natural consequence of the rise in inequalities that had occurred in the US since the 1980s. The strong rise in profits, and in particular of profits and earnings in finance, had been associated with the real wages semi-stagnation for the large majority of workers, which had compressed the growth both of their savings and their consumption, and therefore the overall dynamics of aggregate demand and GDP. All this induced the government, the FED, and the banking system to try to stimulate aggregate demand encouraging the rise in households' debt. This caused the rapidly growing recourse of many people, including the very poor, to consumer credit and credit cards and to mortgages for the purchase of houses.
5. The housing sector was the central detonator of the financial crisis. A long boom in housing prices had begun in the 1980s, had accelerated in the mid-1990s, and had continued in the beginning of the 2000s. From 2000 to the first quarter of 2007, the US housing prices had increased by about 62% at current prices and by almost 36% in real

terms. In zones such as Miami, Los Angeles, and San Francisco, the rise was even stronger, with almost a doubling of housing prices. The boom could not go on endlessly, since the prices of houses had indeed become too high. Therefore, in the first quarter of 2017, the housing structural bubble exploded. From the mid-2007 to the end of 2011, this caused a very severe fall in US housing prices, of about 26%.[4]

What were the main reasons for the housing prices boom and the consequent ruinous fall of the years 2007–2011?

The boom had been fed by a simple mechanism. In the 1990s and in the 2000s, most banks and specialized financial institutions, spurred by the government policy, began to easily grant mortgages for the purchase of houses to all sorts of customers and also to households with low and precarious income. In a period of rapidly rising housing prices, the risks of the banks seemed to be low because if the customer did not pay the installments of the loan, the property of the house rapidly went back to the banks and they could sell the house without losses or even at a profit, given the rapid rise in housing prices. Moreover, the banks could alternatively choose to sell the credits based on the mortgages to specialized semi-public institutions, such as Freddie Mac or Fanny Mae, or to investment banks, which included these credits in composite financial packages that were sold to commercial banks, investment funds, pension funds, and their clients all over the world. This procedure, called *securitization*, provided new liquidity to the bank that had originally granted the mortgages, which hence could further expand the volume of its mortgages.

In addition, the 1977 *Community Reinvestment Act*, later revised and extended in various occasions and especially in the 1990s, had contributed to increase banks' loans to disadvantaged communities.

In the attempt to reduce insolvency risks, the distinction was introduced between *prime* mortgages (to richer and solvent people), *Alt-a* (for middle-income, possibly solvent, people), and *sub-prime* (for people with poor credit rating, who could have serious problems in repaying their loans). In March 2007, the value of the stock of sub-prime mortgages had risen to the enormous amount of about $1.3 trillion. As we already know, many of these credits had been incorporated in complex financial packages and the risk for potential buyers, such as investment funds, pension funds, firms, and households, was very difficult to assess.

The policy of easy concession of mortgages, together with the persistence of low interest rates in the years 2002–2005, had powerfully contributed to rapidly increase the demand for houses. Therefore, the *housing structural bubble* became larger and larger, before exploding in the first quarter of 2007.

The housing prices collapsed and the big *financial crisis* leading to the *great recession* began.[5]

Thus the first important stock-flow negative feedback or *vicious circle* came into being. The rapid fall in the prices and in the total value of housing (an enormous stock) determined heavy losses for all the banks and other financial institutions involved in the mortgages market, putting at risk their liquidity, the prices of their shares in the stock exchange, and their contribution to GDP (a flow concept). The fall in GDP contributed to a further reduction in the housing and shares prices and thus in the US total wealth and so on, in a prolonged vicious circle.

The sub-prime crisis also obliged to sell a huge quantity of houses whose property had returned to the banks when the borrowers had not been able to pay their mortgages (*foreclosures*). The consequent excess in the supply of houses greatly reduced the housing prices. Hence, the construction and real estate industries went into a ruinous crisis and this heavily contributed to further reduce GDP and employment, thus nourishing both the financial and the real crisis.

The sub-prime crisis had devastating social effects. Most mortgages had been granted at adjustable interest rates. Consequently, when in 2004–2005 the interest rates began to rise, many people could not afford to pay rapidly increasing sums for the service of their debt to the banks. Over nine million poor and middle-class people lost or risked losing their house in foreclosures,[6] while many workers in the building and real estate sector remained jobless, and most of them badly needed some sort of public assistance.

The financial crisis, detonated by the sub-prime crisis, was like a big fire spread by a strong wind.

Many banks or *shadow banking* institutes failed or were saved thanks to public interventions. The financial packages that included sub-prime credits became *toxic assets*. Not knowing which financial institute possessed large quantities of these very risky assets, in 2007–2008 the mutual trust between banks fell, the inter-bank credit market collapsed, and thus a great *liquidity crunch* ensued. Many banks lacked liquidity and were in bad waters, or even failed, and so the bank credit to enterprises was briskly curtailed. Many firms ran into difficulties and had to cut down investment, employment, and sometimes wages. In this way, the financial crisis rapidly led to a real crisis, with a fall in aggregate investment, consumption, total GDP, and employment and a strong rise in unemployment.

9.3 The Great Recession

The failure of Lehman Brothers on September, 15, 2008, badly worsened the financial and real crisis already raging in the US economy. The recession had soon spread to the European Union and to several other countries heavily connected with the US financial system.

The US stock exchange market fell by almost 50% from September 2008 to March 2009.

The response of the US monetary and fiscal authorities had been, for several months, weak and excessively delayed.

Since September 2007, the FED had begun to timidly reduce the rate of interest, gradually lowering the FED funds rate from 5.25% in June 29, 2006, to 4.25% in December 11, 2007, and to 2% at the end of April 2008. Yet, since the crisis continued to worsen after the Lehman Brothers failure, the FED finally decided on a much more aggressive expansionary monetary policy by reducing the FED funds rate down to 0.25% in December 16, 2008, and recurring to reiterated measures of *quantitative easing*.[7]

On October 3, 2008, the Bush administration also sought to react to the financial crisis with a program called *Troubled Asset Relief Program* (TARP), which was then partly carried on during the Obama administration. This program tried to save the main financial institutions in difficulty and stabilize the financial market, planning to purchase "troubled assets" with public funds up to $700 billion.

Several giant US financial institutions in severe difficulty, such as Bear Stearns, Fannie Mae, Freddie Mac, and AIG, were saved. Yet, after Lehman Brothers, also a giant savings bank, Washington Mutual, with about $300 billion in assets, failed in 2008, and 477 smaller banks went into bankruptcy in the years 2008–2012.[8]

Besides the severe banking and liquidity effects already recalled, the deepening of the financial crisis led to several other important stock-flow *vicious circles or transmission mechanisms.*[9]

1. *Negative wealth effects.* Total wealth is mainly composed of real wealth (houses, other buildings, etc.) and financial assets (shares, bonds, etc.). If the prices, and hence the total value, of the stock of buildings severely decrease and, soon after, the value of financial assets also collapses, total wealth will fall by an enormous amount—often superior to the value of an entire annual gross domestic product.[10] The fall in wealth will determine a fall in consumption and so a decrease in profit expectations of the firms and a heavy reduction in investment. All this will lead to a decrease in aggregate demand and GDP, to a depressive effect on the prices of housing and shares, to a further reduction in wealth, and so on.
2. *The collaterals effect.* The fall in total wealth will reduce the value of collaterals offered by the firms and the households as guarantees for the loans obtained from the banks. The banks will thus reduce their credit, and this will produce many failures of industrial or services firms and a further fall in investment, GDP, wealth, and so on.
3. *Employment and total wages effects.* The heavy reduction in investment, caused by the fall of wealth and the failure of many firms, produces a large decrease in employment and thus a great rise in unemployment. It also causes stagnation or even a reduction in unit wages, because of the pressure on the labor market coming from the swift rise in unemployment. Thus, total wages diminish and this determines a further reduction in consumption, investment, GDP, the value of wealth, and so on.
4. *The human capital effect.* The economic crisis will cause a reduction of the expenditure in education, in training, and in R&D and the employment crisis will reduce the processes of training and *learning by doing* in the firms. The rising youth unemployment will sterilize the knowledge acquired by a part of the young people graduated from high schools or universities, while the loss of jobs of mature workers will reduce the stock of skills used in the productive process. The stock of knowledge of the country will therefore diminish or become partly obsolete.

5. The *public finance effect*. The economic crisis will contribute to a reduction in tax revenues and an increase in social expenditures (such as unemployment subsidies, aids for homeless people, etc.). All this will increase public deficit and public debt and thus weaken the possibility of investing in new infrastructures, new schools, and new hospitals. The health and wealth of the nation will be in danger.
6. *The non-performing loans effect*. As long as the economic crisis gets deeper and longer, the stock of non-performing loans will continue to grow. The banks will be obliged to recapitalize and to further reduce their credit to firms, especially to small or medium size enterprises, and all this will contribute to reduce GDP and the national wealth.

By all these mechanisms, the financial crisis powerfully contributed to lead to the worst real crisis in the US and in several other industrialized countries of the post-Second World War period.

The US *great recession* started in the fourth quarter of 2007 and greatly worsened in 2008 and in the first half of 2009.

Real GDP lost over 4.2% from the last quarter of 2007 to the second quarter of 2009. In the second half of 2009, real GDP began to recover, but only in the second half of 2011 could the US economy return to the 2007 level for total GDP.

The fall in real investment and in the rate of unemployment was even more severe, and the recovery was delayed and more difficult than that of the GDP. Fixed capital formation fell by 22.7% from the second quarter of 2007 to the first quarter of 2010 and returned to the former level only in the second half of 2013. Civilian employment lost over 8.6 million people from November 2007 to December 2009 and could return to the former level only in September 2014. The US civilian unemployment rate more than doubled from March 2007 (4.4%) to December 2009 (9.9%) and could revert to the March 2007 level more than ten years later, in June 2017. However, during the decade 2007–2017, the employment rate and the labor force participation rate had substantially decreased and a relevant part of new jobs were "bad jobs", that is, low-paid and often precarious jobs, and were mainly concentrated in the tertiary sector.

The great recession also caused a worsening in the US public finance. The federal public deficit in % of GDP rose from 1.1% in 2007 to almost

Table 9.1 The great recession in the US and in selected EU countries

	Real GDP (2007 = 100)			Real Gross Investment (2007 = 100)			Unemployment rate (% of the labor force)		
	2007	2011	2016	2007	2011	2016	2007	2011	2016
US	100.0	101.0	112.4	100.0	87.1	104.2	4.62	8.95	4.87
EU	100.0	99.8	105.7	100.0	89.8	95.3	7.12	9.59	8.53
Germany	100.0	102.9	109.9	100.0	102.6	99.9	8.66	5.82	4.12
UK	100.0	98.4	109.5	100.0	90.5	123.6	5.26	8.04	4.81
France	100.0	101.2	105.3	100.0	95.5	100.6	7.66	8.81	10.06
Spain	100.0	96.5	99.8	100.0	71.3	72.9	8.23	21.39	19.63
Portugal	100.0	97.2	96.3	100.0	78.6	68.8	7.96	12.68	11.07
Italy	100.0	95.6	93.1	100.0	85.4	71.4	6.08	8.36	11.69
Greece	100.0	81.9	73.6	100.0	46.3	33.0	8.4	17.86	23.54

Source: World Bank (2018)

10% in 2009, it gradually went down to 2.4% in 2015, but then it rose again to 3.5% in 2017.

The federal gross public debt as % of GDP increased from 62.2% in the first quarter 2007 to over 100% at the end of 2012 and to 105.4% at the end of 2017.

Though the US was the major responsible and the prime mover of the great recession, the impact of the financial and real crises in several European economies, such as Greece, Italy, Spain, and Portugal, was longer and much deeper than in the US.

In fact, the US did recover sooner its 2007 level in GDP and in unemployment rate and then grow more rapidly than the EU and several European countries (see Table 9.1).

This was mainly due to the less delayed US expansionary monetary policy, associated to an effective industrial and innovation policy and the post-Keynesian fiscal policy of the Obama administration, versus the *austerity policy* prevailing in the European Union.[11]

The models more widely used in economic literature before the crisis greatly overlooked the importance of stock-flow relations, of capital gains and capital losses, and of crucial psychological mechanisms, such as confidence or trust.[12]

There is also another important element, badly undervalued in most economic analyses. It consists in the fact that in face of risky financial decisions the behavior of individuals would be very different if they risked their own money or other people's money.

The top managers of banks or other financial and non-financial institutions are incentivized by large bonuses and stock options that they can obtain if their hazardous financial choices are a winning bet. They are also usually sheltered by *golden parachutes* and by the sheer size of their accumulated wealth if they should lose their jobs because of great losses to their institutions or to the institutions' clients. So, as managers, they are often reckless risk takers: they know that the worst risks are on other people's back. Moreover, the top bank managers can dispose of the firepower of their banking or financial consultants to convince the customers of the bank to subscribe to any dubious financial asset and so timely transfer part of the risk from the portfolio of the banks to the customers' portfolio.

9.4 The Inadequacy of Controls

The financial institutions are usually subject to regulations and controls, but these controls are often inadequate. In particular, in the 2000s, the US financial system was in danger in the case of a severe and prolonged crisis because of the enormous *financialization* of the economy, the high and growing leverage, and the 1999 abolition of the separation between commercial banks and investment banks. Moreover, while commercial banks were subject to rigid ratios and to the controls of the FED and, if listed, of the ones of the SEC, *the shadow finance* sector was almost completely unregulated. As we will see in Chap. 10, the Obama administration could only partially attenuate the problem by means of the Dodd-Frank's Act.

The *rating* on banks and other financial institutions is provided by private *rating agencies*, as Moody's, Fitch, and Standard & Poor's, which on principle could provide a correct evaluation of the trustworthiness and solvency of the financial and non-financial institutions.

Yet, the rating agencies have great *conflicts of interests*. They are in fact paid by the banks or firms they evaluate with their ratings and risk losing their client if their evaluation is too strict. Moreover, they often offer consultancy on the configuration of financial structured assets to the same firms they evaluate. No surprise if just one week before its failure the Lehman Brothers' rating was very good. Even though the 2010 Dodd-Frank's Act and the EU institutions have tried to improve the set of regulations of the rating agencies, they remain subject to extremely dangerous conflicts of interests.

Also, the balance sheets of banks and enterprises can be manipulated. The risks associated to their financial operations in order to obtain better stock exchange values and so higher compensations and stock options for the top managers and higher dividends for the share-holders can be undervalued. A Business Week survey of the 1990s had shown that 67% of financial directors had been asked by their bosses to manipulate the balance sheets or the budget and that 12% had done it. There is no evidence that the situation has improved thereafter.

The accounts of banks of other corporations are usually controlled by auditing companies, but also the latter have large *conflicts of interest*. Not only are they paid by the firms they audit, but they often act as business or financial consultants of the firms they control. So, the controls are not always accurate, as in 2001, in the case of the failure of the US giant corporation Enron and in 2008, in the case of Lehman Brothers.

Finally, in various countries, several investment funds are directly or indirectly controlled by big banks and this can lead to manipulations in the management of their financial assets and to other forms of conflicts of interests.

9.5 Possible Remedies

The possible remedies to a severe financial crisis and its consequences on the real economy are numerous. First of all, in absence of a high inflation, it is crucial to timely apply a vigorous monetary and fiscal anti-cyclical expansionary policy, with a return to Keynesian policies. At the start of the great recession, this policy was possible also because the US had a low inflation and the public debt was relatively contained. Apart from the TARP promoted by Bush in Autumn 2008 aiming at saving the banking system, vigorous expansionary monetary and fiscal policies were attempted only during the Obama administration in 2009–2010, but with a delay of over one year from when the first signs of the crisis occurred at the end of 2007.

There is also the necessity of a deep reregulation of the financial markets, with a return to the separation between commercial banks and investment banks and a drastic reduction of leverage, of too risky structured derivatives, of the incentives to top managers, and of potential conflicts of interest.

The abolition or the full transparency of fiscal paradises to avoid massive tax evasion and dirty money recycling is also necessary.

As regards auditing and rating, a radical reform is essential. It would be wise to assign the choice and the payment of auditing and rating companies to public institutions, such as FED and SEC, on the basis of a public fund financed by the banks and corporations subject to controls.

The estimation of the values of derivatives or of other financial assets in the balance sheets are usually made at current prices and this can push upward the stock exchange values in the booms and depress them in the busts. It would be better to use an evaluation based on appropriate mobile averages.

Moreover, it could be useful to establish a temporary progressive increase in patrimonial indexes during the years of economic expansion in order to reduce speculative booms and to reinforce patrimonial reserves for the period of crisis.

A radical, though politically very difficult, reform in international economic organizations would also be important. A fusion between the IMF and the World Bank might provide an authentic global bank. The new organism, better financed and democratized, might issue an international currency, a sort of Bancor as in the 1944 Keynes' proposal. It might function as a lender of last resource, which would be able to powerfully contribute to regulate and stabilize the world monetary and financial systems.

It would also be essential to regulate and reduce the dangerous short circuit existing between big finance, large corporations-mass media-politics we have described in paragraph 7.9 on the erosion of democracy. These relations have strongly contributed to the deregulation of the financial system and to the advent of the great recession.

9.6 A Comparison with the Great Depression

Several economists have compared the *great recession* to the *great depression* of the 1930s. Yet, a careful scrutiny shows some similarities, but also important differences between the two great crises.

Figure 9.1 and Table 9.2 show that in the US the great depression had been much longer and deeper than the great recession.[13]

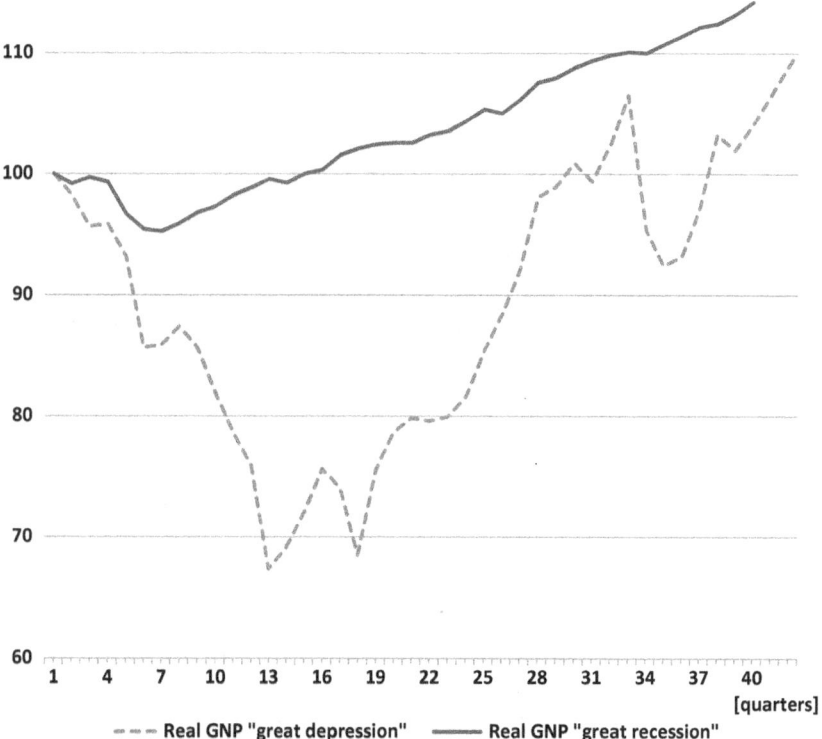

Fig. 9.1 Real GNP in the great depression and in the great recession
Great depression: 3° Quarter: 1929 = 100. Great recession: 4° Quarter 2007 = 100.
Notes: The X axis indicates the first 42 quarters following the beginning of the GNP fall in the two crises: third quarter of 1929 for the great depression and fourth quarter 2007 for the great recession. We used Constant Dollar of 1939 for data about the great depression and Constant Dollar of 2009 for data about the great recession
Sources: NBER (2018), Department of Commerce-BEA (2018), our elaboration

Table 9.2 Real GDP and real per capita GDP in the two US great crises

Great depression years	Real GDP 1933 = 100	Real per capita GDP	Great recession years	Real GDP 2009 = 100	Real per capita GDP
1929	135.8	140.0	2007	103.1	105.0
1930	124.2	126.7	2008	102.8	103.8
1931	116.3	117.7	2009	100.0	100.0
1932	101.3	101.9	2010	102.5	101.7
1933	100.0	100.0	2011	104.2	102.5
1934	110.8	110.1	2012	106.4	104.1
1935	120.6	119.1	2013	108.3	105.1
1936	136.2	133.6	2014	111.0	107.0
1937	143.3	139.6	2015	114.2	109.2
1938	138.5	133.9	2016	115.9	110.0
1939	149.6	143.5	2017	118.5	111.8

Sources: Department of Commerce-BEA (2018) for columns 2, 5, and 6 (chained index 2009 USD), NBER (2018) for column 3

While the fall in stock exchange index had been strong in both cases, in the great depression the fall in real per capita Gross National Product (GNP) had been much deeper than in the great recession. Moreover, the per capita GNP level of the year before the crisis was reached after about ten years in the great depression and after about six years in the great recession.

This has been partly due to the different timing in economic policies. In the great depression, expansionary countercyclical policies began after the change of presidency from Hoover to Roosevelt, about three-four years later than the beginning of the crisis. Instead, in the great recession they started much earlier, about one year after the outbreak of the crisis, and they were considerably reinforced when Obama rose to presidency.

Moreover, the world diffusion of the financial and real crisis for some aspects had been wider during the great recession than during the great depression, but in 2008 three giant emerging economies (China, India, and Indonesia) had been able to better absorb the depressive shock than the US and the European economies, continuing to register large positive rates of growth, though gradually slowing down in the case of China.

While in the period of the great depression the principal drivers of the world economy were the US and the major European economies, in the recent decade also the two great Asian powers and other emerging economies have played an important role.

Moreover, after the outbreak of the great depression, the return to protectionism had been large and widespread, while, up to now, it has remained contained during and after the great recession (see Table 9.3). This has mainly depended on the strong influence of international (WTO) or regional organizations (EU, MERCOSUR, ASEAN, etc.) and on the frequent summits of the industrialized countries (G7 and G20), but even more on the widespread and resilient inter-country economic connections created or consolidated during the third globalization wave. However, as we will discuss in Chap. 11, the economic policy of Donald Trump might inject various forms of neo-protectionism and dangerous trade wars in the world economy.

Table 9.3 A comparison between the great depression and the great recession

Main similarities	Main differences
Origin of financial crisis in the US, then propagated to many other countries.	The fall in per capita and total real GDP, real investment and employment is much larger and lengthy in the great depression than in the great recession.
Financial bubble and then bank crisis and strong fall in the New York stock exchange index and in most other world financial markets.	The great depression starts from the 1929 Wall street crash, while the great recession originates from the sub-prime crisis to which the financial crisis, the stock exchange crash, and the real crisis follows.
Passage from the financial to the real crisis in the US and then in many other countries.	In the great recession, the financial crisis leads to a real crisis in many countries, but in the US, its consequences, if compared with the great depression, have been attenuated by the expansionary monetary policy, the post-Keynesian fiscal policy, and the lower recourse to protectionist measures.
Movements in favor of protectionist policies.	In the great depression tough protectionist policies in the US and in most other countries.
	In the great recession, up to May 2018, contained expansion of protectionist measures during the Trump administration and relatively moderate responses by the EU and China.

Notes

1. See Fratianni (2008) and Kindleberger (1978).
2. See Fratianni (2008), pp. 5–6.
3. See Attali (2008), pp. 57–59.
4. After 2011, with the economic recovery and the following expansion, there was also a gradual recovery of housing prices in current terms, which in 2017, returned in several zones to levels close to those prevailing in the first quarter of 2007.
5. On the financial and real crises, see, for example, Roubini (2008), Krugman (2009), Stiglitz (2010) and the interesting psychological approach of Akerlof and Shiller (2010).
6. In 2009, Obama's administration introduced some important measures in favor of people who risked losing the house due to foreclosures, but the implementation of these measures was partial, difficult, and fragmented.
7. Quantitative easing (QE) is a strong and unconventional expansionary monetary policy aiming at rapidly expanding money supply and reducing interest rates to very low levels. The central bank buys enormous volumes of securities (government bonds and other securities) trying to expand banks' liquidity and lending.
8. Washington Mutual and Bear Stearns had been then acquired by JP Morgan Chase, while a part of Lehman Brothers was bought by the Japanese bank Nomura. Since 2007–2008, also in Europe, there was a long series of bank failures but some giant banks, such as Bradford and Bingley, Northern Rock, Fortis, Hypo real estate, ING, were saved through public interventions.
9. See, for a more detailed analysis, Valli (2013).
10. From 2007 to 2009, in the US, per capita wealth decreased by 26%, while the net national wealth to net national income ratio declined from 5.4 to 4.3. See WID World (2017), http://wid.world/country/usa/.
11. See for a comparative analysis between the US and the European Union, Valli (2017).
12. Some of the psychological mechanisms operating in the great recession were, for example, explored in Akerlof and Shiller's volume on *Animal Spirits* (2010) and in several of Richard Thaler's contributions.

13. However, in some European countries, such as Greece, Spain, Portugal, and Italy, the great recession has been longer than the consequences of the great depression in such countries.

References

Akerlof, G.A., and R.J. Shiller. 2010. *Animal Spirits, How Human Psychology Drives the Economy, and Why It Matters for Global Capitalism*. Princeton: Princeton University Press.
Attali, J. 2008. *La crisi, e poi?* Roma: Fazi.
Department of Commerce-BEA. 2018. Accessed May 10, 2018. http://www.bea.gov.
Fratianni, M. 2008. Financial Crises, Safety Nets and Regulation. Report Held at the *49th Annual Meeting of the Italian Society of Economists*, Perugia, 24–25 October.
Kindleberger, C.P. 1978. *Manias, Panics and Crashes: A History of Financial Crises*. New York: Basic Books.
Krugman, P. 2009. *The Return of Depression Economics and the Crisis of 2008*. New York: W.W. Norton.
NBER. 2018. Accessed May 10, 2018. www.nber.org.
Roubini, N. 2008. The Rising Risk of a Systemic Financial Meltdown: The Twelve Steps to Financial Disaster. *RGE Monitor*, February 5.
Stiglitz, J. 2010. Risk and Global Economic Architecture: Why Full Financial Integration May Be Undesirable. *NBER Working Paper No. 15718*.
Valli, V. 2013. New Economic Policies in a Changing World: A Stock-Flow Approach. *Annali della Fondazione Luigi Einaudi*, Firenze, Olschki, XLVII: 37–53.
———. 2017. Economic Policies during the "Great Recession" in the United States and in the European Union: A Comparative and Critical View. *Annals of the Fondazione Luigi Einaudi* LI (2): 159–182.
WID World. 2017. http://wid.world/country/usa/.
World Bank. 2018. www.worldbank.org.

10

Obanomics

10.1 Obama's Ideas on Economics

The ideas of Obama in the field of economics and economic policy can be evinced from his famous autobiographic books and, in particular, from the second one, *The Audacity of Hope*,[1] but even more from his speeches and his concrete political actions.

In *The Audacity of Hope*, Obama illustrated the main points of his economic vision. On state-market relations Obama's position was very clear. He did not deny the essential role of the market in the US economic development, but he also stressed the great importance of the state in the economic process.

Not only had the state to build infrastructures, provide education to the labor force, contrast market failures but it had also to create the basis for economic development and help structuring industrial relations.[2]

The approach suggested by Obama was an intermediate way between the state and the market. He proposed some examples going in this direction, such as large public investment in science, education, health, technology, and those associated to energy independence, which could improve both welfare and international competitiveness.[3]

Obama attributed a great importance to the work and quality of teachers, to research and innovation, to energy saving policies, and to the improvement of the environment.

He also proposed, and as a president partly realized, a policy of incentives and more severe efficiency standards for automobiles, which could lead the big US car makers to produce automobiles, for example, smaller cars, or hybrid or electric cars, that would consume and pollute less than the existing models. This policy could contribute to increase the US competitiveness in foreign markets, and to better penetrate into the rapidly growing Chinese market, where consumption standards were already more severe than in the US.

According to Obama, the globalization process had to be slowed down, not arrested, but the advantages of this process had to be more equally distributed among the workers. The State had to take charge of the rising risks of the losers in the continuous process of restructuring, reshuffling, streamlining, and off-shoring associated to globalization, making a more inclusive and penetrating social security system.

Finally, Obama advocated a notable improvement in the pension system and, above all, a great reform in the health system (*Obamacare*).

However, in the presidential campaign in 2008 and in his two presidential mandates, Obama had above all to face the great financial and real crises and their consequences, so that the next paragraph will be mainly focused on his policy in the period of the great recession. Afterwards, we will highlight Obama's approach as regards four important economic and social problems: industrial and innovation policy, health care, energy, and the environment.

10.2 Obama's Response to the Great Recession

Obama had inherited a very difficult economic and financial situation from the Bush administration. As we already know, the financial crisis had reached its peak during the last months of George W. Bush's presidency and, in particular, after the failure of Lehman Brothers in mid-

Table 10.1 Annual % rate of change of real GDP in selected areas or countries (2007–2017)

Country or area	2007	2008	2009	2010	2011	2012	2013	2014	2015	2016	2017
World	5.6	3.0	−0.1	5.4	4.3	3.5	3.5	3.6	3.5	3.2	3.8
US	1.8	−0.3	−2.8	2.5	1.6	2.2	1.7	2.4	2.6	1.6	2.1
Euro area	3.0	0.3	−4.5	2.0	1.6	−0.9	−0.2	1.2	1.5	1.8	2.4
Germany	3.4	0.8	−5.6	3.9	3.7	0.7	0.6	1.6	1.5	1.8	2.0
France	2.4	0.1	−2.9	1.9	2.1	0.2	0.6	0.7	1.2	1.1	1.3
Italy	1.3	−1.1	−5.5	1.6	0.7	−2.9	−1.7	0.2	0.7	1.0	1.0
Spain	3.8	1.1	−3.6	0.0	−1.0	−2.9	−1.7	1.4	3.2	3.2	2.8
UK	2.6	−0.6	−4.3	1.9	1.5	1.3	1.9	3.1	2.2	1.8	1.6
Japan	1.6	−1.1	−5.4	4.2	−0.1	1.5	2.0	0.3	1.1	1.0	1.4
Russia	8.5	5.2	−7.8	4.5	4.3	3.5	1.2	0.7	−2.8	−0.2	1.4
China	14.2	9.7	9.4	10.6	9.5	7.9	7.8	7.3	6.9	6.7	6.6
India	9.8	3.9	8.5	10.3	6.6	5.5	6.5	7.2	7.9	7.1	7.3
Brazil	6.1	5.1	−0.1	7.5	4.0	1.9	3.0	0.5	−3.8	−3.6	0.7
Mexico	3.1	1.2	−4.5	5.1	4.0	3.8	1.6	2.3	2.6	2.0	1.9

Sources: IMF, *World Economic Outlook*, April (2018) for the world estimate and OECD (2018) for all the other data

September 2008. The crisis in real variables (GDP, investment, consumption, and employment) had begun at the end of 2007, but had worsened in the second part of 2008 and in 2009, notwithstanding the TARP financial package decided by Bush in October 2008 and subsequently, in large part, maintained by Obama in 2009–2010.

As Table 10.1 shows, the crisis, measured in terms of total GDP growth rates, occurred earlier in the US than in the Euro area and in the world, but it was less deep and prolonged than in the Euro area and in most other countries.

Yet, as we have anticipated in Chap. 9, in the US, the fall in investment, employment, and wages had been much more severe, and the recovery had been longer and more painful than the one for real GDP. While real GDP could recover the 2007 level about 3–4 years later, total gross capital formation came back to the 2007 level about 6 years later and real full-time wages could return to the 2009 maximum after 6 years. The employment situation was even worse. The unemployment rate more than doubled from 2007 to 2010 and could return to the 2007 level only ten years later (see Table 10.2), but with an employment rate

Table 10.2 Harmonized % unemployment rates in selected areas or countries (2007–2017)

Country or area	2007	2008	2009	2010	2011	2012	2013	2014	2015	2016	2017
World	5.5	5.7	6.2	6.1	6.0	6.0	5.9	5.8	5.7	5.7	5.8
US	4.6	5.8	9.3	9.6	9.0	8.1	7.4	6.2	5.3	4.9	4.4
EU 28	7.2	7.0	9.0	9.6	9.7	10.5	10.9	10.2	9.4	8.6	7.6
Euro area	7.5	7.6	9.6	10.2	10.2	11.4	12.0	11.6	10.9	10.0	9.1
Germany	8.5	7.4	7.6	7.0	5.8	5.4	5.2	5.0	4.6	4.1	3.8
France	8.0	7.4	9.1	9.3	9.2	9.8	10.3	10.3	10.4	10.1	9.4
Italy	6.1	6.7	7.8	8.4	8.4	10.6	12.1	12.7	11.9	11.7	11.2
Spain	8.2	11.3	17.9	19.9	21.4	24.8	26.1	24.5	22.1	19.7	17.2
Greece	8.4	7.8	9.6	12.8	17.9	24.5	27.5	26.6	25.0	23.6	21.5
Portugal	9.1	8.8	10.7	12.0	12.9	15.8	16.5	14.1	12.7	11.2	9.0
UK	5.3	5.6	7.6	7.8	8.1	7.9	7.6	6.1	5.3	4.8	4.4
Japan	3.8	4.0	5.1	5.1	4.6	4.4	4.0	3.6	3.4	3.1	2.8

Sources: OECD (2018) and World Bank (2018) for line 1

substantially diminished, a strong reduction in manufacturing jobs and a greater proportion in total employment of low-paid *bad jobs* mainly concentrated in the services sector.

The response of the Obama administration and the FED was based on some neo-Keynesian interventions and on some long-term strategic projects. The short-term measures mainly consisted in a more aggressive expansionary monetary policy (*quantitative easing*) and the continuation of the TARP program, which contributed to save many important US banks and insurance companies, such as AIG, avoiding the total collapse of the financial system.

Moreover, President Obama, winning the opposition of most republicans and of a part of the Democratic party, extended the TARP also to some big failing industrial corporations, such as General Motors and Chrysler.

After their bankruptcy, the US Treasury took over General Motors and Chrysler in March 2009. It invested $51 billion into GM, but later recovered about $39.7 billion from the sale of its shares, so that its total direct costs for GM were about $11.3 billion.[4] Moreover, the Treasury also saved the financial branch of General Motors, GMAC, which became Allis financial, but in this case, it disbursed about $17.2 billion in

December 2008, recovering $19.6 billion in December 2014, with a net profit of $2.4 billion. It was estimated that, on the whole, the bailouts preserved 1.2 million jobs and about 39.4 billion in tax revenues.[5]

Chrysler was saved in a different way, with a gradual sale of the shares owned by the Treasury and by the UAW labor union retiree health-care fund to the Italian FIAT automaker group. All this led, in October 2014, to the merger of the two corporations and the constitution of FCA (Fiat Chrysler Automobiles). The Treasury invested $12.5 billion in Chrysler later recovering more than $11.2 billion with a direct loss of about $1.3 billion, but the intervention allowed the fast recovery of the firm and the activation of new investment and car models and so saved many jobs while preserving substantial tax revenues and the health care and pension funds of the Chrysler employees.

On the whole, the US Treasury invested about $80 billion in the automobile sector, recovering about 90% of the public funds in six years, but it was very successful in speeding up the recovery of the sector, in saving jobs and in maintaining tax revenues for an amount abundantly superior to the net cost of its intervention.

While General Motors and Chrysler had been rescued after bankruptcy by public Federal aids, the other giant US car maker, Ford Corporation, was able to independently resist to the crisis. Ford was able to refuse TARP money by means of a better industrial policy and having obtained $26 billion in banking loans in exchange for the mortgage of all its assets in 2006. However, sizable public financial aids were also extended to the Ford Corporation in two ways. Generous incentives were given to all US automakers for research expenditures regarding greener cars. Moreover, a $3 billion *Cash for Clunkers* program was introduced in July–November 2009. This program gave consumers the possibility of receiving financial incentives if they bought new more fuel-efficient vehicles, scrapping their old fuel-inefficient ones.

President Obama could so revitalize the automobile sector and prompt the three biggest US car makers to switch a part of their research and productive efforts in favor of less consuming and less polluting vehicles.

Obama's administration also made other important interventions in the fiscal and financial fields. They were: the February 2009 *American Recovery and Reinvestment Act*, the *Financial Stability plan*, and the

Dodd-Frank Act (Wall Street Reform and Consumer Protection Act), approved on July 21, 2010.

The American Recovery and Reinvestment Act was an important Keynesian-type fiscal stimulus package of $787 billion. It was constituted for about one third by tax reductions and for about two thirds by public expenditure increases. The latter principally regarded energy saving and renewable sources, improvements in education and transportation infrastructures, larger unemployment subsidies, the extension of health coverage to the recipients of unemployment subsidies, R&D and education expenditure, transfers to state and local authorities for collective services, and so on.

The fiscal stimulus was criticized as excessively dangerous for the US public finance by most Republican representatives and several mainstream economists. On the contrary, many other economists, including two Nobel laureates, Joseph Stiglitz and Paul Krugman, judged the stimulus package not big enough, excessively focused on tax cuts and too timid as regards unemployment, social expenditure, and the fight against the rise in inequality.

Yet, the Obama neo-Keynesian approach, even though its impact on investment, employment, and inequalities was largely insufficient, was much more fruitful than the rigid and ill-conceived austerity policy maintained during the same period in the European Union.

Naturally, Obama's stimulus package contributed, together with the consequences of the crisis, to a worsening of public finance accounts.

As Table 10.3 shows, the Federal receipts in percentage of GDP went down, mainly because of the crisis, from 17.9% in 2007 to 14.5% in 2009, while the total outlays went up from 19.1% to 24.4%. The increase in outlays was partly due to the rise in war expenditures mainly associated to the second Iraq war unfortunately launched by George W. Bush. It was also due to TARP disbursements and, since 2009, to Obama's expansionary budgetary policy. Consequently, the public deficit in percentage of GDP increased from −1.1% in 2007 to −9.8% in 2009 and in the same period the Federal debt in percentage of GDP went up from 65.2% to 91.4%.

The huge and growing public debt generated increasing expenses for the service of the debt, but the sharp reduction of interest rate due to the

Table 10.3 Federal receipts, outlays, deficits, and debt as percent of GDP: 2007–2019

Fiscal year	Receipts	Outlays		Deficit	Federal debt (end of year)	
		Total	Defense		Gross	Held by public
2007	17.9	19.1	3.8	−1.1	62.5	35.2
2008	17.1	20.2	4.2	−3.1	67.7	39.3
2009	14.5	24.4	4.6	−9.8	82.4	52.3
2010	14.6	23.4	4.7	−8.7	91.4	60.9
2011	15.0	23.4	4.6	−8.5	96.0	65.9
2012	15.3	22.1	4.2	−6.8	100.1	70.4
2013	16.8	20.9	3.8	−4.1	101.2	72.6
2014	17.5	20.3	3.5	−2.8	103.2	74.1
2015	18.1	20.5	3.3	−2.4	100.8	72.9
2016	17.7	20.9	3.2	−3.2	105.8	76.7
2017	17.3	20.8	3.1	−3.5	105.4	76.5
2018 (f)	16.7	20.8	3.2	−4.2	107.2	78.8
2019 (f)	16.3	21.0	3.3	−4.7	108.1	80.3

f = forecast
Source: White House (2018), p. 553

quantitative easing monetary policy contributed to contain the Treasury's disbursements. This strongly contributed to the continuation of the rise of the federal debt/GDP ratio up to 105.8% in 2016, even though the recovery in GDP and in tax receipts since 2010 had attenuated the increase of the ratio. In 2017, with the advent of the Trump's administration, there was a small decrease in the ratio, to 105.4%, but the official estimates for 2018 and 2019 foresee a rise up to 108.1% in 2019. This means that most Republicans who, in the name of sound public finance, were eager to restrain Obama's expansionary efforts when Obama was president, soon changed their position on public debt during Trump's presidency, favoring large tax cuts.

The *great recession* contributed to the deterioration also of the state and local budget deficits in percentage of GDP, which rose from about −0.5 in 2007 to about −2% in 2009. Several state and local authorities, lacking tax revenues or federal transfers, decided to reduce social expenditures in a period in which poverty and social needs were escalating.

The trends in public deficit and in public debt were at the center of the political debate during the midterm elections of November 2010. In the

Republican party, the advent and the growing influence of the right-wing *tea party movement*, and the harsh campaign against *Obama care* and against "too much taxation, too much public deficit, too much public debt, too many immigrants", greatly contributed to the defeat of the Democratic party and to the success of the republicans. With a large majority, the Republicans took over the House of Representatives and the state governorships and reduced almost completely their gap with the Democrats in the Senate. Therefore, in the following years, Obama had to confront a largely hostile House and a fragile situation in the Senate and this heavily conditioned his political and economic choices. Almost immediately, there was a harsh confrontation with the Congress on the increase of the *federal debt limit*, that is, "the total amount of money that the US government is authorized to borrow to meet its existing legal obligations, including Social Security and Medicare benefits, military salaries, interest on the national debt, tax refunds and other payments."[6] The annual approval of Congress had historically been a pure formality, but in 2011 and in the following years of Obama's terms it became a nightmare.

A Congress refusal to approve the increase in the debt limit could have catastrophic consequences, like the default of the country or the impossibility to pay part of the salaries of the public Administration and to honor other vital legal obligations.

Each year, there was a difficult political battle in which President Obama could finally obtain the Congress approval, but after a series of painful compromises with the Republican majority of the Congress, usually in terms of strong reductions in public expenditures and of several tax cuts.[7]

The bipartisan compromises reached by Obama on the debt limit introduced austerity measures and strongly contributed to reduce the recovery and then the pace of the economic expansion of the US economy in the 2011–2016 period while fostering great economic and social inequalities. Yet, after his re-election in 2012, President Obama was able to regain more freedom of manoeuver in economic policy matters and could activate some other expansionary measures.

The *Dodd-Franck Act Plan* attempted at better regulating the financial system in order to avoid the recurrence of other major financial crises. In particular, the July 2010 Dodd-Frank Act reregulated the financial system, including part of the previously unregulated *shadow banking* sector, trying to protect savers and consumers against financial frauds and malpractices. Yet it was too lengthy, complex, and of difficult application and there was no return to a full separation of commercial banks and investment banks, as the former FED president Volker and many economists had suggested. Moreover, the Dodd-Frank Act extended the capital requirements of the financial intermediaries, but it did not fully obstruct the huge and extremely dangerous financialization of the economy, the excessive leverage, the problem of the existence and consolidation of "banks too big to fail", and the return to very high salaries and bonuses easily conceded to the top managers of the banks.

10.3 The Industrial and Innovation Policy

President Obama, in addition, had some medium- and long-term strategic programs. One of them was to slow down the rapid deindustrialization of the US economy and to structurally sustain total employment, increasingly eroded by globalization and rapid technological changes, such as the widespread use of robots and the e-economy.

We have already analyzed Obama's crucial interventions in favor of the financial system, the automobile sector, and the construction sector, but industrial policy has been principally made through a complex set of technology or innovation policies. These policies had been carried out by government departments, such as Defense, Energy, Health, and so on, or by a vast network of decentralized federal agencies or programs.

Defense Advanced Research Projects Agency (DARPA) has exercised a crucial role in the introduction of inventions and innovations later largely used by several firms active in the civilian high-tech sectors, but also National Science Foundation (NSF), National Health Institute (NHI), National Aeronautics and Space Administration (NASA), National Nanotechnology Initiative (Nni), and so on have greatly contributed to support the technological growth of important US industrial and tertiary groups, such as Apple, H.P., Google, and so on.[8]

In particular, for most of its products Apple has greatly benefited from State financed research, which has contributed to the creation and diffusion of internet, of touch screen technologies, of GPS, SIRI, and so on; NASA has produced important innovations and spin-offs, such as Fairchild Microelectronics; the pharmaceutical and bio-medical sectors have largely profited from the NHI and other public research funds, and so on.

Moreover, many university research centers or agencies, heavily financed by public money, have decisively contributed to create and help the growth of a number of successful start-ups, science parks, or even entire high-tech areas, such as the Silicon Valley in California.

Finally, the Small Business Administration (SBA) through their Small Business Innovation Research (SBIR) has supported the technological and economic expansion of many small- or medium-size enterprises or start-ups.

The total value of the public funds directly or indirectly conceded to these agencies or university institutions have been increased in the crucial recession years 2009–2010, acting in a countercyclical way and hence helping in the recovery and the international competitiveness of the US economy.

In the medium and long-run perspective, public policy has therefore been a fundamental factor in fostering and shaping the US economic development. Nonetheless, it could only slow down, but not arrest, the basic trends of the last four decades toward continuing deindustrialization, growing financialization, and the rise in income and wealth differentials.

10.4 Obama and the Environment

Before his election to presidency, Barack Obama, in his books and speeches[9] and in his political activity as senator and presidential candidate, had already clearly shown that he wanted to create a sharp discontinuity with the environmental policy of President George W. Bush. In particular, he wanted to associate a policy of strong reduction in the US foreign energy dependency with an important improvement of the environment.

In his two presidential terms, Barack Obama accomplished a relevant part of his electoral programs. His policy contributed to reduce the total and per capita consumption of energy and of electricity, and even more the associated emission of CO_2 and other pollutants.

In 2016, the total and per capita US consumption of energy had fallen with respect to the 2008 level, even though, in that period, total and per capita GDP had increased.[10]

From 2008 to 2016, total and per capita energy-related CO_2 emissions diminished and the CO_2 emissions/GDP ratios fell even more. This was mainly due to coal-to-gas switching, to the growing use of renewables in electricity production and to the reduction in US energy consumption.

In the same years, the energy dependency ratio of the US, that is, the net import/consumption rate, also diminished. On the consumption side, this was mainly due to vast changes in the industry/mix and to more vigorous regulations and energy conservation policies and, on the production side, to the rapid increase in the US production of shale oil and shale gas.

The electricity generated from solar panels had grown from 0.9 million megawatts/hours in 2008 to 37 million megawatts/hours in 2016, while the electricity produced from wind had increased from 55 million megawatts/hours to 227 million. Although, in 2016, wind and solar together generated only around 6.4% of total electricity and all renewables (including hydro, bio-mass, etc.) generated just about 15% of total power, the rise of solar and wind net generated power had been very rapid. During the same period, the use of coal in the production of electricity, which was the cheapest but more polluting energy source, had been considerably reduced.

A comprehensive ecological indicator, such as the *ecological footprint* (see Fig. 10.1), shows that the US' situation had fairly improved during the Obama administrations, but yet remains one of the worst in the world. Obama's environmental policy was very wide-ranging. Some of the principal measures can be summarized in the following points.[11]

1. A *clean-power plan*, which has given states the tools to reduce carbon pollution and other dangerous pollutants from power plants, thus helping to improve people's health.

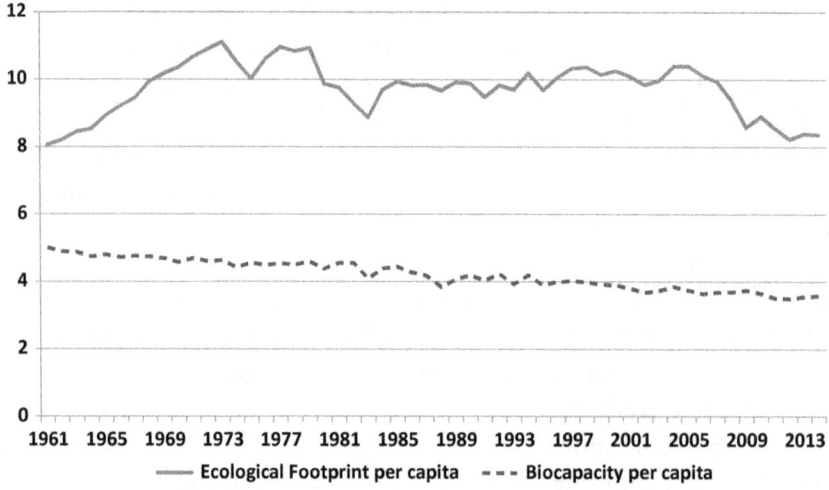

Fig. 10.1 Ecological Footprint and Bio-capacity in the US: 1961–2014 (global hectares/person)
Note: The Ecological Footprint is the measure of how much area of biologically productive land and water an individual, population, or activity requires to produce all the resources it consumes and to absorb the waste it generates, using prevailing technology and resource management practices. Bio-capacity is the ecosystems' capacity to produce biological materials used by people and to absorb waste material generated by humans under current management schemes and extraction technologies
Source: Global Footprint Network (2018)

2. *The introduction of a set of new standards or incentives* to cut fuel consumption in vehicles, energy consumption in appliances and equipment, carbon pollution in industry, methane emissions, greenhouse gas emissions in firms, universities, federal activities, agriculture.
3. A set of measures aimed at the *expansion of the clean energy economy*, including $90 billion investment provided through the American Recovery and Reinvestment Act for the growth of the clean energy sector. It was estimated that it could leverage about $150 billion in private and other non-federal capital, leading to a relevant growth of new jobs and new technologies, to over a tripling of wind power and an increase of solar power by 30-times. In 2008–2015, the intervention helped also to decrease the cost of solar by 64%, the cost of wind power by 41%, and the cost of LEDs by 94%. There were also mea-

sures to introduce solar and wind power, or energy saving up-grades, in Federal land, military sites, off-shore windy areas, two million houses, and to foster electric car diffusion, bio-fuel technologies, hydro-electric production, and so on.
4. During the Obama presidency the US also tried to foster international progress in the war against global warming. It signed, together with other 193 countries and the European Union, the 2015 Paris Agreement on Climate Change.[12] It also led a coalition of countries favorable to amend the Montreal Protocol to phase down hydrofluorcarbons (HFCs), which are very damaging greenhouse gases.

   Moreover, the US established important bilateral agreements with China, India, Brazil, Indonesia, Canada, Mexico, UK, and Norway to reduce various forms of pollution. In particular, in the agreement with China, the two presidents announced that by 2025 the US would reduce its greenhouse emissions from 26% to 28% below 2005 levels, while China would peak carbon emissions in 2030 and increase the share of zero carbon energy capacity by 20 percent.
5. There were also several measures to limit the power plants' emissions of mercury, arsenic, and other toxic air pollutants; vehicular emissions; toxic chemical and ozone emissions; the potential pollution from off-shore oil and gas extraction and exploration; and so on. Stricter standards for drinking water and *the clean water rule* tried to better protect US water resources.
6. The Obama administration introduced many incentives, new standards, and regulations in order to cut energy waste. It also released important reports to assess the impact of climate change on the US.
7. Finally, the US tried to better protect its national treasures, extending public lands and waters and Federal wilderness, fighting illegal fishing, financing the restoring of iconic natural sites and the Gulf coast, announcing more recoveries of endangered species and the protection of precious pollinators such as honeybees and Monarch butterflies, and so on.

While the Obama administration could take important steps toward a better environment, it did also permit a rapid worsening of the environment and of deep water resources in the zones of extraction of shale gas and shale oil, even though the government had tried to introduce more severe regulations to the sector. There was indeed a conflict between Obama's two major objectives: to reduce US energy dependence and to respect the environment. In this case the trade-off seems to have largely privileged the first objective, although the availability of abundant low-cost gas has contributed to reduce the use of more polluting energy sources, as coal, and to slow down the deindustrialization process.

10.5 Obamacare

One of the major objectives of the Obama 2008 program was the attempt at giving a decent health coverage to the whole US population, including the people who could not buy the costly private health insurances. The Obama health reform, often called *Obamacare*, was extremely difficult, since it was fiercely opposed by the large majority of the Republican Party and by a section of the Democratic Party under the great pressure of powerful interest groups, such as the big health insurance companies and a relevant part of the health system.

During the Bill Clinton presidency, a health reform, partly designed by Hillary Clinton, had aborted, and also Obama's attempt encountered many obstacles.

Yet, in the early 2000s, the American health system was considered by many economists and health experts too costly, socially unjust, and with adverse economic and demographic effects.[13]

In 2008, US health expenditures in percent of GDP were 15.3%, versus the 10.1% of France, which the World Health Organization in a 2000 report had ranked as the country with the best health system in the world, while the US held only the 37th position.[14]

In 2008, the US health system was mainly based on private insurance policies subscribed by individuals or by medium and large firms for their employees, but it also had two public programs, *Medicare* and *Medicaid*, introduced by President Lyndon Johnson in 1965. *Medicare* is a federal program for people of 65 years or older, or for people with severe disabilities, while *Medicaid* is a state and federal program for people with a very low income. In 2008, the final year of the George W. Bush presidency, private health expenditures were over half of total health expenditure, one of the highest percentages in industrialized countries. The whole population was not covered by private insurance policies or by the public programs. About 46 million people were without any coverage, and so they were liable to dramatic health and bankruptcy risks in the case of major illnesses.

Infant mortality rate was higher than in several other industrialized country. Defining the infant mortality rate as the number of children under five years of age died in a year per 1000 live births of the same year, we can see that in 2016 the US had a rate of 6.5, over the double than countries such as Japan (2.7) and Sweden (2.9) and much higher than Italy (3.3), Germany (3.8), France (3.9), and so on.

Moreover, a rough synthetic indicator of health conditions, *life expectancy at birth*, in the US was almost 3–4 years lower than in Japan and in most Western European countries, while the total cost of health per person in the US was much higher.

Naturally, life expectancy depends not only on the overall efficiency of the health system, but also on other problems, such as the immediate and the indirect consequences of wars, easy access to weapons, abuse of drugs, smoking and/or drinking, car crash casualties, on-the-job deaths, suicide rates, obesity, life style, and so on.

Some of these problems can be tackled by social and medical prevention, but a great part of the question is associated to the very expensive and exceedingly unbalanced health organization prevailing in the US. Several people could pay, or their firms or Administrations could pay for them, high-cost insurance policies and thus receive extensive and high-quality services, but a large part of the population could only afford much cheaper policies and hence they obtained less extensive and lower quality services. Moreover, almost 16% of the population had no health coverage at all and little or no prevention of major illnesses.

The health reform proposed by president Obama during the 2008 presidential campaign had three main objectives: (a) to extend health coverage to the greatest possible part of the population, with the aim of ultimately reaching a universal health service, (b) to reduce the level and the rapid rate of growth of total and per capita cost of health care introducing a sound competition between public and private health institutions and health services; (c) to continue to increase the quality and the technological level of the health system not only in its top institutions and for a relatively few people but for the entire population.

The bill proposed by president Obama in July 2009 aimed at reaching a coverage of at least 97% of American citizens with an expenditure of $1500 billion. It was based on seven major pillars: (a) obligatory health insurances, (b) the choice of the citizen among the various private health insurances or the subscription to a public plan, (c) private companies were forbidden to refuse the insurance coverage on the basis of preexisting health conditions of the citizens, (d) firms over a certain size were obliged to offer health insurance to their employees or to contribute to their cost, (e) financial aids were given to poorer citizens for the subscription of health insurances, (f) there were extensions in the Medicaid programs, (g) citizens could add their children up to 26 years to their health insurance plan.

The Obama project had to face a fierce political opposition and a loud mass-media campaign, which spoke of "socialist" measures, which were costing a fortune to the tax payers and killing the freedom of choice of the citizens.

So, in order to have the *Affordable Care Act* approved by the Congress, President Obama had to make various and heavy compromises with the opposition and also with some members of the Democratic Party. In particular, he had to renounce the public pillar, that is, the possibility of choosing public hospitals and public care instead of private insurance policies. In this way, the possibility of introducing more competition into the health system and of reducing the monopolistic gains of insurance companies and the too rapid growth in the prices of health policies was severely curtailed.

The reform, that was finally approved on March 25, 2010, introduced a complex system of public subsidies for the subscription of private health policies by low-income people and penalties for the people who did not acquire a health policy. The reform obliged also the insurance companies to concede policies also to people with major and costly diseases, obliged firms with over 50 employees to contribute to the costs of health insurance policies, widened the coverage of Medicaid and allowed the parents to add their children up to the age 26 on their health insurance plan.

In this way, it was possible to reduce the people without health coverage in percent of the population from 16% in 2010 to 8.9% in 2016, obtaining a result much inferior to the objective of the initial Obama project (3% or less).

The reform also allowed important improvements in the activity of prevention of major diseases and on the conditions previously imposed by the companies to the subscribers of a large number of low-cost policies, such as upper limits of costs or other restrictions. However, some companies ceased to offer health policies, or raised their prices conspicuously.

The total health spending in percent of GDP increased from 16.4% in 2010 to 17.2% in 2016, but the annual rate of growth in health care expenditures at constant prices went down considerably from 4.4% in the years 2000–2010 to 2.8% in the years 2010–2016,[15] although, after the reform, the health coverage had been considerably expanded. The share of government/compulsory spending on GDP rose from 7.9% in 2010 to 8.5% in 2015, while the share of voluntary/out of pocket spending on GDP increased from 8.5% in 2010 to 8.8% in 2016.[16]

On the whole, we can say that Obamacare is a useful, but halved reform, if compared to the original project. While it could provide important basic health coverage to over 20 million more people, it did not lead to a fully universal health system, nor did it solve the problem of the too high level of US health spending and of the strongly unequal quality of health services provided to the population.

10.6 Inequality, Taxation, and the Middle-Class Crunch

In his eight years as president, Barack Obama achieved a fairly good success in his economic policy against the great recession, and partially in his environmental and social policies. However, in international politics, where the legacy of his predecessor was very heavy, he had reached mixed and often unsatisfactory results. Moreover, as regards medium- and long-term economic problems, his policy was probably too weak.

He was able to attenuate, but not reverse, the basic negative trends shaping the economic and social environment since the late 1970s and the 1980s. Inequality in income and in wealth continued to rise and taxation continued to privilege the very rich and the big owners of financial assets versus the poor and the declining middle class. As we have seen in previous chapters, off-shoring, deindustrialization, robotization, financialization, and the rise of the e-economy continued to compress the employment opportunities and the real wages of middle-income people. These trends extended the number and the wealth of very rich people while impoverishing a substantial part of the middle class and enlarging the number of people living in urban or rural ghettos, often with precarious "bad jobs" and exposed to the competition from migrant workers. So a large area of middle-class or poor "angry white men" rose, who strongly contributed to the electoral success of Donald Trump, though his policy will most probably worsen their economic and social destiny.

Notes

1. See Obama (2006, 2008). Besides *The Audacity of Hope*, Obama's main writings were *Dreams from My Father* (1995, 2004) and a selection of his speeches, *Words That Changed a Nation* (2009). On Obama's personality and his policies, see, for example, David Maraniss (2012) and Mario Del Pero (2017).
2. See Obama (2006, 2008), pp. 213–224 in the 2008 first Vintage edition.
3. See Obama (2006, 2008), pp. 188–201 of the 2008 first Vintage edition.
4. See U.S. Department of the Treasury (2015). https://www.treasury.gov/initiatives/financial-stability/TARP-Programs/automotive-programs/Pages/default.aspx.
5. See Healy (2013). Government Sells Last of Its GM Shares, *USA Today*, December 9, 2013. Accessed on November 20, 2017 at Government Sells Last of its GM Shares.
6. See U.S. Department of the Treasury (2017). Accessed on November 27, 2017 at https://www.treasury.gov/initiatives/Pages/debtlimit.aspx.

7. For an in-depth political analysis, see, for example, Del Pero (2017), pp. 213–218.
8. See Mazzucato (2013), chaps. 4–6. See also Di Tommaso and Schweitzer (2013) for a general overview of the US industrial policy.
9. See Obama (2006, 2008).
10. See IEA (2018).
11. See, for a detailed list of interventions, the official White House Document on Environmental Policy at https://obamawhitehouse.archives.gov/the-record/climate, accessed on December 2, 2017. See also the analysis of US environmental policy presented in Zachary. A. Smith, *The Environmental Policy Paradox* (2017).
12. Signatures up to April 2018. However, one of the first moves of president Trump, strongly disapproved by US environmentalists, was to announce the unilateral withdrawal from the Paris Agreement in 2020.
13. See, for example, Krugman (2007) and Gordon (2016), who advocated a universal public health system.
14. See WHO (World Health Organization), *World Health Report*, Genève, 2000. WHO tried to estimate a ranking of the health system in 191 countries on the basis of a complex set of indicators, taking account of both the level and the distributive aspects of the health systems.
15. See OECD (2017). The 2016 data are provisional estimates.
16. OECD (2017).

References

Del Pero, M. 2017. *Era Obama*. Milano: Feltrinelli.
Di Tommaso, M., and S.O. Schweitzer. 2013. *Industrial Policy in America: Breaking the Taboo*. Cheltenham, UK: Edward Elgar Pub.
Global Footprint Network. 2018. *NFA: 2018 Edition*. Oakland, CA.: http://www.footprintnetwork.org.
Gordon, R.J. 2016. *The Rise and Fall of American Growth: The U.S. Standard of Living Since the Civil War*. Princeton: Princeton University Press.
Healy, J.R. 2013. Government Sells Last of its GM Shares, December 9. Accessed November 20, 2017. https://eu.usatoday.com/story/money/cars/2013/12/09/government-treasury-gm-general-motors-tarp-bailout-exit-sale/3925515/.
IEA. 2018. https://www.iea.org.

IMF. 2018. *World Economic Outlook.* Accessed April 2018.
Krugman, P. 2007. *The Conscience of a Liberal.* New York: W.W. Norton.
Maraniss, D. 2012. *Barack Obama: The Story.* New York: Simon & Schuster.
Mazzucato, M. 2013. *Lo stato innovatore.* Roma and Bari: Laterza.
Obama, B. 1995. *Dreams from My Father: A Story of Race and Inheritance.* New York: Times Books.
———. 2006, 2008. *The Audacity of Hope: Thoughts on Reclaiming the American Dream.* Lake Arbor, MD: Crown Books. 2006. First Vintage Books edition, 2008.
———. 2009. *Words that Changed a Nation: The Most Celebrated and Influential Speeches of Barack Obama.* Boston: Beacon Hills.
OECD. 2017. http://stats.oecd.org/Index.aspx?DataSetCode=SHA.
———. 2018. www.oecd.org.
Smith, Z.A. 2017. *The Environmental Policy Paradox.* 6th ed. Abingdon-on-Thames, UK: Routledge.
U.S. Department of the Treasury. 2015. https://www.treasury.gov/initiatives/financial-stability/TARP-Programs/automotive-programs/Pages/default.aspx.
———. 2017. Accessed November 27, 2017. https://www.treasury.gov/initiatives/Pages/debtlimit.aspx.
White House Document on Environmental Policy. 2017. Accessed December 2, 2017. https://obamawhitehouse.archives.gov/the-record/climate.
White House. 2018. *Economic Report of the President.* Washington, DC.
WHO (World Health Organization). 2000. *World Health Report.* Geneva.
World Bank. 2018. www.worldbank.org.

11

The Economic Consequences of Donald Trump

11.1 Populism and Trumpism

It is probably too early to attempt an assessment of the full economic consequences of the ascent of Donald Trump to the presidency. While some of the main aspects of his economic policy are already clear, the full impact of his choices can be judged only after the final days of his mandate.

It is also important, in order to better evaluate Trump's economic views, to try to understand his peculiar version of *populism*, which we have called *Trumpism*.[1]

Populism is a particularly elusive and vague concept, since it has been defined by political scientists, economists, and politicians in a large variety of ways.[2] Yet, it has been usually associated to the presence of a charismatic leader, or a group of persons, leading a movement that directly appeals to the people, harshly criticizing the "establishment" or the elites. In democracies, when they are at the opposition, populists also attack the government, a large part of the political parties and of members of parliament, while proclaiming that they only are the true and direct defenders of the people's will. In recent times, there have been right-wing populisms as those led by Marine Le Pen in France, Nigel Farage in the UK, Silvio Berlusconi and Matteo Salvini in Italy, and Donald Trump in the US. There have also been left-wing populisms, such as the ones of Chavez in Venezuela or Evo Morales in Bolivia; or more complex ones as Peronism in Argentina or the Five Star Movement in Italy.[3]

In his book *What is Populism?* Jan-Werner Muller stresses the importance of some central elements in populism: *anti-elitism, exclusivity*, and *the rejection of pluralism*.

Donald Trump's policy contained all these aspects. His anti-elitism was bluntly clear. In his presidential campaign, he trumpeted against the Washington establishment "who betrayed American workers" and against expertise, academic, political, and media elites. Truly, he seemed to forget that he belonged to the economic elite of the super-rich, living in luxury and using the connections with the privileged class and that part of the political body that was in various ways associated to his building and T.V. activities and his family wealth. Yet, Donald Trump was able to use his wealth as a political asset. He fully utilized the envy and fascination that success and the exhibition of wealth have on a part of the population, while harshly criticizing the Washington and New York elites.

In some way, he attempted at appearing as the king that in ancient times presented himself as the prime protector of the people against the abuses of the feudal lords.

Usually, populists pretend to be the exclusive representatives of the people. Even if they are, as it was in the case of Trump, a minority, albeit a large one, of the entire population, they present themselves as the true interpreters of popular will, excluding the possibility that other leaders or parties could feel, as they do, the true heart and pulse of the people. In doing so they are against pluralism and this can be, and in some historical cases has been, a deadly danger for democracy.

The rejection of pluralism is a typical element of most right-wing populist movements, and in Donald Trump it takes the form of a strong nationalistic, macho, racist, anti-immigrant, and anti-science inclination.

In his presidential campaign, Donald Trump could appeal to many white poor or middle-class workers on the basis of his *America first*, antiglobal, anti-immigrants, apparently anti-establishment, platform. His simplified, often rude, but easy to understand, language, was so different from the one used in the cultivated speeches of Hilary Clinton or Barack Obama, and powerfully contributed to his electoral success.

Also, his long presence as host in a popular NBC T.V. series *The Apprentice*, was very useful to his political career, not only because it gave him a large renown among the general public, but also because his bossing role gave the idea that he was a man who could make prompt and strong decisions, that he was a man with charisma.

Yet, several observers have pointed out that his after-election economic moves have been more conservative than populist. In his electoral campaign, he attacked "them", the elites, but not so much Wall Street, the great corporations, their top managers, and the super-rich. He has, for example, inserted several exponents of the financial elite in his government. Moreover, as we will see in next paragraphs, Donald Trump has greatly supported the industrial-military complex and the construction sector, reduced taxes in particular for the rich and big business, deregulated the financial and energy sectors and cut public expenditure in health care and in welfare.

In his campaign and in the first part of his mandate, he adopted a double-face policy: a tough conservative one in favor of the rich and affluent, and a populist one which seemed to be in favor of a neglected part of the working class. He could thus obtain both the votes of a large part of the traditional conservative electorate and a portion of the votes which had traditionally mainly gone to the Democratic Party.

Following his electoral promises to the workers in the manufacturing industry, he has tried to contain US Corporations' off-shoring, to attract foreign investment, to cancel or modify multilateral international agreements.

Finally, risking heavy foreign retaliations, he has introduced protectionist measures, such as tariffs on steel and aluminum and on European and Chinese exports. However, most of his moves have been more favorable to the economic and financial elite than to the middle class and the poor, who have also been damaged by large cuts in health care and welfare.

11.2 Donald Trump's Victory in the 2016 Presidential Election

Donald Trump extensively used his populist appeal to defeat his opponents in the primaries of the Republican Party and then to win the presidential elections against Hillary Clinton. Although he lost the popular vote (about 46% of votes versus 48% for Hillary), he captured more electoral votes than Hillary Clinton (304 versus 227), also gaining narrow victories in traditionally Democratic industrial states, such as Pennsylvania, Michigan, and Wisconsin, finally winning the presidency in November 2016. Without Trump's marginal success in those three states, the presidency would have gone to Hillary Clinton.[4] A relatively restricted number of distressed workers in former industrialized zones of the *rust belt*, who had been heavily hit during the great recession by the rise in unemployment and the reduction in real wages, responded to Trump's anti-globalist, protectionist, anti-immigrant populist promises, and thus contributed to change the destiny of the election.[5]

However, other factors were also very important, and perhaps decisive, in Trump's success. Three of them are well known: the announcement made by the FBI's director just a few days before the election of further inquiry about Hillary Clinton's use of her private e-mail server while serving as Secretary of State; the pro-Trump interference of Russia in the US presidential campaign by means of hackers and manipulated information; the use of Facebook's information on over 50 million voters illegally obtained by Trump's campaign assistants through Cambridge Analytica. A fourth factor was also central: in the last days of the campaign the capacity to concentrate a great volume of media ads and of personalized big data, such as those provided by Cambridge Analytica, on the crucial categories of voters in the crucial states.

So, although, in his primary and general electoral campaigns Trump's fund-raising had received much less money than Hillary Clinton from donors ($335 million to Trump versus $623 million to Hillary),[6] he was able to use them in a more concentrated and productive way.

11.3 The Relations with Economic and Financial Power

Donald Trump obtained large contributions and political support from big interest groups that were also very influential among the conservative voters, such as the National Rifle Association and the US Chamber of Commerce.

Trump's campaign also received substantial funds by a nonprofit association, which was not obliged to reveal the names of the original donors.

Among Trump's individual big donors for his campaign and his inauguration fund there were a hedge fund Co-CEO, Robert Mercer; Las Vegas Casino owners, the Adelson family, who had advocated the moving of the US embassy to Jerusalem; the owner of Mac Mahon Ventures, Linda Mac Mahon; a coal baron, Robert Murray; the owner of The New York Jets, Robert Woods Johnson, and so on. Some of the big donors had later received ambassadorial posts, as Robert Woods Johnson, who was appointed ambassador to the UK, or important positions, as Linda Mac Mahon, who was nominated administrator of the US Small Business Administration.[7]

Several other big donors to Trump or the Republican Party had an easy access to Trump's inner circle, where they tried to influence some elements of the president's policy, such as the industrial and energy policy, or the environmental and financial regulations.

In his presidential campaign, Donald Trump often attacked Hillary Clinton because of her contacts with the Wall street establishment, and in particular for the compensations of the speeches given by Hillary Clinton in Goldman Sachs's conferences and for the donations received by the Clinton Foundation from several big banks. So he even declared that Goldman Sachs "owned" Hillary Clinton, but one of the first moves he did as President was to appoint Goldman Sachs' former exponents and other "big finance" men to crucial positions in his Administration.[8]

For example, he appointed Gary Cohn, the former Goldman Sachs president, as Director of the National Economic Council and as his chief economic advisor. Although Cohn was very influential on several 2017 economic moves of the Trump administration, he resigned in March

2018, since he had failed in his opposition to the President's decision to impose import tariffs on steel and aluminum. Cohn was soon replaced by Larry Kudlow, from 1987 to the mid-1990s chief economist and managing director of another big business bank, Bear Sterns, then TV anchor and author of several works in favor of tax cuts and supply-side economics.

Also Dina Powell, another Goldman Sachs exponent, for about a year held a post as deputy national security advisor in the Trump White House, before returning to Goldman Sachs in a manifest representation of the "revolving doors" often existing in the US between big finance and political power.[9]

In general, the military-industrial complex; the big oil, coal, and gas corporations; the electrical power industry; the steel and aluminum companies; the big business banks, such as Goldman Sachs; some investment or hedge funds; several games, sport and entertainment tycoons; selected construction groups, and so on were particularly generous in their financing of Trump's political machine before and after his rise to presidency and could obtain favors from his economic policy.

11.4 America First

One of the strongest slogans of Trump's campaign was *America first*. It was a nationalistic message, with profound political and economic consequences. Politically, it gave the sense of a more isolationist approach, of an anti-migration position and of some detachment from traditional international obligations. The emphasis on the completion of the anti-immigrant wall at the Mexican border and the pressure on NATO partners to contribute more to its budget, thus reducing the burden of US spending, were two signals in this direction.

One of the basic issues of the *America first* approach was the immigration policy.

Trump had proposed a rapid completion of the US-Mexican border wall, which "had to be paid by Mexico…" as a barrier against illegal immigrants; the tripling of border control agents; the ban of immigrants coming from seven dangerous Muslim countries; mass deportation of undocumented immigrants and the phasing out of an Obama 2012 executive order regarding about 800,000 young adults, who, as children, had been illegally brought to the US and that could legally work in the country. As president, on these matters Trump issued several executive orders, which encountered many legal or financial difficulties. These measures somewhat reduced new immigration inflows, but contributed to a large number of deaths along the Mexico-US border and badly worsened the human and social conditions of about 12 million undocumented immigrants who have lived and worked in the US.

On the field of economics, the anti-globalization and protectionist stance was a reversal of American policy since Bretton Woods. As we know, Obama, with caution and some welfare compensations to the losers of globalization, had tried to proceed with the international economic policy which had begun at Bretton Woods in 1944. This policy had favored international multilateral agreements, trade liberalization, and economic and financial globalization. Yet for several goods and services, the US had patiently built a complex network of bilateral agreements, attempting at maintaining some protection for critical sectors.

In 2015, Obama had signed the TTP multilateral trade agreement with several Asian countries, but at the end of his mandate such agreement had not yet been ratified by the Congress and was then repudiated by Donald Trump. Obama had also been negotiating the controversial TTIP agreement with the European Union.[10]

Unregulated globalization had contributed to accelerate off-shoring, deindustrialization, and the strong rise of income differentials, but when the competition on manufactured goods mainly came from Germany and other Western European countries, where the labor costs were not so distant from the American ones, it did not worry the US firms and the US public opinion too much. A real external shock had instead come after the rapid penetration into the US market of Japanese goods in the 1970s and 1980s, the delocalization in Mexico of several manufacturing activities after the 1994 NAFTA agreement, and, above all, the massive entry of Chinese goods (partly produced in China by US multinationals) since the mid-1990s.[11]

This trend had met with increasing protests by the *no-global movement* active in the US and in several other industrialized countries from the end of the 1990s. This movement was mainly leftist, but some of its concerns on the loss of American jobs and the rapid rise in inequalities were also shared by Democratic exponents such as Bernie Sanders, who had opposed NAFTA, TPP, and TTIP. With partially different, often nationalistic or racist motivations, several right-wing groups were also opposing the widening and deepening of globalization.

Trump capitalized the discontent of unemployed or marginalized workers in the *rust belt* and in other areas of the country, the worries about security in the degraded city districts, the widespread dissatisfaction about unregulated globalization in several young people and in a part of the suffering middle class, the support of supremacist circles, and so on. He blended all this with a strong nationalistic appeal: *Make America great again.*[12]

As far as economic policy is concerned, he worked in three main directions, all respecting, in his view, the *America first* principle: (a) a neo-protectionist policy, (b) a reduction in taxes, (c) the dismantling of Obama's health and environmental policies.

11.5 The Neo-Protectionist Policy

A traditional protectionist policy is mainly based on restrictions on imports: higher tariffs, the application of quantitative limits to the imports of selected goods or services, extra-tariff barriers, the long maintenance of a sizable undervaluation of the currency, and so on.

Trump is attempting to pursue a *neo-protectionist policy*, which, though using some of the traditional protectionist tools as well, is essentially founded on the asymmetric balance of powers between countries, on the large use of incentives and disincentives and on commercial threats aimed at obtaining advantages from another country through a bilateral country-to-country negotiation.

For example, Trump threatened to withdraw from NAFTA, probably in order to obtain better conditions from Canada and even more from Mexico in terms of trade conditions and of immigration flows. Trump also withdrew from the Trans-Pacific Partnership (TPP), promising to replace it with a series of bilateral agreements. He cancelled the negotiations with the European Union on TTIP and tried to negotiate directly with Germany on the issue of its huge trade surplus with the US Truly, he perfectly knew that trade policy is a competence of the European Union, not of a member country as Germany, but he also knew that the US had many convincing means to put pressure on German government and on German companies, and thus indirectly on EU international economic policy. Moreover, he imposed tariffs on steel (25%) and aluminum (10%) to try to revive the ailing American steel industry and put pressure on the big foreign exporters of these products to the US, Germany and other EU countries included. Then he announced to Canada and Mexico that he was ready to waive these import duties for them if they accepted to make a new NAFTA agreement, namely an agreement more favorable to US interests. It must be reminded that in 2017 Canada was the biggest steel and aluminum exporter to the US (17% of steel total US imports) and Mexico was the fourth exporter of steel to the US (9%).[13]

In the same way, in his November 2017 state visit to South Korea, which was the third big steel exporter to the US (10% of US imports), Trump was ready to suspend the import duties on steel and aluminum in exchange for other trade and political advantages,[14] including a South Korean mediation with North Korea on the latter's nuclear program.

In international negotiations, Trump systematically used first the stick and then the carrot. In addition, he largely preferred bilateral trade agreements to multilateral ones because in bilateral negotiations the US could better exploit its greater economic, financial, and military power.[15]

With the other economic giant, China, the moves of Trump were more cautious, as the asymmetry in power was lower.

As usual, he began to use the stick, acting in three main directions:

(a) The US administration imposed a huge $1.2 billion fine to ZTE, the largest Chinese telecommunication company, which had evaded the sanctions against North Korea and Iran; then it forbade to employ the Google-Android technology that ZTE used in its services when ZTE violated the agreement on the fine; (b) the generalized import tariff on steel and aluminum severely hit China, which was the second largest exporter of aluminum to the US and the 10th largest exporter of steel; (c) the US threatened to introduce over 1300 import duties in order to reduce by about $100 billion its huge deficit in the US-China trade balance.

As expected, in April 2018, the Chinese trade authorities also introduced tariffs on 128 categories of US goods in retaliation to the US moves.

Yet, in May 2018, Trump conceded to return to supply the US technology to ZTE on account of his good relations with President Xi and of the number of jobs that these technology exports could provide to the US economy.

Moreover, he sent a high level US delegation to Beijing to discuss a comprehensive US—China trade agreement.

Generally, in its relations with foreign countries, after whirling the big stick of the rise of tariffs, Trump offered the carrot: suspension of the measures as regards the new tariffs and other trade or political concessions in exchange for benefits for the American trade balance or for vital political issues. In the case of China, for example, the pressure that China could exercise on North Korea's nuclear policy was essential.

He also offered incentives to the investors on the American soil. He promised to grant substantial incentives to US firms which reshored, returning to open new plants in the US instead of in Mexico or in China or in other low wages countries.

In addition, Trump presented a tax bill which included a sizable reduction on corporate taxes and therefore could contribute to some increase in domestic investment.

However, Trump's tough neo-protectionism might lead to a growing number of retaliations, US responses to retaliations, and finally to large trade wars.

History has shown that trade wars are extremely dangerous since they might lead to real wars, or, at least, to profound hates and divisions among countries and people.

Yet, to ignore, or easily forget, the lessons of history, and go on repeating the same errors over and over again has frequently occurred in world history, and this is a possible sign that each generation wants to be free to make the same mistakes as their fathers and ancestors.

11.6 The Reform Tax Bill

On December 22, 2017, Trump signed a comprehensive tax reform bill he had promised in his electoral campaign and that had been sustained by the majority of the Republican Party.

The bill widely reduced corporate tax rates (from 35% to 21%); regulated the multinationals' taxation on the basis of the territorial principle; from 2018 to 2026, modified the income levels and reduced the tax rates of six of the seven tax brackets of income tax; introduced several other measures to incentivize investment for five years, to increase inheritance exemption levels, to repatriate foreign profits, to weaken Obama's health care reform; and so on.

The large reduction in corporate tax can strongly increase corporate profits. It might have some positive effects on economic growth and on America's competitiveness, but these effects might differ very much according to the use the companies will make of the corporate tax cut. The companies might increase real investment, or buy financial assets, or distribute bonuses to the managers and to other employees, or increase the dividends distributed to shareholders, or make a partial buy-back of the companies' shares, or make a complex combination of some of these choices.[16] The corporate tax cut might thus stimulate the economy in different ways and different degrees, but also increase inequality, in particular in favor of rich people. Top managers and the owners of big packages of shares or investment funds might in fact greatly benefit from the rise in dividends and from the increase in the values of shares in the stock market.

Many analyses have shown that the majority of gains might go to the rich, while a smaller part, in terms of a limited rise in employment and/or wage increases, might go to the workers but at the cost of a rise in public deficit and public debt and of drastic cuts of public spending and thus a reduction in the quality and quantity of public services. In 2017, the Tax Policy Center estimated that the top 1% income group will receive 34% of total benefits of corporate tax cuts, the top fifth will receive about 70% of benefits, the fourth fifth 15%, the middle fifth 9%, the second fifth 4% and the poorest fifth only 1% of the benefits.[17]

As regards income tax, from 2018 to 2026 the bill establishes a rise in the income levels of most of the seven tax brackets and, above all, a sizable cut of tax rates, plus an increase in the standard deduction for lower taxable income and an increase in child tax credit. On the whole, the bill provides a small income tax cut to the majority of the low or middle-level income earners, but much more generous tax advantages in favor of the rich and super-rich people.

Therefore, the combination of the cuts in corporate tax, in income tax, and in inheritance taxation contributes to increase the already high level of income and wealth inequality existing in the US economy.

We already know that Donald Trump has a double face: in his populist version Trump presents himself as a sort of Robin Hood, who cuts taxes and creates new jobs for the working class, while in his truer conservative version he looks more like the Sheriff of Nottingham, who robbed from the poor and gave to the rich.

The macroeconomic impact of Trump's tax bill is very difficult to assess since it depends on the assumptions of the model used for its estimation. The effects in terms of an increase in GDP are limited. The estimates vary between 0.1% and 0.4% per year in the first three years and are close to zero in most ten-year simulations.[18] Yet, in the long run, the severe consequences of the deterioration in public debt and of the economic and social effects of the rise in inequality and of the cut of spending in essential public services, such as health care, public education, and the protection of the environment, will probably be worse than the short-time positive macroeconomic effects.

11.7 Trump's Policy on Health Care and Environment

One of the main objectives declared by Donald Trump in his electoral campaign was the demolition of Obama policies about health care and the environment.

As president, Donald Trump swiftly worked in this direction. His first frontal assault to Obamacare was unsuccessful. In July 2017, the attempt at repealing Obama's ACA (the 2010 Affordable Care Act) did not pass at the Senate, since two Republican senators voted against such repeal together with Democratic and independent senators. However, Trump will try again to get a full repeal of ACA if the 2018 mid-term elections provide the Republican Party with a larger majority both in the House and at the Senate.

In the meanwhile, Donald Trump has attempted at undermining some important aspects of Obamacare. In his reform tax bill he inserted the abolition of the federal fine imposed for not obtaining health insurance coverage. Moreover, by means of presidential executive orders and other administrative means he tried to expand the recurs to associations and short-term health care plans outside Obamacare and to reduce the federal funds going to ACA.

However, some of the main provisions of Obamacare, such as the Medicaid expansion, insurance subsidies, and the protection for preexisting conditions, still remain and in several States Obama's health reform has found a growing popularity. On the whole, Trump's health policy is going to increase the number of people without health coverage and increase the average cost of insurance policies.

As regards environment, Donald Trump is contrary to the view sustained by a large majority of scientists, that the rise in global warming is associated to human activities and to the growing use of fossil sources, such as coal, oil, and gas. His anti-scientific approach here is evident, as well as his closeness to the oil, coal, and automobiles industries.

In his tax reform bill, Trump maintained some tax credits for electricity produced from wind, biomass, solar, hydropower and other clean sources, but his central policy was to return as much as possible to coal, the most polluting source, and other fossil fuels, such as oil and gas. His 2017 *America first energy plan* essentially focused on fossil fuels.

Trump also tried to dismantle Obama's regulations on water and power (*Clean Water Rule* and *Clean power plan*) and on automobiles' emissions and the use of fossil fuel. In February 2017, he appointed Edward Scott Pruitt as administrator of the crucial regulatory anti-pollution body, *the Environmental Protection Agency* (EPA). Pruitt had been a fierce opponent of EPA' s policy during Obama's administration. In 2010, Pruitt's successful election campaign to Attorney general of Oklahoma had been heavily financed by fossil fuel companies. Like Trump, Pruitt is against the scientific consensus that human activities have a strong effect on global warming. As EPA administrator, Pruitt has considerably weakened the observance of some regulations, reducing fines and controls, and has tried to repeal several regulations, but he has often encountered the opposition of courts and environmental experts.

Trump appointed Mike Pompeo as new secretary of State after the exit of Rex Tillerson, Rick Perry as the head of the Department of Energy, Ryan Zinke as secretary of the Interior, and several other people to important posts in his administration. All of them were contrary to the Paris Agreement on Climate Change and to Obama's environmental policies. Some of them had been close to the oil, coal, and automobile interest groups.

Donald Trump also announced the US exit (effective in November 2020) from the Paris Agreement on Climate Change; plans to allow offshore drilling in most American oceanic waters; cuts of EPA funds and of the funds to preserve endangered species; the relaxation of regulations on dangerous chemical substances, and so on. In addition, he favored the revival of the plans for two pipelines, which Obama's administration had stopped because of the pollution dangers to the soil, and in the case of Dakota's access pipeline, also to the water reserves of Sioux tribes.

The environmental policy of the Trump administration is therefore mainly an anti-environmental policy, which will increase air, water, and soil pollution.

On the whole, Trump's economic policy has aggravated public finance, health care, environment and, above all, it has exacerbated the social, racial, religious, and economic disparities. Moreover, Donald Trump has created profound international trade, environmental, and political tensions. Up to now he has been a very divisive president.

Notes

1. Trumpism is a term with two major meanings: one is based on Trump's, often outrageous, statements; the second is used in political philosophy to define his particular mix of populism, nationalism, militarism and

white supremacism. I will use the term in its political philosophy version, mainly focusing on his economic populist approach.
2. See, for example, the political studies by Tuggart (2000), Taguieff (2007), Albertazzi and Mcdonnel (2008), Laclau (2005), Muller (2016), Urbinati (2014), Parmar (2017), Rovira Kaltwasser (2018). Several economists have also studied the problems of the relations between populism and economics. See for example the classical studies by Sachs (1990) and Dornbusch and Edwards (1991) on the Latin American populism and the more recent insightful works by Acemoglu et al. (2013), Boeri et al. (2018), Rodrik (2018), Guriev (2018).
3. Initially, Peron had the support of a large part of the labor unions, but in the following decades he also gained the support of important right-wing nationalistic interests favored by his protectionist policies. In Italy, in the March 2018 political elections the Five Stars Movement captured many votes from both right-wing and left-wing sections of the population on the basis of a mixed populist program promising large, but very costly, widespread income subsidies and a fight against corruption and bad administration. The movement made an agreement (contract) with Lega, the right-wing populist party, to set up the government. Yet, the contract risks to aggravate the already high public debt of the Italian economy, the country's financial stability, and relations with the European Union.
4. Trump's success in Pennsylvania (20 electoral votes) was by only 44,298 votes, in Michigan (16 electoral votes) by 10,704 votes, in Wisconsin (10 electoral votes) by 22,748 votes. With only 77,750 votes more than Hillary Clinton in these three crucial states, Trump gained all the 46 electoral votes, and so conquered the presidency. Failing in these states, he would have accumulated only 258 electoral votes versus 273 for Hillary Clinton, barely sufficient for the Democratic candidate to become president (270 electoral votes were necessary to win).
5. Bernie Sanders, the other Democratic candidate defeated by Hillary Clinton in the Democratic primary, was more open to the problems of these workers and in general to social problems than Hillary Clinton and probably, he would have captured more votes than Hillary in Wisconsin and Michigan.
6. See Narayanswamy et al. (2017). On December 31, 2016, Hillary Clinton's campaign had spent 98% of the funds it had raised, Trump's campaign 99%.

7. See Janetsky (2018).
8. Trump inserted two other former Goldman Sachs exponents besides Gary Cohn and Dina Powell in his administration. First, Steve Bannon, who had been in Goldman Sachs before directing Breitbart News and who was Trump's main strategist in the electoral campaign and then, for a few months, Trump's chief adviser; secondly, the Secretary of the Treasury Steve Mnuchin.
9. Also Dina Powell had to resign from Trump's administration in February 2018, as had many other influential men and women of the inner circle of the President. For some hints on the power battle and its victims in Trump's administration see, for example, Michael Wolf (2018). Several exponents of both the populist wing (Bannon, etc.) and of the globalist one (Cohn, etc.) were fired or had to resign in just a year and half of Trump's presidency.
10. TPP (Trans-Pacific Partnership) was a trade agreement between the US and 11 other countries bordering the Pacific ocean, China excluded; TTIP was the US-EU "Transatlantic Trade And Investment Partnership" proposed in the years 2013–2016, but aborted in 2016 and definitively buried by Trump's hostile declarations in 2017.
11. NAFTA (North America Free Trade Agreement) is a comprehensive 1994 trade agreement between US, Mexico, and Canada.
12. In 2012, Trump had trade-marked this slogan, which he used extensively in his 2016 presidential campaign, selling million "make America great again" caps.
13. See International Trade Administration, Global Steel Trade Monitor (2018). In volume, the major steel exporters to the US were Canada (17% of exports to the US), Brazil (14%), South Korea (10%), Mexico (9%), Russia (8%), Turkey (6%), Japan (5%), Germany (4%), Taiwan (3%) and China (2%). As regards aluminum, in 2017, the top ten exporters to the US in dollar value are Canada (36.3%), China (15.1%), Russia (7%), United Arab Emirates (6.5%), Mexico (2.7%), Bahrain (2.7%), Argentina (2.4%), Germany (2.4%), India (2.1%) and South Africa (1.5%). Only Canada and Mexico have been temporarily exempted from the US 10% tariff decided by Trump. In 2017, the total value of US import of steel was $29 billion, and the total value of aluminum imports was $23.4 billion. For aluminum imports see World's Top Exports (2018).
14. Donald Trump had threatened to leave or renegotiate, the 2012 KORUS trade agreement with South Korea and this induced South Korea (which

has a big trade surplus with the US) on March 27, 2018 to agree on the revision of the trade bill. South Korea restricted of about one third its steel exports to the US in exchange for the exemption from the 25% steel tariff, accepted the rise of US automobile exports to South Korea from 25,000 to 50,000, and so on.

15. Though not pushing the US to leave the World Trade Organization (WTO) Trump's policy is deeply weakening the world influence of this international organization, whose action is essentially based on large multilateral agreements.
16. Stephen Gandel (2018), p. 1 has estimated that "about 60 per cent of the gains are going to shareholders, compared with 15 per cent for employees". In the first year of tax and spending changes for the companies he surveyed, out of the $54.5 billion tax saving, about $21.1 billion went to stock buybacks or increasing dividends, $12.3 billion to business investment, $8.1 billion to employees as wages, benefits, bonuses, $1.4 billion to philanthropy.
17. See Chye-Ching Huang and Brandon DeBot (2017).
18. In the official forecasts the federal deficit/GDP ratio will rise to –4.7 in 2019 and the federal gross debt/GDP ratio to 108.1 (see Table 10.3).

References

Acemoglu, D., G. Egorov, and K. Sonin. 2013. A Political Theory of Populism. *Quarterly Journal of Economics* 128 (2): 771–805.
Albertazzi, D., and D. Mcdonnel. 2008. *Twenty-First Century Populism: The Spectre of Western European Democracy*. London: Palgrave Macmillan.
Boeri, T., P. Mishra, C. Papageorgiou, and A. Spilimbergo. 2018. A Dialogue between a Populist and an Economist. *AEA Papers and Proceedings* 108 (May): 191–195.
Dornbusch, R., and S. Edwards. eds. 1991. *The Macroeconomics of Latin America Populism*. Chicago: University of Chicago Press.
Gandel, S. 2018. *Five Charts That Show How Companies are Spending Their Tax Savings*. Bloomberg, March.
Guriev, S. 2018. Economic Drivers of Populism. *AEA Papers and Proceedings* 108 (May): 200–203.
Huang, C.-C., and Brandon DeBot. 2017. *Corporate Tax Cuts Skew to Shareholders and CEOs, Not Workers as Administration Claims*. Center of Budget and Policy Priorities, August 16.

International Trade Administration. 2018. *Global Steel Trade Monitor.* Accessed May 26, 2018. https://www.trade.gov/steel/countries/pdfs/imports-us.pdf.

Janetsky, M. 2018. *Trump's Top Donors: Where are They Now?* Center for Responsive Politics, January 18. https://www.opensecrets.org/news/2018/01/trump-donors-1year-later/.

Laclau, E. 2005. *On Populist Reason.* London and New York: Verso.

Muller, J.W. 2016. *What is Populism?* Philadelphia: University of Pennsylvania Press.

Narayanswamy, A., D. Cameron, and M. Gold. 2017. How Much Money is behind Each Campaign? *Washington Post*, February 1. Accessed June 9, 2018. https://www.washingtonpost.com/graphics/politics/2016-election/campaign-finance/?.

Parmar, I. 2017. Elites and American Power in an Era of Anti-elitism. *International Politics* 54 (3): 255–259.

Rodrik, D. 2018. Is Populism Necessarily Bad Economics? *AEA Papers and Proceedings* 108 (May): 196–199.

Rovira Kaltwasser, C. 2018. Studying the (Economic) Consequences of Populism. *AEA Papers and Proceedings* 108 (May): 204–207.

Sachs, J. 1990. *Social Conflicts and Populist Policies in Latin America.* San Francisco: ICS Press.

Taguieff, P.A. 2007. *L'illusion populiste.* Paris: Flammarion, new edition; first edition, Berg (2002).

Tuggart, P.A. 2000. *Populism.* Maidenhead: Open University Press.

Urbinati, N. 2014. *Democracy Disfigured.* Cambridge, MA: Harvard University Press.

Wolf, M. 2018. *Fire and Fury, Inside the Trump White House.* New York: Henry Holt and Company.

World's Top Exports. 2018. Accessed May 26, 2018. www.worldtopexports.com/us-aluminum-imports-by-supplying-countries.

12

America's Decline? Toward an Imperfect Multipolar World

12.1 America's Decline?

As we have seen in Chap. 6, before the dissolution of the Soviet Union, there was an *asymmetric bipolarism* in the world. Two leading global powers, the US and the Soviet Union, dominated the world scenery, but the US had a much larger economy than the Soviet Union.

After 1991, the world saw a sort of *imperfect hegemony* of the US. However, the gradual expansion of the European Union, the rapid economic rise of China and other major countries, and the recovery of Russia are rapidly changing the situation in the direction of an *imperfect multipolarism*. *Multipolarism*, because there are several important actors in the world scenery and *imperfect* because of the uneven powers of the major actors. At present, the US is, and for several years will remain, the world's most powerful and influential country in the economic, political, and military spheres, but its leadership is being gradually eroded by the rise of China and other important global or regional powers.

Much has been written on the American decline.[1] It is true that every empire soon or later declines. In the past, it occurred to the Roman Empire, to the Chinese, Arab, Mongol, Turkish, and Moghul empires.

More recently, it has happened to the vast colonial British and French empires, and some decades later, to the vast and mighty Soviet Union.

Could it happen also to the US? A brief comparison with the British experience can be useful. As Marcello De Cecco in his important book, *Money and Empire*, had sustained,[2] a great part of the strength of Great Britain in the years 1890–2013 was based on its dominance within its empire and in the *gold standard system* prevailing in the world financial market. The gold standard actually was a *gold-pound sterling system*. Great Britain exported consumer goods to its Asian colonies and imported capitals from these countries, and in particular from India and Malaysia. The latter were obliged to export raw materials to Great Britain and to accumulate net exports toward other extra-empire countries in order to be able to buy British manufactured goods and to send capitals to London. Other colonies, such as Australia, New Zealand, and Canada, populated by European immigrants, were instead importing British goods and importing capitals, mainly in the form of direct investments, which could later provide abundant flows of profits to the center of the empire. At the beginning of the nineteenth century, this system was gradually undermined by the economic ascent of the US and Germany. These two states rapidly increased their net exports to the countries outside the British Empire, accumulating a large surplus in their balance of current accounts. Germany had therefore growing inflows of gold money. The US, lacking a central bank up to December 1913, had to deposit its gold values in the London financial district, but could freely dispose of them and thus could destabilize British monetary strategy in the international financial market.

The gold-pound sterling system went therefore gradually into crisis, finally collapsing at the beginning of the First World War. In the mid-1920s, some countries, such as Germany and the UK, decided to return to the convertibility of their currency to gold, but in 1931, after the explosion of the great depression, the gold standard was definitively suspended, to be replaced by the Bretton Woods system in the years 1944–1971. This system sealed an epochal change which had been already evident at the end of the First World War, that is, the gradual shift of global financial power from Great Britain to the US, from London to New York.

The transition of a country which had a dominant power in commerce and industry to a dominant position in financial power had been fairly frequent in history,[3] but usually such process had taken several decades. The reasons for this great delay are essentially two. It is a long and complicated task to create well-functioning financial institutions and build their worldwide reputation and the necessary trust in their behavior. Secondly, reputation is essentially built on wealth and on its correct use and not on temporary income results, and a country and its financial institutions need several decades of good economic and financial results to build up a sufficient stock of wealth and a worldwide trust.

As we have seen in Chap. 1, at the end of the nineteenth century, the US had already a much larger economy than Great Britain, but it could fully reach a financial hegemony only in the 1940s.

What can these historical events teach us?

First, in the long run, economic power is usually associated to the dominance of a country in industry and commerce. Such country can thus gain a strong competitiveness in international markets and a long sequence of surpluses in the balance of payments. All this can assure to the country a strong currency and a great abundance in gold, or in hard currencies or financial assets, and a rapid expansion in its financial capital.

Secondly, an economic predominance usually leads to a phase of rapid expansion of financial capital at the expense of productive capital and this signals the crisis that in the end will cause a change in economic and, later, in world financial supremacy. Using the words of a great French historian, Fernand Braudel, the phase of financial expansion "... announces its maturity, ... *it is a sign of autumn*".[4]

Giovanni Arrighi in *The Long Twentieth Century* suggested that the first phase of rapid expansion of financial capital gives the signal of the beginning of a crisis, and the final phase leads to a change of leadership as regards the center of world capital accumulation. He also discussed the possible future transition from the US financial dominance to the Chinese one, noting that this change might create an unprecedented and risky situation, with the world military supremacy maintained by the US and the financial supremacy gradually going to China.

Let us go back to the basic trends of the US economy as regards its economic and financial dominance in the post-Second World War period.

In Chap. 7, and in particular in Table 7.1, we have seen that the US economy had experienced a *relative economic decline*, growing less in per capita GDP than the rest of the world, both in the years 1953–1973 and 2003–2017. In the years 1973–2003, though reducing its rate of growth if compared to the 1950–1973 period, the US had done a little better than the rest of the world. Yet this had been essentially due to the misfortune of other economies: to the severe transition crisis of Eastern Europe and of the former Soviet Union countries in the 1990s and to the devastating economic depression of several poor African, Asian, and Latin American countries in the 1980s and 1990s.

From the 1980s up to now, the US, has, in particular, grown much less than China and India and other emerging countries, but a little faster than the European Union. However, in the 1990s and in the 2000s, the EU has gone through a considerable enlargement, incorporating several other countries, mainly from Central and Eastern Europe, but had lost the UK because of the June 23, 2016, referendum on the *Brexit*.

Since the 1970s, the deep structural transformations in the US economy, partly caused by the process of globalization in a growing part of the world economy, have contributed to accelerate the US deindustrialization process and the shift from a structurally positive balance of current accounts to a structurally negative one and from a creditor net position to a huge negative international position. Yet, in the US, from the 1970s onwards, an enormous expansion of financial capital has taken place. The main reasons for this phenomenon were the rapid increase of corporate profits and of the compensations of managers and professionals; the tax cuts on higher incomes and on financial assets; the introduction of derivatives and other innovative financial tools; the periods of easy money policy and the large widening of investors' choices made possible by the financial globalization. Moreover, the US was able to attract many FDI and huge amounts of portfolio capitals from other countries, the latter coming mainly from the oil-rich countries in the 1970s and in the 1980s, from Japan in the 1990s, and from China in the 2000s.

However, in a country, if many individuals, corporations, investment funds, pension funds, asset managers, and so on, decide to invest more in financial assets than in real productive investments and to invest more off-shore and less inland, they pave the way toward a decline of their economy. Rapid deindustrialization ensues as well as growing difficulties in the balance of current accounts and a rise of inequalities between the winners and the losers of globalization.

In the US, the critical final phase of expansion of financial capital has probably begun and it can prelude to the shift of the leadership in world finance to China. However, such transition phase might last for decades, as it was true in the case of the shift of financial power from Great Britain to the US in the first decades of the twentieth century.

If China is the primary candidate to the future succession to the US as the first world economic and financial power, also the European Union, Russia, India, Brazil, Indonesia, and a few large emerging countries will probably have an increasing, albeit mainly regional, role in the world economy and in world finance.

In the next decades, the US' major problem will be a great internal political and psychological question, that is, the gradual acknowledgment of the slow decline of its huge power and the acceptance, without convulsions or abuse of military force, of the necessity to share the power with China and other global and regional partners.

12.2 China: The Other Economic Giant

The extraordinary economic growth of China since 1978, after the sweeping economic reforms of Deng Hsiao Ping and his successors, has projected the giant Asian country to become the first largest economy in the world in terms of total GDP in purchasing power parities (PPP).

Table 12.1 shows, for example, that in 2017, China had surpassed by 20% the US in terms of total GDP in PPP, though its GDP is still largely inferior if the comparison is made on the basis of official rates of exchange.

Table 12.1 The US and China: selected indicators

Indicators for China (US = 100)	2008	2017
Total GDP in PPP EKS (US = 100)	68.8	120.4
Population (US = 100)	432.7	421.9
Per capita GDP in PPP EKS (US = 100)	15.9	28.5

Source: Our elaborations on Conference Board (2018) data. The data on China in PPP refer to estimates based on official data and not adjusted to ICT prices

In 2017, China had also surpassed the US for exports of goods; for the total number of people employed in R&D (but not yet for total spending in R&D); for total capital formation; for manufacturing production; for total employment; for the production of steel, cement, electricity, ships, automobiles, TV sets, PCs, mobile phones, solar panels; for the total use of mobile phones, internet, e-commerce; and so on.

However, in per capita terms, the gap between the two countries remains substantially in favor of the US. In 2017, the US had a per capita GDP level about 3.5 times the one of China, though the distance had been rapidly diminishing.

Labor productivity and average wages were also over four times higher in the US than in China, although the gap has continued to decrease.

As regards the level of science and technology, the US is by far the world leader, and China remains at a sizable distance. However, the gap is diminishing year after year, because China is very rapidly increasing the technological level of its products and its services, thanks to a much faster rise in its capital stock (which incorporates also advanced foreign technology), to its rapidly growing R&D expenditures, to the rising quality of its schools and Universities, and so on.

In the 2000s, real per capita GDP has grown in China almost four times faster than in the US, although the advantage in the rate of growth has considerably diminished since 2010 and probably will continue to diminish in the next decades.

The causes of the phase of very rapid growth and of the impressive catching up of the Chinese economy from 1978 up to now are manifold.

Several radical economic reforms have triggered the gradual shift from a centrally planned, public and centralized economy to *an economy of the triple mix*: a complex mix between the plan and the market, the public and the private ownership of the means of production, and the centralization and decentralization of main economic decisions.[5] The last four decades have, in fact, seen a gradual shift toward more market, more decentralized activities (the responsibility principle in agriculture, the expansion of TVE, i.e., the township and village enterprises), more private activities, more decentralization, more openness to international trade and foreign direct investments. All these trends have liberated many hidden public and private abilities and the drive to initiate new economic activities to innovate and to raise production and productivity.

There has also been the vast exploitation of the advantages of *latecomer countries*[6] and of *the third wave of* the *Fordist model of development*, accompanied by some Toyotist and post-Fordist elements. The first set of advantages comprises: first, the possibility of gradually moving an enormous mass of labor force from low-productivity agricultural activities to higher productivity activities in the industrial and services sectors; second, the opportunity of purchasing, adapting, imitating, and assimilating more advanced foreign technologies, thanks to the import of large amounts of capital goods and the attraction of massive Foreign Direct Investments (FDI) inflows, mainly localized in special economic zones (SEZs).

The second set of advantages is associated to the crucial adoption of some aspects of the *Fordist-Toyotist model of development*.[7] In the 1980s, this mainly regarded domestic electrical appliances, fertilizers, and the related sectors, such as steel, plastics, electricity, and chemicals. In the 1990s, it mainly regarded PCs, phones, mobile phones, communication services, ships, and the energy and steel industry. Finally, in the 2000s, it concerned automobiles, trucks, fast trains, housing and infrastructures, airplanes components, internet services, e-commerce, and so on.[8]

In the 1970s and in the 1980s, the Fordist-Toyotist model of growth has been mainly associated to the rise of the internal market, while since the 1990s, it has received a growing and very important impulse by the rapid increase of exports and of FDI inflows, favored by the expansion of the SEZs and by the policy of greater openness of the Chinese economy. This trend has been additionally favored by the Chinese entry into the WTO in 2001. In the 2000s, there was also the rapid growth of Chinese outward FDI, whose flow in 2016 surpassed the inward FDI flow, while in 2017 the outward FDI stock almost reached the level of the inward FDI stock, which had been accumulated in a much longer period of time.[9]

The period of exceptionally rapid growth of China's real GDP reached its top in 2007 (+ 14.2%). Then, the *great recession* slashed the rate of growth of China's exports and reduced the inflow of FDI. So, there was a considerable slow-down in China's rate of growth of real GDP, which fell to 6–7% in the years 2015–2017. In these three years, China's government tried to change its growth model reducing the role of exports and increasing the internal demand, but the country, though slowing down, was able to maintain a GDP rate of growth which was almost four times higher than those of the US and of the European Union.

Yet, the phase of very rapid economic growth of the Chinese economy was accompanied by important economic, social, and environmental problems.

First, there was a very strong increase in income and wealth inequalities among the households, among the different provinces, and between the rural and urban areas. For example, the Gini index on income inequality rose to 0.49 in 2008 and then went down to 0.47 in 2016, close to the level of the US and much higher than those of Japan, South Korea, and most EU countries.

Secondly, there was an enormous and increasing number of people living in the cities without *hukou* (a sort of internal passport) and thus deprived of most welfare benefits.

Thirdly, there was a rapid and enormous worsening of the environment, with air, water, and soil being heavily polluted in most cities, in industrial areas, and in numerous rural zones.

Finally, social tensions exploded on several occasions, as it happened in the case of Tiananmen Square on June 4, 1989, in the Tibetan and Uighur zones on various occasions, and in labor strikes and suicides, often due to distressing labor conditions.

Three additional problems are becoming more and more severe in China's economy.

China is relatively rich in a variety of raw materials, including oil and coal. Yet, the extremely rapid economic expansion has increased the consumption of energy so much that since the mid-1990s China has become a net importer of oil and in 2015 had surpassed the US as the highest net importer of oil in the world. China has also become an important net importer of gas, though in its territory there are relevant reserves of shale gas, which China is beginning to exploit. Since 2009, China has also become a net importer for coal, though it is the top producer in the world and has the third highest level of reserves in the world.

The net foreign energy dependence of China increased up to 15% in 2014, while the US had reduced its dependence from almost 30% in 2005 to 7% in 2015.

The large and rapidly growing dependence on foreign energy has contributed to induce China's government and its oil companies to try to get the control of a large amount of oil provisions from African countries such as Sudan, Nigeria, Angola, as well as from some Middle East and Latin American countries.

From the 1990s to the *great recession*, China had chosen to continue the fast, striking industrialization process and to become an export-led economy. Therefore, exports had showed a very rapid rate of growth, superior to that of its imports. China's balance of current accounts passed from negative to positive values from 1994 onwards. The accumulation of very large surpluses in the following years, and especially due to China's entry in WTO in 2001 up to 2007, had permitted it to rapidly become a net creditor country and to buy large volumes of financial and real assets of the US and of other industrialized countries.

More generally, there has been the gradual creation of an enormous and intricate network of economic and financial relations between China and the US.

The US multinationals had made massive foreign direct investments in China in order to exploit the lower labor cost of Chinese workers or to enter the giant Chinese market. More recently also, several big Chinese companies have rapidly increased their FDI in the US, trying to enter the vast American market or to obtain more advanced technologies or management techniques. Up to 2017, the stock of US outward FDI to China was still much higher than the Chinese outward FDI stock to the US, but the Chinese FDI outflows were rapidly increasing.

There has almost been a symbiosis between the two economies. The US consumers bought an enormous volume of Chinese goods, so that the US–China trade balance in goods reached a huge deficit, up to $375.6 billion in 2017.

Although in 2017, the US had a surplus of $38.5 billion for services, the overall trade deficit was enormous. However, a substantial part of the

US dollars gained by Chinese producers was invested in US financial assets (Treasury bonds, etc.), or in real US assets, or kept as international reserves by the Chinese central bank. So, while Chinese exporters were becoming largely dependent on the American market, the US Treasury and the US finance were increasingly influenced by China's investors, but also China had become strongly interested to what happened to the value of the dollar. Moreover, many big American corporations, such as the giant retailer Walmart, have obtained large benefits from the sale of Chinese products in the US market and American multinationals, such as Apple, Boeing, GM, and so on, have also greatly profited from their FDI in China. Such FDI aimed at the production of components or at the assemblage of their products in Chinese plants, while their goods were sold all over the world and also in the US and in the huge Chinese market. China has become a central part in their *global value chain*.

Even if in recent years the Chinese government has tried to reduce its excessive dependence on exports and to increase its domestic demand, there remains a strong trade imbalance between China and the US. On the other hand, China's holdings of US Treasury securities were close to $1185 billion in 2017.

Moreover, China is rapidly increasing the stock of outward FDI to the US and also the value of US buildings bought by China's investors.[10]

12.3 The Role of the European Union

One of the major actors in the World Economy is the European Union, which, if it were truly unified, would be the real great competitor of the US and of China.

In January 2017, the EU 27 (EU 28 minus the UK) had about 446 million people, third in the world after China and India and over one third more than the US population. In 2016, in terms of total GDP in PPP, the European Union (UK excluded) reached almost the 82% of China's level and the 94% of the US GDP.[11] Finally, in 2016, in terms of per capita GDP in PPP, the EU 27 reached almost two thirds of the US' level, and over 2.4 times the one of China.

Within the European Union, there are larger internal differences than within the US in terms of per capita GDP, labor productivity, wages, and welfare services. Yet, in most EU states, welfare provisions are more extensive and articulated than in the US and China.

The European Union has three great points of strength. One has a priceless value: the capacity to conserve a long-lasting peace among its member states. The second one is the progressive reduction of physical and cultural barriers between the EU citizens. The third one is the possibility of creating large economies of scale in different productive sectors enabling EU economies to become valid competitors of the two giant world economies—the US and China.

Unfortunately, in its present conditions, the European Union has rather weak institutions. It is an invertebrate giant, a great organism without a backbone or solid unitary institutions. It has no real head—it looks like a mythical creature with multiple heads—because the executive power is primarily given to the council of prime ministers and the various councils of ministers, supported by the European commission, and not to a real EU president and a real government voted by the European Parliament. The president of the European Council and the high representative of the Union for foreign affairs and security policy have limited powers, probably even more restricted than those of the president of the Commission. In the EU internal and international policy, they are much less influential than the prime minister or the president of major EU countries, such as Germany or France. Also the European Parliament and its president have an important but limited role. The European Parliament exercises the legislative power together with the Council and the Commission and it is the only European institution that is directly elected by the citizens. Yet, the candidates to the European parliament are usually chosen by national parties in national electoral districts, so they often represent more the interest of their countries and of their national parties than true European interests. The European parliament also has rather limited powers. It has partial legislative powers and it cannot directly choose the EU executive or the president of the Commission. The latter is proposed by the Council and then voted by parliament, when the agreement on the names is in fact already made.

The European Union directly controls a limited budget, only amounting to about 1% of the total GDP of the EU member States, while, for example, the US federal government budget amounts to about 20% of the GDP of the country.

Such a limited budget does not permit the EU to make an effective anti-cyclical policy, or a solid industrial and development policy.

While the EU has a unified policy on international economic relations, it has not yet an effective common fiscal policy, but basically tries to coordinate national policies and to implement rigid parameters, which don't allow to carry out a flexible anti-cyclical policy in the case of a severe recession.

The EU has no fully comprehensive central bank and a common currency. There are the European Central Bank (ECB) and the euro,[12] but presently, only 19 of the 27 member states have entered the Euro area. However, as a consequence of the great recession, belated, but useful, financial stability mechanisms and a banking union have been established.

Moreover, the statute of the European Central Bank primarily takes into account the objective of the control of inflation, not the employment conditions as well, as the FED's statute in the US, for example, does.

Finally, the EU has neither a Constitution nor a unified army, nor a solid common international policy. A constitutional project was rejected in 2005 after two negative referendums in France and the Netherlands. As regards defense policy, the European Union primarily relies on NATO, where the US has an essential role. In international politics, there are often consistent differences between the positions of member states, so that the role of the high representative of the Union for foreign affairs and security policy is considerably weakened.

From the political point of view, the European Union is therefore a half-built construction, a work-in-progress, with complex and poorly designed institutions. A big push toward more solid federal institutions, a common immigration policy and a budget of at least 10% of EU's total GDP would be badly necessary, but, at present, strong local and nationalistic pressures are against these objectives.

In the present conditions, the economic and financial strength of the European Union, which is potentially very high, is fragmented and lessened with respect to truly unified countries such as the US and China.

Yet, despite its severe institutional weaknesses, its relatively slow rate of growth in the 1990s and 2000s, and the shock of the Brexit, the European Union maintains a very important position in the world economy and a capacity to attract other European countries, such as Serbia, other Balkan States, and some former USSR republics.

Economic inequalities between member states are relevant, but the internal inequalities in each member state are lower than the ones prevailing in the US and in China.

The EU unemployment rate is usually higher, and the employment rate lower than those of the US and China, but there are profound employment and wage differences between the various EU member states.

Finally, the European Union has a deep demographic and migration problem.

In the 2000s, its population grew very little, and in some countries, such as Germany, Italy, and Greece, the population increased only slightly because of the large immigration inflows, while other poorer EU countries registered net migration outflows and a negative rate of population growth.

In the 2007–2017 years, the EU population, excluding the UK, has grown at an annual rate of 0.2% versus the 0.8% of the US.

In most EU countries, this has determined a rapid *aging* of the population, with severe consequences on public costs for pensions and health and in the dynamism of the economy.

In some EU countries, the demographic problem has required a continuous flow of immigrants to cover several sections of the labor market. This was partly provided by important migration inflows from other European countries and partly from Africa, East and South Asia, the Middle East, and Latin America.

A large mass of refugees and other immigrants were forced to emigrate to Europe by cruel wars, bloody local conflicts, famine and mass poverty, or by the dream of getting a decent job and somewhat improve the quality of life of their family. The migration problem has become a crucial and divisive political issue in several EU countries, especially during the great recession and in the following years. In this period, the lack of decent job opportunities for young and lower-middle-class native citizens, the accrued competition for low-paid jobs and low-cost housing, and fears provoked by Islamic terrorism have contributed to the expansion of populist and racist anti-immigration movements and to a political shift to the right in several EU countries, as it has happened in the US with Trump's election.

12.4 Russia, Japan, India, and Other Emerging Powers

In the years 1999–2008, the Russian economy exhibited a vigorous recovery after the dissolution of the Soviet Union and the dramatic transition crisis of the 1990s. In 2006–2007, it regained, and later surpassed, the per capita income level of 1989. In the following years, the economy has, however, registered a marked slow-down in its rate of growth. Yet, Russia could recover a great part of its economic weight, thanks mainly to its huge exports of oil, gas, and other important raw materials. All this, together with the regained strength of its military force and nuclear arsenal, allowed Russia to return to play an important role in world economy and in world politics.

So, the Russian Federation has been able to return to a ruthless expansionary policy. In 2014, it annexed the Crimean peninsula, which since 1954 had been a territory of the Republic of Ukraine and, after the dissolution of the Soviet Union, had been a part of independent Ukraine since 1991. In addition, Russia further menaced the integrity of Ukraine, trying to take control of a large section of Eastern Ukraine, where a part of the population considers Russian as its mother language.

The Russian government has also attempted to win back a large economic and political influence in former republics of the Soviet Union, such as Belarus and Georgia, and in most central Asian countries, driving them away from the possible attraction of the European Union or of Turkey.

Finally, Russia has militarily intervened in the Syrian war, contributing to defeat ISIS, saving the position of Assad, greatly amplifying Russian influence in the Middle East and improving its relations with Turkey, Iraq, Iran, and Egypt.

Yet, from the purely economic point of view, the progress of Russia has been meager. The country had returned to the level of real GDP of 1991 only in 2006 and it has grown thereafter only by about 1.7% a year. Moreover, Russia has lost a sizable part of its population, decreasing from 148.4 million people in 1991 to about 143.8 million in 2017. The country had also registered a marked decline in life expectancy at birth during the great transition crisis of the 1990s and at the beginning of the 2000s. Since 2005, life expectancy recovered and then had a little expansion up to 71 years in 2017, but in that year Russia still resulted only 154° in the world ranking.

Finally, Russia has not succeeded in achieving an adequate diversification of its production system. The economy has remained too dependent on the production and export of weapons, oil, gas, and other raw materials and on the import of a large variety of civilian goods.

Nonetheless, while recovering a strong position in the production and exports of oil, gas, and many kinds of weapons, Russia also has been able to increase the production of some other industrial products, such as machine-tools, steel, electricity, housing, chemicals, pharmaceutical products, some electric domestic appliances, and so on. It has also expanded and slightly modernized its services sector and partially improved its fragile and corrupt banking and financial system. However, Russia has remained relatively weak in the production of important goods, such as machinery, ICT products, automobiles, pharmaceuticals, plastics, and so on, which were in 2006–2007 largely imported from foreign corporations (Figs. 12.1 and 12.2).

Japan has a larger economy than Russia, though less natural resources and a much more limited military power. It is also more populated and has a fairly larger economy than Germany, the UK, and major EU countries. In the production of several civilian goods, Japan has reached a very high position for quality, technological level, and export levels. Yet, in the 2000s, it has gradually lost ground in the world market for some goods, such as ships, fast trains, PCs, smart phones, TV sets, and other electrical domestic appliances, under the fierce competition of South Korean, Taiwanese, and Chinese corporations and of some American and European multinationals.

Japan had reached an extraordinary economic growth performance in the years 1950–1973, with an annual rate of growth of real GDP of

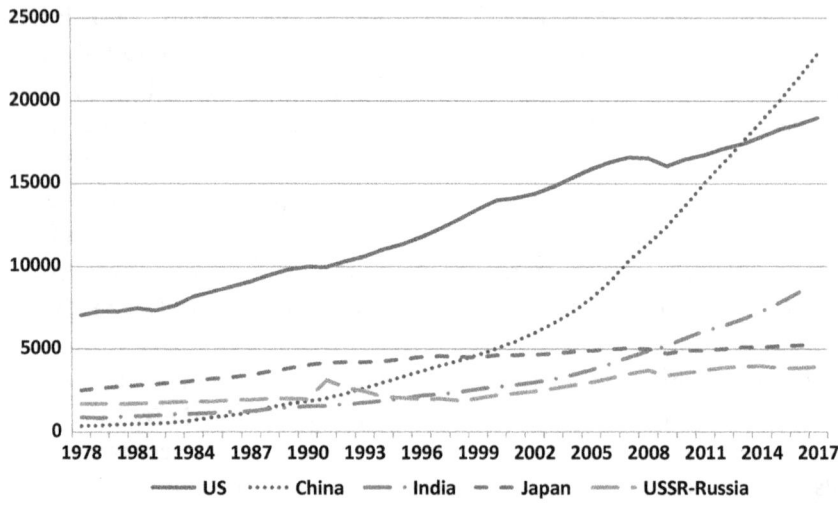

Fig. 12.1 Total GDP in China, Russia, and India: 1978–2017
Levels of GDP in PPP of China, Russia, and India in comparison to the levels of US and Japan. GDP in billions of 2016 US$, converted to the 2016 price level with updated 2011 PPP. Notes: At present borders in PPP EKS except for USSR; USSR 1978–1990 data in GK, Russia 1991–2017 data in EKS
Sources: Maddison Project Database (2010), Conference Board, Total Economy database: output, labor and labor productivity (November 2017)

9.1%. In the 1973–1991 period, the Japanese economy had considerably slowed down but had maintained a yearly rate of growth of real GDP of 3.7%, much higher than the ones of the US and of other major industrialized countries.

However, in the 1990s and in the 2000s the Japanese economy fell into a deep structural crisis. After a severe financial and real slump in 1992–1993, the Japanese economy registered a difficult recovery and then a very slow and widely fluctuating pattern of growth. In the years 1991–2017, the annual rate of growth of real GDP fell to less than 0.9%. The main causes for this long structural crisis were numerous.[13] However, the most important reason was probably the progressive breakup of the powerful mechanism of capital accumulation of the preceding decades. This model was essentially based on long-term stock-flow relationships. Rapid GDP growth led to a continuous rise in the value of buildings and

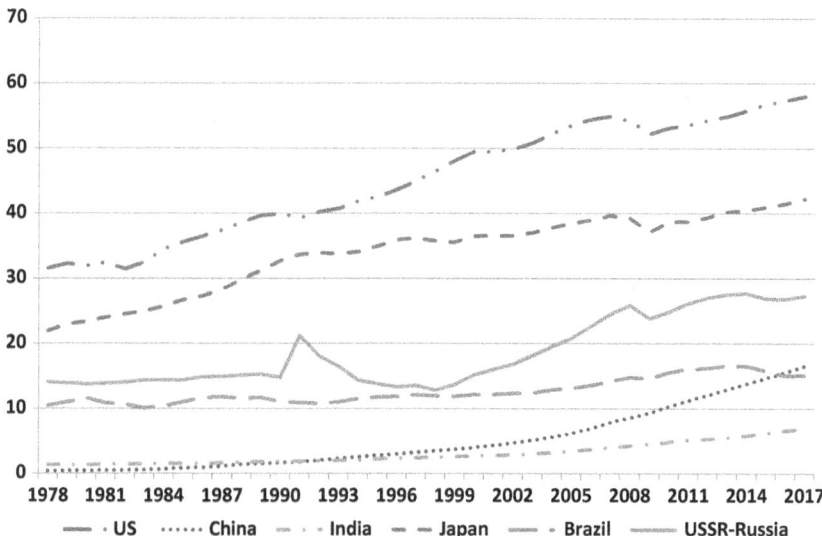

Fig. 12.2 The economic ascent of selected emerging countries: 1978–2017 Levels of GDP per capita in PPP of China, Russia, India, and Brazil in comparison to the levels of US and Japan. GDP per capita in thousands of 2016 US$, converted to 2016 price level with updated 2011 EKS PPP. Notes: At present borders in PPP EKS except for USSR; USSR 1978–1990 data in GK, Russia 1991–2017 data in EKS Sources: Maddison Project Database (2018), Conference Board, Total Economy database: output, labor and labor productivity (November 2017)

shares, which were used as collaterals by the Japanese firms to obtain abundant financial means from their main banks. This allowed the firms to make very large investments and so to speed up the growth, generating a further increase in real GDP, in the prices of shares and buildings, and so on. The slowing down of the economic growth in the 1980s, the increasing liberalization of capital movements and, in 1990–1991, the explosion of the cyclical and structural bubbles as regards the prices of shares and of buildings, provoked the great 1992–1993 crisis, and consequently the final collapse of the mechanism of rapid capital accumulation. Many capitals went abroad—to the US or to Europe. Many banks failed or went into crisis and had to severely cut lending. Most Japanese firms were obliged to greatly reduce investment and so the Japanese model of growth collapsed. From the 1990s up to now, no expansionary fiscal or monetary policy attempted by the Japanese government has been able to contrast the phenomenon in an effective and durable way.

The Japanese economy has nonetheless been extremely resilient, maintaining a fairly good international competitiveness and a structural surplus in its balance of current accounts. This has been mainly due to its high level of human capital, to its great technological achievements, favored by the maintenance of large expenditures in R&D activities, and to a huge volume of outward FDI.

Let us consider India, the third largest economy in the world.

Since the mid-1980s, India has followed some aspects of the post 1978 Chinese model of development, such as a growing openness of the economy and a partial application of the Fordist-Toyotist model of development to the *formal sector of the economy*. Yet, there are many important differences. India has a multiparty democratic regime, with very complex internal social and political equilibria among the different castes, ethnic, and religious groups, rural and urban areas, rich landowners and poor peasants. Moreover, India has an enormous *informal economy*, with several million micro-enterprises or self-employees often getting very low and precarious incomes. Structural changes and industrialization processes have been less deep than in China,[14] while the tertiary sector is very wide. It includes a vast range of traditional low-paid services, but also several modern activities, like the production of software and sophisticated banking and financial operations. In India, per capita income and the average level of education are lower than in China, pollution and economic inequalities are also lower, while absolute poverty is much higher.

The phase of rapid growth of the Indian economy started in the second half of the 1980s and has accelerated since 1992. It has led to a brisk speeding up of the rate of economic growth. Real per capita GDP in PPP increased yearly by 3.1% from 1984 to 1991 and by 5.2 from 1991 to 2017 notwithstanding the Indian recession of 1991, the South East Asian financial crisis of 1997–1998 and the consequences of the great recession.

In terms of real GDP, the phase of fast growth has been less rapid than that of China, with the exception of the years 2016–2017. Yet, even in those two years, the rate of change of real per capita GDP continued to be slightly inferior to the one of China, given the Indian higher rate of growth of population. India will surpass China as the most populous country in the world around 2024, though having a gradually declining rate of population growth.

Finally, India has a considerably younger population than China, which begins to suffer from an acute problem of aging.

In India, the period of rapid growth has been associated to a smaller increase in inequalities among regions and households than in China and to a slower growth of pollution, partly due to the lower level of industrialization and economic development. From the 1990s up to 2017, the rise of international trade and foreign direct investments between India, the US, and the rest of the world was remarkable, though inferior to that of China. In the 2000s, India has also accelerated its FDI outflows toward the rest of the world, including the US, China, and the European Union.

An increasing proportion of Indian exports has regarded software services, but they often depend on sub-contracting to American multinationals.

In any case, India, thanks to its huge demographic and economic size and the rapid rate of growth, is going to become a great world power.

According to the estimates on the size of total GDP in PPP of both the Conference Board and the World Bank, India has already reached third position in the world ranking, after China and the US and before Japan, though still registering widespread poverty and low levels in per capita GDP and in the human development indicator.

Also, Brazil has become a very large economy, although in the years 2014–2017 its rate of economic growth badly worsened. Yet, Brazil's total GDP in PPP has surpassed the level of the UK, France, and Italy, and in 2017, its population has exceeded 208 million people.

Large countries such as Brazil, but also Indonesia, Mexico, Turkey, Iran, Saudi Arabia, Egypt, Vietnam, and so on aspire to obtain a stronger position in the world and also to increase their regional influence. Other countries, such as Pakistan, North Korea, and perhaps in the future, Iran, count on the nuclear bomb as an instrument of power, while South Korea, Taiwan, and Singapore mainly rely on their high technological achievements.

From the economic, military, and political point of view, the world is rapidly changing and the US will have to deeply redesign its role in the world scenery.

12.5 The Nongovernmental Powers

Up to now, we have almost solely dealt with macroeconomic trends: the rise or decline of major economies.

Yet, other mighty nongovernmental powers, which we have called NGPs, have been very influential in shaping the economic destiny of the world.

Large commercial or business banks, big multinational corporations, huge pension and investment funds, wealthy foundations, nongovernmental organizations (NGOs), a restricted number of super-rich people, big criminal organizations, terrorist groups, and so on have heavily influenced the world economic affairs. They have done so directly or indirectly, by means of their economic decisions or by means of their influence on governments, on media or on powerful politicians and bureaucrats.

In the 2000s, the global scenery of giant companies has seen rapid and important transformations reflecting the deep changes taking place in world economy.

In the 2017 Fortune global 500 list,[15] the US had 133 companies, China 109, Japan 51, France and Germany 29 each, the UK 21, South Korea 16, and so on. Instead, in 2000, China had only 10 companies, while the US had almost 40% and Japan over 20% of the top 500 companies.

In 2017, just after the US giant retailer, Walmart, there were three Chinese companies, while in 2000, American and Japanese groups, and a few European ones, dominated the top 20 ranking and Chinese companies appeared only after the 57th position.

Moreover, in 2017, in terms of total profits, after Apple, four Chinese giant banks and three US financial institutions were leading the Fortune ranking, while in 2000 top profits went mainly to US, Japanese, and European industrial companies such as automobile or oil companies.

Finally, in the 2000s, in major stock exchange markets, the capitalization (total values of outstanding shares) has seen a marked trend in favor of technology companies such as the US groups Apple, Alphabet (Google), Microsoft, Amazon, Facebook, and the Chinese groups Tencent and Alibaba, as well as of financial institutions such as Buffett's fund Berkshire Hathaway and the giant US banks JP Morgan Chase and Wells Fargo.

The owners of important packages of shares and, more directly, the top managers of these companies have therefore an enormous impact on the world economy by means of their choices on investment, employment, wages policy, and the localization of their companies' activities. In addition, as we have underlined in the paragraph on the erosion of democracy in Chap. 7, they can have a deep influence on politics and society. Their powers are, however, limited in the countries where a dominant party, as in China, or strong presidents, as in Russia or in Turkey, or autocrats, as in several Middle Eastern, African, and Latin American countries, can deeply influence, for good or evil, their economic and financial decisions.

With very different objectives and means, NGOs, humanitarian Foundations, criminal organizations, and terrorist groups can also have a deep impact on society and politics, the first two promoting solidarity, the third spreading drugs and violence, the fourth spreading terror, distrust, and hate, but each governing a very large volume of economic assets and financial means.

12.6 The Fragility of International Organizations

Perhaps the major problem of the current economic international situation is the following: globalization has made a substantial and growing part of economic and financial activity global, while the mechanisms of regulation and control have remained national or regional (EU, NAFTA, MERCOSUR, ASEAN, etc.).

So, there is a severe gap between the difficulties caused by the imperfections, incompleteness, or failures of the market, which is more and more global, and the action of the mechanisms of regulation and control, which, being mainly national, are increasingly unable to face these difficulties. Moreover, the situation has worsened since the dominant economy, the US, has seen a gradual reduction of its influence on major international economic decisions.

Therefore, it would be necessary to increasingly recur to the regional and international organizations in order to face global problems with global actions.

Yet, the regional organizations, such as the EU, have still limited powers, while the international organizations have severe weaknesses. They are, in fact, hardly effective and scarcely democratic.

They are poorly effective in their action mainly because they have been conceived and structured on the basis of the world situation of more than 70 years ago. Their statutes and the distribution of voting rights have been only marginally modified and are far from representing the current situation.

They are costly and dismembered in a great number of different organizations and agencies difficult to direct in a coordinated and efficient way.

Finally, the international organizations are perceived by many people as scarcely democratic. The UN has a general assembly where countries with a very small population have the same voting right as countries such as China, India, and the US, and it has a Security Council in which the veto of one country can paralyze any controversial initiative.

The International Monetary Fund and the World Bank have voting rights based on wealth and not on population and associated to the situation of several decades ago, only partly reformed thereafter. The almost complete dominance of the US and of the major Western European countries as regards the main representatives of the two organizations is incongruous in the present world situation, where several very populous emerging countries are asking for a more important role.

Summits such as G7 or G20 try to respond to some of the deficiencies of major international organizations, but even these Conferences have a very indirect and weak democratic basis, especially when they attempt to tackle problems concerning also a great number of countries that are excluded from these meetings.

There is no doubt that without radical reforms, which would reorganize, simplify, and inject more democracy into the existing international organizations, the capacity of regulation and control of world financial and real markets will be totally inadequate, so that severe events such as *the great recession* or even worse economic and financial crises will continue to periodically reappear.

12.7 Conclusions

The destiny of any dominant power is to rise, triumph, and then decline, but it is very difficult to predict the exact timing of these great historical changes.

From the economic, political, and military point of view, the US have gone through the first two phases (rise and triumph) from the end of the nineteenth century to the beginning of the twenty-first century. Now we can perceive the beginning of a slow and gradual decline, or better, the loss of a proud, solitary supremacy and the forced acceptance of dominance shared with other great powers, such as China.

As we have already underlined in the preceding sections, there is a trend toward an *imperfect multipolarism* among powers with different economic sizes and uneven levels of economic and technological development, military strength, and width and depth of political and cultural influence. In the absence of major wars, for some decades the American empire will remain the prevailing global power, but with growing fractures and increasing worries under the vigorous rise of China and other old or emerging powers.

In the American economy, the main fracture has been the growing divide between the very rich and both the declining middle class and the poor, as well as between good jobs for high-skilled workers and bad jobs, or no jobs, for the semi-skilled or unskilled workers. This has opened the way to the populist appeal of a populist-conservative president as Donald Trump. However, his policy will ultimately raise the divide between the poor and the very rich and will increase other fractures between white, black, and Hispanic people, between American citizens and new immigrants, between the US and most other countries.

American wisdom will be great if the country is able to compose its fractures and to accept its gradual relative decline without brutal political or military backlashes.

Yet, at present, global equilibrium is unstable and precarious. Imperfect multipolarism can be even more difficult and unstable to manage than the imperfect bipolarism prevailing in the years of the cold war. The major difficulty consists in the fact that the present global economic and financial trends require supranational rules and regulations, while the political context is able to introduce and implement regulations principally at the national or regional or local level, not at the world level.

This is the original sin implicit in the construction of modern States, namely, the fact that most of them are fundamentally based on the concept of nation, with its frequent corollary, nationalism. A country can become strong and powerful only if there is internal cohesion and a widespread political consensus. A dangerous, but widely used, shortcut to reach these objectives is a strongly nationalistic policy, which will magnify the domestic virtues and minimize the domestic defects, while denigrating the results of other nations and even despising poorer or weaker countries. This is the main incubator of a number of conflicts and of atrocious wars.

There is an alternative: the gradual shift of power to reformed and democratized international organizations, both at regional and world level. But this requires from the US, China and the other major countries, and from all the people in the world, a higher level of wisdom.

Notes

1. See, for example, Arrighi (1994, 2010), Gordon (2016), Wallerstein (2004). Payne (2009), pp. 54–55.
2. See De Cecco (1974). See also the beautiful note in memory of Marcello De Cecco written (in Italian) by Joseph Halevi (2016). In this note, Halevi also observes that De Cecco's interpretative scheme might also have been partially applied to the crisis of the Japanese empire before Second World War.
3. See Braudel (1984), Arrighi (1994, 2010) and Payne (2009), chap. 2.

4. See Braudel (1984), also quoted in Giovanni Arrighi (1994, 2010).
5. See Valli (2015), chap. 2. On the Chinese reforms, see, for example, also Perkins (2015), Naughton (2006) and Musu (2011).
6. See Gerschenkron (1962) for the introduction of this concept.
7. See Valli (2015), paragraph 2.13.
8. See Valli and Saccone (2009) and (2015) for economic development and structural change in China, compared with the Indian case. The second paper tries also to explain the relations between structural change and globalization in the two countries.
9. See UNCTAD (2018).
10. See Morrison (2018), pp. 3–30.
11. The UK decided to leave the European Union as a consequence of the Brexit referendum of June 23, 2016, but the exit process has not yet been completed and will probably end in 2019. The PPP estimates are extracted from World Bank (2018) and are a little different from the Conference Board estimates.
12. On the theoretical and applied problems of the Euro see, for example, the in-depth analyses of De Grauwe (2016) and of Marelli and Signorelli (2017).
13. For a more detailed analysis, see Valli (2017), chap. 3.
14. See for example, Basu and Maertens, eds. (2012), Valli (2015), chaps. 3 and 4.
15. The Fortune list regards the ranking of major companies by total revenues.

References

Arrighi, G. 1994. *The Long Twentieth Century: Money, Power, and the Origins of Our Times*. London and New York: Verso, new edition 2010.
Basu, K., and A. Maertens. 2012. *The New Oxford Companion to Economics in India*. Oxford: Oxford University Press.
Braudel, F. 1984. *Civilization and Capitalism, 15th–18th Century: The Perspective of the World*. New York: Harper & Row.
Conference Board. 2017. Total Economy Database: Output, Labor and Labor Productivity, November.
Conference Board. 2018. Total Economy Database: Output, Labour and Labour Productivity. Accessed May 10, 2018. https://www.conference-board.org/data/economydatabase/index.cfm?id=27762.

De Cecco, M. 1974. *Money and Empire*. Oxford: B. Blackwell.
De Grauwe, P. 2016. *Economics of Monetary Union*. Oxford: Oxford University Press.
Gerschenkron, A. 1962. *Economic Backwardness in Historical Perspective*. Cambridge, MA: Harvard University Press.
Gordon, R.J. 2016. *The Rise and Fall of American Growth: The U.S. Standard of Living since the Civil War*. Princeton: Princeton University Press.
Halevi, J. 2016. Joseph Halevi ricorda Marcello De Cecco. http://www.syloslabini.info/online/jospeh-halevi-ricorda-marcello-de-cecco/.
Maddison Project Database. 2010. Accessed May 10, 2018. https://www.rug.nl/ggdc/historicaldevelopment/maddison/releases/maddison-database-2010?lang=en.
———. 2018. Accessed May 10, 2018. https://www.rug.nl/ggdc/historicaldevelopment/maddison/releases/maddison-project-database-2018.
Marelli, E., and M. Signorelli. 2017. *Europe and the Euro*. London: Palgrave Macmillan.
Morrison, W.M. 2018. *China-U.S. Trade Issues*. Congressional Research Service, CRS Report, April 2016. Accessed June 9, 2018. http://fas.org/sgp/crs/row/RL.33536.pdf.
Musu, I. 2011. *La Cina contemporanea: economia e società di fronte alle nuove sfide*. Bologna: Il Mulino.
Naughton, B. 2006. *The Chinese Economy: Transitions and Growth*. Cambridge, MA: The MIT Press. Second edition. 2018.
Payne, R.J. 2009. *Global Issues: Politics, Economics and Culture*. New York: Pearson.
Perkins, D.H. 2015. *The Economic Transformation of China*. Singapore and London: World Scientific Publishing Co.
UNTCAD. 2018. www.untcad.org.
Valli, V. 2015. *The Economic Rise of China and India*. Torino: Accademia University Press.
———. 2017. *The Economic Rise of Asia: Japan, India and South Korea*. Torino: Accademia University Press.
Valli, V., and D. Saccone. 2009. Structural Change and Economic Development in China and India. *European Journal of Comparative Economics* 6 (1): 101–129.
———. 2015. Structural Change, Globalization and Economic Growth in China and India. *European Journal of Comparative Economics* 12 (2): 133–163.
Wallerstein, I. 2004. *World-Systems Analysis*. Durham, NC: Duke University Press.
World Bank. 2018. www.worldbank.org.

Statistical Appendix

Table A1 Population in the US and in the selected countries (million)

Countries	1870	1913	1952	1973	1990	2008	2017[c]
China	358.0	437.1	568.9	881.9	1,135.2	1,318.6	1,380.9
India	253.0	303.7	372.0	580.0	839.0	1,125.3	1,282.2
USSR-Russia[a]	88.7	156.2	185.9	249.7	150.0	143.5	143.8
US	*40.2*	*97.6*	*157.5*	*211.9*	*250.1*	*304.7*	*327.3*
Germany[b]	39.2	65.1	69.1	78.9	79.4	82.1	83.9
France	38.4	41.5	43.2	53.3	58.2	64.2	67.1
Japan	34.4	51.7	86.5	108.7	123.5	127.8	125.9
UK	31.4	45.6	50.4	56.2	57.5	62.1	66.1
Italy	27.9	37.2	47.7	54.8	56.7	58.8	60.7
Brazil	9.8	23.7	56.6	103.5	151.2	194.4	209.8

Source: Maddison Project Database (2018)
[a]From 1870 to 1973 the data concern borders of the USSR; from 1990 to 2017 borders of the Russian Federation
[b]Borders of Unified Germany
[c]Preliminary estimates Conference Board (November 2017)

Table A2 Total GDP in PPP, not adjusted to ICT prices, in the US and in selected countries (US = 100)

Countries	1870	1913	1952 GK[a]	1952 EKS[b]	1973	1990	2008	2017
China	192.9	46.7	18.8	2.7	4.7	18.8	68.8	120.4
India	137.1	39.5	14.4	13.3	11.7	15.8	29.5	47.3
UK	101.8	43.4	22.0	25.0	19.7	16.7	15.4	14.9
US	100.0	100.0	100.0	100.0	100.0	100.0	100.0	100.0
USSR-Russia[c]	85.0	44.9	33.6	33.6	42.8	33.2	22.4	20.7
France	73.3	27.9	14.8	17.2	20.3	18.6	15.7	14.7
Germany	73.3	45.9	19.4	26.7	33.4	27.2	22.2	21.5
Italy	42.5	18.5	11.7	15.3	19.5	18.8	14.4	11.9
Japan	25.8	13.8	12.4	13.9	35.6	40.5	30.3	28.0
Brazil	7.1	3.7	6.1	8.8	14.8	16.7	17.4	16.7

Sources: Maddison Project Database (2010), Conference Board, Total Economy database: output, labor and labor productivity (November 2017)

[a]The data are in PPP GK (million 1990 International Geary-Khamis dollars) until 1952

[b]The data are in PPP EKS (Eltoto-Kovacs-Szulc; expressed in 2016 PPPs obtained by extrapolating 2011 benchmark PPPs using the changes of the US GDP deflator) from 1952 to 2017. The data of the two periods are not fully comparable

[c]Only for USSR-Russia: from 1870 to 1973 the data concern borders of USSR and they are measured by the GK method (million 1990 International Geary-Khamis dollars), while from 1990 to 2017 the data concern the borders of Russian Federation and are measured by the EKS method

Statistical Appendix 209

Table A3 GDP per-capita in PPP, not adjusted to ICT prices, in the US and in selected countries (US = 100)

Countries	1870	1913	1952 GK[a]	1952 EKS[b]	1973	1990	2008	2017
UK	130.5	92.8	68.7	70.7	74.2	72.9	75.5	73.7
US	*100.0*	*100.0*	*100.0*	*100.0*	*100.0*	*100.0*	*100.0*	*100.0*
France	76.7	65.7	53.9	56.7	80.8	80.0	74.7	71.5
Germany	75.2	68.8	44.1	55.1	89.6	85.8	82.6	83.8
Italy	61.3	48.4	38.7	45.8	75.3	83.1	74.5	64.3
USSR-Russia[c]	38.6	28.0	28.5	28.5	36.3	56.1	47.6	47.2
Japan	30.0	26.2	22.6	22.9	69.4	82.0	72.3	72.8
Brazil	29.2	15.3	17.0	22.2	30.4	27.7	27.3	26.1
India	21.8	12.7	6.1	5.1	4.3	4.7	7.9	12.1
China	21.7	10.4	5.2	0.7	1.1	4.1	15.9	28.5

Sources: Maddison Project Database (2010); Conference Board, Total Economy database: output, labor and labor productivity (November 2017)
[a]The data are in PPP GK (million 1990 International Geary-Khamis dollars) until 1952
[b]The data are in PPP EKS (Eltoto-Kovacs-Szulc; expressed in 2016 PPPs obtained by extrapolating 2011 benchmark PPPs using the changes of the US GDP deflator) from 1952 to 2017. The data of the two periods are not fully comparable
[c]Only for USSR-Russia: from 1870 to 1973 data concern the borders of USSR and are measured by the GK method, while from 1990 to 2017 the data concern the borders of Russian Federation and are measured by the EKS method

Table A4 Macroeconomic indicators in the US and in selected countries: 1952–2017 (average annual % rates of change)

Countries	Population			Real GDP in PPP			Real GDP per capita in PPP		
	1952–1973	1973–2003	2003–2017	1952–1973	1973–2003	2003–2017	1952–1973	1973–2003	2003–2017
US	1.4	1.1	0.8	3.8	3.0	1.8	2.3	1.9	0.9
China	2.1	1.3	0.5	6.9	11.2	9.3	4.7	9.8	8.7
India	2.1	2.0	1.4	3.6	5.2	7.6	1.5	3.1	6.1
Japan	1.1	0.5	−0.1	9.0	2.6	0.8	7.8	2.1	0.9
Germany	0.6	0.1	0.1	5.4	1.7	1.4	4.7	1.5	1.3
USSR-Russia[a]	1.4	0.5	−0.1	5.0	0.1	2.9	3.5	−0.4	3.0
UK	0.5	0.2	0.7	3.1	2.2	1.5	2.5	2.0	0.8
France	1.0	0.5	0.5	5.1	2.2	1.1	4.1	1.7	0.6
Italy	0.7	0.1	0.4	5.5	2.2	0.0	4.8	2.0	−0.4
Brazil	2.9	1.9	0.9	6.9	3.1	2.4	3.9	1.2	1.4

Sources: Maddison Project Database (2010), Conference Board, Total Economy database: output, labor and labor productivity (November 2017)

[a] In the periods 1952–1973 and 1973–2003 the data concern the borders of former USSR (the data of GDP and per capita GDP are measured by the GK method); from 2003 to 2017 borders of Russian Federation (the data of GDP and per capita GDP are measured by the EKS method)

Table A5 Macroeconomic indicators for the US in the period 1980–2017

Years	Real GDP (%)	Real gross private domestic investment (%)	Civilian unemployment rate (%)	Inflation, consumer prices (%)	Average hourly earnings (in 1982–1984 US$)
1980	−0.2	−10.1	7.2	13.5	8.26
1981	2.6	8.8	7.6	10.3	8.14
1982	−1.9	−13	9.7	6.2	8.12
1983	4.6	9.3	9.6	3.2	8.22
1984	7.3	27.3	7.5	4.3	8.22
1985	4.2	−0.1	7.2	3.6	8.18
1986	3.5	0.2	7.0	1.9	8.22
1987	3.5	2.8	6.2	3.7	8.12
1988	4.2	2.5	5.5	4.0	8.07
1989	3.7	4.0	5.3	4.8	7.99
1990	1.9	−2.6	5.6	5.4	7.91
1991	−0.1	−6.6	6.9	4.2	7.83
1992	3.6	7.3	7.5	3.0	7.79
1993	2.7	8.0	6.9	3.0	7.78
1994	4.0	11.9	6.1	2.6	7.79
1995	2.7	3.2	5.6	2.8	7.78
1996	3.8	8.8	5.4	2.9	7.81
1997	4.5	11.4	4.9	2.3	7.94
1998	4.5	9.5	4.5	1.6	8.15
1999	4.7	8.4	4.2	2.2	8.27
2000	4.1	6.5	4.0	3.4	8.30
2001	1.0	−6.1	4.7	2.8	8.38
2002	1.8	−0.6	5.8	1.6	8.50
2003	2.8	4.1	6.0	2.3	8.55
2004	3.8	8.8	5.5	2.7	8.50
2005	3.3	6.4	5.1	3.4	8.44
2006	2.7	2.1	4.6	3.2	8.50
2007	1.8	−3.1	4.6	2.9	8.59
2008	−0.3	−9.4	5.8	3.8	8.56
2009	−2.8	−21.6	9.3	−0.4	8.88
2010	2.5	12.9	9.6	1.6	8.90
2011	1.6	5.2	8.9	3.2	8.77
2012	2.2	10.6	8.1	2.1	8.73
2013	1.7	6.1	7.4	1.5	8.78
2014	2.6	5.5	6.2	1.6	8.85
2015	2.9	5.2	5.3	0.1	9.07
2016	1.5	−1.6	4.9	1.3	9.20
2017	2.3	3.3	4.4	2.1	9.22

Sources: Department of Commerce-BEA (March 2018), FRED of St. Louis (2017), Economic Report of the President-CEA (2018)
aAnnual rates of change for columns 2, 3 and 5
bFRED (2017) is the source for the 2017 estimates of column 6
cPreliminary estimates from White House, Economic Report of the President-CEA (2018), Washington D.C for the 2017 data

Statistical Appendix

Table A6 Other indicators for the US in the period 1980–2017

Years	Exports of goods (million currents $)	Balance on current account (million currents $)	FDI outward stock (% GDP)	Output per Hour Worked (%)	Population (thousands)
1980	224,250	2,318	7.5	0.3	227,726
1981	237,044	5,029	7.1	2.3	229,966
1982	211,157	−5,537	6.7	−0.4	232,188
1983	201,799	−38,691	7.5	2.3	234,307
1984	219,926	−94,344	6.7	2.1	236,348
1985	215,915	−118,155	8.8	1.6	238,466
1986	223,344	−147,176	11.5	2.2	240,651
1987	250,208	−160,655	12.1	0.8	242,804
1988	320,230	−121,153	13.1	1.2	245,021
1989	359,916	−99,487	14.6	0.7	247,342
1990	387,401	−78,969	12.2	1.6	250,132
1991	414,083	2,897	13.3	1.2	253,497
1992	439,631	−51,613	12.1	3.6	257,037
1993	456,943	−84,805	15.3	0.4	260,449
1994	502,859	−121,612	15.2	0.7	263,662
1995	575,204	−113,567	17.7	0.6	266,821
1996	612,113	−124,764	19.7	2.0	269,944
1997	678,366	−140,726	21.7	1.8	273,203
1998	670,416	−215,062	24.9	2.3	276,417
1999	698,524	−288,365	29.2	2.9	279,609
2000	784,940	−403,450	26.0	2.5	282,738
2001	731,331	−389,689	21.6	2.2	285,550
2002	698,036	−450,797	18.3	3.1	288,212
2003	730,446	−518,744	23.5	3.3	290,700
2004	823,584	−631,591	27.2	2.6	293,402
2005	913,016	−745,234	27.6	1.8	296,119
2006	1,040,905	−805,964	32.1	0.8	298,988
2007	1,165,151	−711,035	36.2	1.0	301,846
2008	1,308,795	−681,389	20.9	0.8	304,714
2009	1,070,331	−372,521	29.8	2.9	307,397
2010	1,290,273	−430,698	31.9	2.6	309,979
2011	1,499,240	−444,589	28.9	0.1	312,299
2012	1,562,578	−426,198	32.1	0.5	314,639
2013	1,592,002	−349,543	37.2	0.4	316,850
2014	1,633,986	−373,800	35.6	0.5	319,213
2015	1,510,757	−434,598	33.1	0.5	321,551
2016	1,455,704	−451,685	34.2	0.2	323,786
2017	1,550,720	−466,246	40.2	1.0	327,292

Sources: Department of Commerce-BEA (August 2017); UNCTAD stat (2018); Conference Board (November 2017)

Statistical Appendix

Table A7 Full-time and part-time employees by industry in the US: 1950–2017 (million)

	Sectors	1980	1990	2000	2007	2016
1	Agriculture, forestry, and fishing	1.7	1.4	1.5	1.4	1.4
2	Mining	1.0	0.7	0.5	0.7	0.6
3	Public utilities	0.7	0.7	0.6	0.6	0.5
4	Construction	4.5	5.4	7.0	7.9	6.9
5	Manufacturing	19.2	17.6	17.5	14.0	12.3
6	Total industry (2–5)	25.4	24.4	25.6	23.2	20.3
7	Wood products	0.5	0.5	0.6	0.5	0.4
8	Nonmetallic minerals	0.6	0.5	0.6	0.5	0.4
9	Primary metal industries	1.1	0.7	0.6	0.5	0.4
10	Fabricated metal products	1.8	1.6	1.8	1.6	1.4
11	Machinery	1.9	1.4	1.5	1.2	1.1
12	Computer and electronic products	1.8	1.9	1.8	1.3	1.0
13	Electrical equipment, appliances, and components	0.8	0.6	0.6	0.4	0.4
14	Motor vehicles, bodies and trailers, and parts	1.1	1.1	1.3	1.0	0.9
15	Other transportation equipment	0.9	1.0	0.7	0.7	0.7
16	Furniture and related products	0.6	0.6	0.7	0.5	0.4
17	Miscellaneous manufacturing industries	0.7	0.7	0.8	0.7	0.6
18	Food and beverage and tobacco products	1.8	1.7	1.8	1.7	1.8
19	Textile mills and textile product mills	0.9	0.7	0.6	0.3	0.2
20	Apparel and leather and allied products	1.5	1.1	0.6	0.3	0.2
21	Paper and allied products	0.6	0.6	0.6	0.5	0.4
22	Printing and publishing	0.7	0.8	0.8	0.6	0.4
23	Petroleum and coal products	0.2	0.2	0.1	0.1	0.1
24	Chemicals and allied products	1.1	1.0	1.0	0.9	0.8
25	Plastics and rubber products	0.7	0.8	1.0	0.8	0.7
26	Total Services	71.3	92.4	112.0	120.4	128.5
27	Wholesale trade	4.7	5.5	5.8	6.1	5.9
28	Retail trade	10.8	13.4	15.6	16.0	16.0
29	Transportation and warehousing	3.0	3.4	4.5	4.6	5.0
30	ICT	2.3	2.7	3.6	3.0	2.8
31	Finance and insurance	4.0	5.2	5.9	6.2	6.2
32	Real estate and rental and leasing	1.3	1.8	2.1	2.2	2.2
33	Professional services, management of companies and enterprises	6.8	11.9	17.4	18.3	20.2
34	Educational services (private)	1.3	1.8	2.5	3.0	3.6
35	Health care and social assistance	6.3	9.8	13.1	15.9	19.2
36	Arts, entertainment, and recreation	6.4	9.1	11.9	13.6	2.3
37	Accommodation and food services	5.5	7.9	10.1	11.5	13.4
38	Other private services	4.9	5.7	6.5	7.0	7.1
39	Public administration	19.3	21.8	23.0	24.5	24.6
40	Federal Government	6.0	6.5	5.2	5.1	5.1
41	Full-time and part-time employees	98.4	118.2	139.1	145.0	148.7

Source: Department of Commerce-BEA (August 2017)

Index[1]

A
Acemoglu, D., 61n1, 177n2
Acocella, Nicola, ix
Advantages of relative economic backwardness, 35, 36
Aggregate demand, 16, 20, 21, 27, 50, 85, 127, 131
Aghion, P., 61n9
Aglietta, M., 13
Akerlof, G.A., 140n5, 140n12
Albertazzi, D., 177n2
Algeria, 81
Allende, Salvador, 120
American dream, 6, 94–96, 117
American Economy (US Economy)
  American growth in the Fordist phase, 7
  American growth in the globalization phase, 84, 111–116, 184
  balance of currents accounts, 84–87, 89, 108, 126, 182, 184, 185
  deindustrialization, vii, 60, 107, 151, 184
  economic and social inequalities, 33, 115, 150
  economic power, 1, 8, 68, 71–76, 79–100, 167–168, 171, 185
  employment structure, 39, 55–57
  financial power, 167–168, 171, 185
  foreign dependence on oil and raw materials, 79–81, 105
  long-run determinants of U.S growth, 45
  military power, vi, 31, 68, 71–72, 87, 171
  military spending, 120

[1] Note: Page numbers followed by 'n' refer to notes.

from a net creditor country to a net debtor one, 126
points of strength, 68–69
political power, 68, 71–72, 87
from a positive balance of current account to a negative one, 184
relative economic ascent, 1, 34, 83
rise in wages differentials, 91
the strength of arms and diplomacy, 118–121
structural changes, 27, 55–57
towards a global economic empire, vi, 84, 103–121
weaknesses, vi, 69, 76, 79–100, 103
American Recovery and Reinvestment Act (Fiscal stimulus), 147, 148, 154
America's Affordable Health Care Act (Affordable Care Act-ACA), 158, 175
America's decline, 181–204
Andreff, W., 122n6
Apple, 42, 58, 108, 111, 118, 121n3, 151, 152, 190, 200, 201
Arena, R., 61n16
Argentina, 178n13
Arrighi, G., 183
Arrow, K., 48
ASEAN, 105, 139, 201
Asian tigers
 Hong Kong, 34, 47, 60, 113
 Singapore, 34, 47, 53, 60, 113
 South Korea, 34, 47, 53, 60, 113
 Taiwan (Taipei), 34, 47, 53, 60, 113
Asset inflation, 126

Asymmetric bipolarism, vii, 181
Atkinson, A., 92
Attali, J., 127
Australia, 33, 34, 82, 182
Austria, 34, 54

B

Backlash, vii, 60, 204
Bahrain, 178n13
Balcet, G., ix, 122n6
Bannon, Steve, 178n8, 178n9
Barro, R., 48
Basu, K., 205n14
Bay of pigs invasion, 120
Beard, C.A., 8n4
Beard, M.R., 8n4
Bear Sterns, 168
Bebchuk, L.A., 91
Becattini, G., 41, 43n5
Belgium, 33, 35, 36
Berlin
 Berlin blockade, 67, 121
 Berlin Wall, 67, 105
Berlusconi, S., 164
Bertola, G., 100n10
Big bang, 116, 122n8
Bilmes, L., 119, 122n10
Bio-capacity, 154
Boeri, T., 177n2
Bosnia, 122n11
Boyer, R., 13, 16n2
Brain-drain, 53
Brazil, 42, 73–75, 110, 145, 155, 185, 197, 199, 207–210
Bretton Woods, vi, 31, 85, 87, 169
Brexit, vii, 90, 184, 193, 205n11
British Empire, 33–34, 182
British pound, 88

Brynjolfsson, E., 51
Buffet, Warren, 92, 201
Bulgaria, 42
Bureau of Labour Statistics, 62n20, 62n22
Bush, G.W., vii, 92–94, 130, 135, 144, 145, 148, 152, 156

C

Canada, 15, 24, 32–34, 81, 95, 155, 170, 171, 178n11, 178n13, 182
Capital accumulation (capital formation), 13, 16n4, 17n5, 45–60, 132, 145, 183, 186, 196, 197
Castro, F., 66
CDC, 100n16
Center-periphery, 2
Chandler, A.D., Jr., 49
Chavez, 164
Chenery, H., ix, 55
China
  Ascent of China's economy, 90
  Chinese Communist Party, 65
Chrysler, 110, 111, 146, 147
Churchill, Winston, 65
Cipolla, Carlo Maria, ix
Clark, C., 55
Clean energy economy, 154
Clean Power Plan, 153, 175
Clean Water Rule, 155, 175
Clinton, B., 156
Clinton, H., 94, 99, 117, 127, 156, 165–167, 177n4, 177n5, 177n6
Cohn, Gary, 167, 168, 178n8, 178n9

Cold war, 32, 65, 67, 119, 204
Community Reinvestment Act, 128
Conference Board, 73, 185, 196, 197, 199, 205n11, 207–210, 212
Conflict of interest, 134–136
Congress, 97, 150, 158, 169
Consumption, 5, 13, 15, 20–22, 24, 28, 32, 37, 41, 42, 66, 67, 79, 98, 104, 127, 130, 131, 144, 145, 153, 154, 188
Contini, B., 43n3
Corporatism, 28, 29
Countervailing power, 6
Cozzi, Terenzio, ix
Cuba, 66, 94, 120
  Cuban missile crisis, 67, 121
Czech Republic, 42

D

Dalmazzone, Silvana, ix
David, P.A., 49
Davis, J., 95
De Cecco, M., 182, 204n2
De Grauwe, P., 205n12
DeBot, Brandon, 179n17
Debt
  external debt, 86
  public debt, 27, 51, 122n9, 132, 133, 135, 148–150, 173, 174, 177n3
Defense Advanced Research Projects Agency (DARPA), 151
Del Pero, M., 160n1
Deng Hsiao Ping, 185
Denison, E.F., 48
Denmark, 54

Department of Commerce (BEA), 107, 137, 138, 211–213
Di Tommaso, M., 161n8
Dodd-Frank Act (World Street Reform and Consumer Protection Act), 147
Dornbusch, R., 177n2

E

Eastern Asia, 35
Ecological footprint, 153, 154
Economic power, vii, 1–8, 71–74, 76, 91, 99, 100, 113, 183
Economies of network, 14
Economies of scale, vi, 6, 7, 12–14, 16, 21, 27, 33, 36–39, 42, 59, 109, 191
Economies of scope, 14
Education
  expected years of schooling, 54
  mean years of schooling, 54
Edwards, S., 177n2
E-economy, 57–59, 126, 151, 160
  e-companies, 59
Egorov, G., 177n2
Egypt, 121, 194, 199
Elasticity of demand, 38
Emerging countries, vii, 7, 14, 47, 60, 68, 111, 114, 115, 122n6, 184, 185, 197, 202
Employment
  bad jobs, 59, 132, 146, 160, 203
  working poor, 57
Energy
  coal, 50, 153, 156, 188
  energy crisis, 13, 34, 39, 41, 47, 51, 84, 88, 107
  oil prices, 39, 81, 107
  shale gas and shale oil, 80, 81, 153
Enron's failure, 135
Environmental problems
  CO_2 Emissions, 82
  Obama environmental policy, 152, 153, 170, 176
  pollution, 153–155, 176
Environmental Protection Agency (EPA), 175, 176
Erosion of democracy, 96–100, 136, 201
EU, vii, 81, 89, 90, 133, 135, 139, 146, 171, 184, 190–195, 201, 202
European Central Bank (ECB), 192
European Economic Community (EEC), 33, 34, 36, 105
European empires, 2
European Free Trade Association (EFTA), 34
Exports, 6, 15, 21, 22, 24, 28, 33, 36, 37, 60, 68, 73–76, 85, 86, 89, 106–109, 112, 114, 165, 172, 178n13, 179n14, 182, 186–190, 194, 195, 199, 212
Extensive development, 34

F

Facebook, 42, 50, 58, 59, 99, 108, 166, 201
Fanny Mae, 128
Farage, Nigel, 164
Fasce, F., ix
Fascism, 28, 29
Federal Reserve (FED), 24, 26, 117, 127, 130, 134, 136, 146, 151, 192

Festré, A., 61n16
Fiat Chrysler Automobiles (FCA), 111, 147
Filippi, Enrico, ix
Finance
  financial bubble, 19, 139
  financial crisis, 20, 25, 27, 57, 84, 91, 117, 125–132, 135, 139, 144, 198
  financial power, 98, 167–168, 182, 183, 185
  stock market crash, 22
  transmission mechanisms, 20, 21, 131
Financialization, 116, 127, 134, 151, 152, 160
Financial Stability plan, 147
Finland, 42
Fisher, I., 125
Five Stars Movement, 164
Flexible production, 37
Flows, 28, 52, 60, 98, 113, 114, 129, 170, 182, 187, 193
Foray, D., 61n9, 61n16
Ford, Henry, 12–14, 24, 40, 147
Fordist model of development
  First Fordist wave, 14
  Second Fordist wave, 14
  Third Fordist wave, 14
Fordist phase, 33, 34, 37
Foreclosures, 129, 140n6
Foreign Direct Investment (FDI)
  flow, 108, 111, 112, 122n6, 187
  inward, 109, 112, 114, 187
  outward, 74, 75, 106, 109, 110, 112, 114, 187, 189, 190, 198
  stock, 109, 112, 187, 189
Foxconn, 121n3

Fragmentation of production, 37, 109
France, 2, 4, 21, 31, 33–38, 40, 47, 73–75, 95, 104, 107, 110, 121, 145, 146, 156, 157, 164, 191, 192, 199, 200, 207–210
Fratianni, M., 125
Freddie Mac, 128, 130
Fried, J.M., 91
Friedman, M., 24, 26
Frontier, vi, 3–8, 8n4, 47, 60

G

Galbraith, J.K., 8n5, 26, 49
Gandel, S., 179n16
GDP (PPP), xviii, 1, 6, 32, 66, 73–75, 83, 185, 190, 196–199, 210
Geary Khamis, 8n7, 208, 209
General Agreement on Tariffs and Trade (GATT), 36, 105, 121n1
General Motors (GM), 90, 110, 111, 146, 147
German mark, 88, 100n9
Germany, 2, 21, 33–36, 38, 40–42, 47, 52, 54, 65, 67, 70, 73–76, 104, 107, 108, 145, 146, 157, 169, 171, 178n13, 182, 191, 193, 195, 200, 207–210
Gerschenkron, A., 43n1, 205n6
Gini index, 73, 74, 76, 93, 188
Globalization
  economic globalization, 106, 112
  financial globalization, vi, 84, 103, 111–116, 169, 184
  globalization waves, 112–115, 125, 139

winners and losers of
  globalization, 185
Global productive networks, 109
Global value chains, 42, 106, 111,
  190
Golden age, 34
Goldin, C., 29n3, 100n10
Goldman Sachs, 167, 168, 178n8
Gold standard system, 182
  gold pound sterling system, 182
Google, 42, 50, 57, 59, 61n13, 97,
  99, 108, 151, 201
Gordon, R.J., 50, 51, 59
Gramsci, A., 11, 12, 16n1
Great compression, 25, 29, 33, 90
Great depression, vi, 16, 19–29, 47,
  72, 83, 90, 127, 137–139,
  141n13, 182
Great recession, vii, 47, 51, 56, 68,
  81, 84, 86, 89, 110, 112, 113,
  116, 125–139, 144–151, 159,
  166, 187, 189, 192, 193, 198,
  203
Greece, 65, 89, 133, 141n13, 146,
  193
Greenhouse gas emissions, 154
Grossman, G.M., 61n4, 61n8
Grossman, Gregory, ix
Gross national product (GNP), 22,
  137, 138
Guriev, S., 177n2

H
Habakkuk, J., 8n4
Halevi, J., 204n2
Hard power, 69
Healy, J.R., 160n5
Heathcock, Clara, x

Helpman, E., 61n4, 61n8
Hewlett Packard (HP), 42, 108, 111,
  151
Hiroshima, 65
Hitler, Adolf, 65
Huang, Chye-Ching, 179n17
Hukou, 188
Human capital, 49, 91, 131, 198
Hungary, 42

I
Iceland, 34
Ichino, A., 100n10
ICT technologies, 40
IEA, 100n1, 100n2
IMF, *see* International Monetary
  Fund
Immigration, vi, 53, 114, 168–170,
  192, 193
Imperfect hegemony, 181
Imports, 6, 21, 34, 79–81, 86, 106,
  107, 112, 114, 153, 168, 170,
  171, 178n13, 187, 189, 195
India, vii, 1, 3, 14, 16n3, 37, 47, 60,
  68, 73–76, 84, 105, 106, 108,
  111, 113–115, 117, 138, 145,
  155, 178n13, 182, 184, 185,
  190, 194–200, 202, 207–210
Indonesia, 16n3, 42, 47, 81, 84,
  113, 115, 138, 155, 185, 199
Industrial cluster, 41
Industrial district, 39, 41, 43n4
Industrial revolutions
  first industrial revolution, 50
  second industrial revolution,
    49–51
  third industrial revolution, 51,
    61n13

fourth industrial revolution (Industry 4.0), 61n13
International Monetary Fund (IMF), 31, 69, 87, 105, 116, 121, 122n9, 136, 145, 202
International organization, 69, 98, 105, 116, 117, 121, 121n1, 179n15, 201–204
International Trade Administration, 178n13
Investment
  extensive, 5, 6, 15, 16n4, 48
  intensive, xv, 4, 15, 16–17n4, 28, 47
Iran, 120, 171, 194, 199
Ireland, 33, 34, 42
Israel, 54, 121
Italy, 12, 33–38, 40, 41, 47, 65, 70, 73–75, 104, 107, 110, 133, 141n13, 145, 146, 157, 164, 177n3, 193, 199, 207–210

J

Janetsky, M., 178n7
Japan, vi, vii, 7, 14, 16n3, 32–40, 42, 45, 47, 52–54, 60, 65, 70, 71, 73–76, 81, 84, 89, 106–108, 113, 121, 145, 146, 157, 178n13, 184, 188, 194–200, 207–210
Japanese yen, 88
JP Morgan, 140n8, 201

K

Kaldor, N., 48
Kaltwasser, C.R., 177n2
Keynes

Keynes and the great depression, 25, 26
Keynesian policies, 13, 28, 135
Keynesism, 13
Kindleberger, C.P., 26, 125
Knowledge, v, 15, 17n5, 27, 28, 45–60, 75, 109, 131
Krugman, P., 95, 140n5, 148
Kuznets, S., 55

L

Laclau, E., 177n2
Landes, D.S., 8n4
Latecomer countries, 36, 187
Law of the three sectors, 55
Lazaric, N., 61n16
Le Pen, Marine, 164
Learning by doing, 48, 49, 52, 54, 131
Lebanon, 122n11
Lehman Brothers failure, 130, 135, 144
Leibenstein, Harvey, ix
Liechtenstein, 34
Lipietz, 13
Lost decade (1929-1939), vi, 47
Lucas, R., 61n4, 61n8

M

Maddison, A., ix, xvii, 1, 4, 8n1, 48, 55, 66, 73, 83
Maertens, A., 205n14
Malaysia, 42, 47, 113, 182
Mammarella, G., 8n4
Marelli, E., 205n12
Margo, R.A., 29n3, 100n10

Marshall Plan, 69, 71, 85, 103, 104
Marshall, A., 43n4
Martellato, Dino, ix
Marxism, 13, 66
Maturity of a market, 38
Mazumder, B., 95
Mazzucato, M., 161n8
McAfee, A., 51
McDonald, 118
Media and internet, 118
Medicaid, 156, 158, 175
Medicare, 150, 156
Melting pot, 117
MERCOSUR, 105, 139, 201
Mexico, 34, 110, 114, 145, 155, 168–172, 178n11, 178n13, 199
Michigan, 166, 177n4, 177n5
Military power, 31, 70–72, 171, 195
Mill, J.S., 96
Minsky, Hyman, 125
Mirllees, J., 61n3
Mishra, P., 177n2
Mistral, 13
Mnuchin, Steve, 178n8
Mohammad Mossadeq, 120
Monetary policy, 19, 88, 117, 126, 127, 130, 133, 139, 140n7, 146, 149, 198
Morales, Evo, 164
Muller, J.W., 164, 177n2
Multipolar world (imperfect), vii, 181–204
Murdoch, 97
Mussolini, B., 65
Musu, I., ix

N
NAFTA, *see* North America Free Trade Agreement
Nagasaki, 65
NASA, *see* National Aeronautics and Space Administration
National Aeronautics and Space Administration (NASA), 151, 152
National Health Institute (NHI), 151, 152
National Nanotechnology Initiative (Nni), 151
National Science Foundation (NSF), 151
NATO, 71, 168, 192
Naughton, B., 205n5
Nazism, 21, 28
NBER, 137, 138
Neo-corporatism, 28, 29
Netherlands, 33, 35, 36, 104, 192
New Deal
  Agriculture Adjustment Act, 25
  Fair Labour Standards Act, 25
  Federal Securities Act, 25
  Glass Steagall Banking Act (Banking Act), 25
  National Industrial Recovery Act (NRA), 25
  Norris-LaGuardia Act, 25, 28
  Recovery, 25
  Reform, 25
  Relief, 25
  Social Securities Act, 25, 28
  Tennessee Valley Authority, 25
  Wagner Act, 25, 28
New Zealand, 182
Nigeria, 189

Nixon, R., 87
No-global movement, 111, 169
Nongovernmental organization (NGOs), 200, 201
Nongovernmental powers (NGPs), 200–201
North America Free Trade Agreement (NAFTA), 105, 169–171, 178n11, 201
North, D.C., 8n4
North Korea, 67, 171, 172, 199
Norway, 34, 155
Nye, J.S. jr., 76n2

O

Obama, Barack, v, vii, viii, 83, 92, 94, 95, 99, 111, 130, 133, 134, 136, 138, 140n6, 143–159, 160n1, 160n2, 160n3, 165, 169, 170, 175, 176
Obanomics
 Obama and globalization, 95, 144, 151, 169
 Obamacare (Obama's health care policies), viii, 144, 156–159, 173–175
 Obama's economic policies in the great recession, 144–151, 159
 Obama's energy policies, 144
 Obama's environmental policies, 153
 Obama's ideas of economics, 143–144
 Obama's industrial innovation policies, 133, 144, 151–152
Oddo, Luigi, x

OECD, 53, 55, 74, 86, 88, 105, 145, 146
Openness degree, 106, 113, 114

P

Pacey, Laura, x
Panama, 122n11
Papageorgiou, C., 177n2
Paris agreement on climate change, 155, 176
Parmar, I., 177n2
Pasinetti, L., 62n18
Payne, R.J., 204n3
Pegatron, 121n3
Pennsylvania, 166, 177n4
Per capita GDP, 1, 2, 6, 8n6, 8n7, 32, 35, 59, 66, 83, 138, 153, 184–186, 190, 198, 199, 210
Perkins, D.H., 205n5
Peron, Juan Domingo, 177n3
Peronism, 164
Perry, R., 176
Petrovich, Giuliano, ix
Physical capital, v, 28, 52
Pianta, M., 8n4
Piketty, Thomas, 92
Piore, M.J., 43n2
Poland, 42
Political power, 68, 71–72, 98, 168
Pompeo, M., 176
Population
 Soviet Union population, 66
 US population, 4, 156, 190
Populism, 163–165, 176n1, 177n2
Porter, M.E., 43n6
Portugal, 33, 42, 133, 141n13, 146
Post-Fordism, 37

Powell, D., 168, 178n8, 178n9
Prices
   GDP deflator, 208, 209
   housing prices, 127–129, 140n4
   inflation, 31
   prices of goods, 15
Productivity, 3, 6, 12–16, 21, 24, 33, 34, 36, 37, 39, 40, 42, 47, 48, 51, 56, 58, 60, 68, 75, 85, 91, 96, 187
   labor productivity, 4–6, 8n7, 14, 17n4, 32, 48, 50, 56, 67, 73, 74, 76, 84, 85, 107, 186, 191, 196, 197
Profits, 4, 12, 13, 15, 21, 24, 26, 27, 48, 58, 60, 91, 94, 96, 114, 116, 119, 121n3, 126–128, 131, 147, 152, 173, 182, 184, 190, 200
Pruitt, E.S., 175, 176
Public deficit as percent of GDP, 132, 148
Pyke, F., 43n5
Pyramid of economic development, 46

Q

Quantitative easing (QE), 130, 140n7, 146, 148

R

R&D
   employed people in R.&D., 73–75, 186
   expenditure in R.&D. (% GDP), 54, 148, 186
   total spending, 54, 75

Rate of unemployment, 24, 132
Rating agencies, 134, 135
Reagan, Ronald, 42, 88, 92, 94
Real crisis, 126, 129, 130, 132, 138, 139
Reddy, Sanjay, ix
Regulation school
   modes of regulation, 13
   regimes of capital accumulation, 13
Revelli, R., 43n3
Rivoli, P., 122n5
Robinson, J., 61n1
Robots, 43, 51, 56–59, 61n13, 151
Rodrik, D., 177n2
Romania, 42
Romer, P., 48, 49
Roosevelt, F.D., 24, 25, 28
Roosevelt, T., v, 21, 65, 138
Rossi, S., ix
Roubini, N., 140n5
Russian Federation (Russia), 68, 73, 76, 194, 208–210

S

Sabel, C.F., 43n2
Saccone, D., 205n8
Sachs, J., 177n2
Saddam Hussein, 93
Saez, Emmanuel, 92
Salvini, Matteo, 164
Sanders, Bernie, 170, 177n5
Saudi Arabia, 81, 110, 199
Schumpeter, J.A., 26, 48
Schwab, Klaus, 61n13
Schwartz, A.J., 24, 26
Schweitzer, S.O., 161n8
SEC, 134, 136

Securitization, 128
Sengerberger, W., 43n5
Serbia, 122n11, 193
Shadow bank, 117, 129, 151
Shiller, R.J., 140n5, 140n12
Signorelli, Marcello, ix, 205n12
SIPRI, 120, 122n12
Slovak Republic, 42
Slovenia, 42
Small Business Administration (SBA), 152, 167
Small Business Innovation Research (SBIR), 152
Social cohesion, 74, 90
Soft power, 69, 71
Solow, R., 48, 49
Somalia, 122n11
Sonin, K., 177n2
South Africa, 178n13
Soviet Union (USSR), vi, vii, 31, 32, 34, 65–68, 70, 73–76, 104, 106, 113, 119, 121, 181, 182, 184, 193, 194, 196, 197
  dissolution of the Soviet Union, vii, 3, 60, 66, 68, 76, 105, 181, 194
Spain, 33, 34, 41, 42, 133, 141n13
Spilimbergo, A., 177n2
Stalin, Joseph, 65
Steindl, Josef, 26, 27
Stiglitz, Joseph, 119, 122n10, 140n5, 148
Stock exchange market, 69, 116, 122n8, 126, 130, 201
Stock-flow feedback
  Frankfurt, 69
  Hong Kong, 69
  London, 69
  Paris, 69

Tokyo, 69
Stocks, 16, 19, 26, 27, 52, 69, 73–75, 86, 89, 90, 92, 100, 106, 108, 109, 113, 114, 122n8, 126, 128, 129, 131, 132, 134–136, 138, 139, 173, 179n16, 186, 189, 190
  wealth, 27, 183
Structural bubble, 126, 128, 197
Student movement, 41
Sub-prime mortgages, 128
Sudan, 189
Suez crisis, 36
Sweden, 33, 42, 54, 157
Switzerland, 34, 53, 127
Sylos Labini, Paolo, ix
Syrquin, Moshe, 55

Taguieff, P.A., 177n2
Targetti Lenti, R., xv
Taylorism, 11–13
Technical progress, v, 15, 34, 46, 48, 49
Teheran, 31, 65–68
Teodori, M., 8n4
Terrorism
  al Qaeda, 93
  Bin Laden, Osama, 93
  ISIL (Daesh), 93, 119
  September 11 (twin towers terrorist attacks), vii, 93, 126
Thailand, 42, 47, 113
Thaler, Richard, 140n12
Tillerson, R., 176
Tito, Josip Broz, 65, 67
Tocqueville, Alexis de, 8n8
Toninelli, Pierangelo Maria, xv

Toniolo, Gianni, ix
Toyotism, 42
   just in time, 39
Trade liberalization, 84, 105–108, 169
Trade war, viii, 28, 139, 172
Trans-Pacific Partnership (TPP), 170, 178n10
Troubled Asset Relief Program (TARP), 130, 135, 145–148
Trump, Donald, v, viii, 53, 83, 94, 99, 105, 111, 112, 139, 149, 160, 163–176, 194, 203
   America first, 164, 168
   anti-immigrant policy, 164, 166
   Cambridge Analytica, 166
   neo-protectionism approach, 172
   populism, vii, viii, 163–165
   presidential election (2016), 166
   reform tax bill, 173–175
   tariffs on steel and aluminum, 165, 168, 171
   Trump and environment, 174–176
   Trump and healthcare, 174–176
Trumpism, 163–165, 176n1
TTIP, 169–171, 178n10
Tuggart, P.A., 177n2
Turin index of economic power (TIEP), 72–76
Turkey, 42, 178n13, 194, 199, 201
Turner, F.J., 8n4

U

Ukraine Republic, 194
UN, 69, 105, 121, 202
UNCTAD, 74, 106, 109, 114
UNDP, 54

United Arab Emirates, 82, 178n13
United Kingdom, 35, 205n11, 207–210
Urbinati, N., 177n2
US Department of the Treasury, 160n4, 160n6
US dollar
   dollar shortage, 87
   fixed exchange rates, 87
   flexible exchange rates, 87
   international monetary seigniorage, 86
USGS, 100n3

V

Valli, V., 16n3, 140n9, 140n11, 205n8
Vaudagna, M., 28
Vicious circles, 126, 131
Virtuous circle of development, 16, 24

W

Wages
   hourly wages, 12
   total wages, 5, 15, 21, 24, 27–28, 131
   wages for employee, 15
Wallerstein, I., 204n1
Wall Street crash, vi, 19–22, 26, 125, 139
   Black Thursday, 19
Wars
   Afghanistan war, xvii, 71, 86, 93, 108
   economic consequence of, 69–71

First World War, 7, 8, 12, 69, 70, 72, 112, 182
Iraq war I, 71, 119, 120
Iraq war II, 71, 119, 120, 148
Korean war, 67, 85, 107, 119, 120
Libya war, xvii, 71, 108
Second World War, vi, 2, 3, 29, 31, 39, 65, 70–72, 80, 82, 90, 104, 119
Syria war, vii, 71, 108
Vietnam War, 41, 67, 71, 77n3, 85, 87, 107, 119, 120
Washington consensus, 116, 122n9
Washington Mutual, 130, 140n8
Wealth effect, 20, 131
Western Europe, 7, 14, 32, 34–37, 39, 41, 42, 60, 92, 104
Williams, W.A., 8n4
Wisconsin, 122n3, 166, 177n4
Wolf, M., 178n9
World Bank, 31, 69, 73, 87, 93, 105, 106, 114, 116, 121, 122n9, 136, 146, 199, 202, 205n11
World Health Organization (WHO), 156
World Inequality Report, 100n15
World's Top Exports, 178n13
World Trade Organization (WTO), 105, 106, 121n1, 139, 179n15, 187, 189
WTO, *see* World Trade Organization

X
Xi Jinping, 172

Y
Yalta, 31, 65–68
You tube, 99
Yugoslavia, 65, 67

Z
Zinke, R., 176
Zucman, G., 92

GPSR Compliance
The European Union's (EU) General Product Safety Regulation (GPSR) is a set of rules that requires consumer products to be safe and our obligations to ensure this.

If you have any concerns about our products, you can contact us on

ProductSafety@springernature.com

In case Publisher is established outside the EU, the EU authorized representative is:

Springer Nature Customer Service Center GmbH
Europaplatz 3
69115 Heidelberg, Germany

www.ingramcontent.com/pod-product-compliance
Lightning Source LLC
LaVergne TN
LVHW040735250326
834688LV00031B/310